THE SEXUAL LABYRINTH
OF NIKOLAI GOGOL

Nikolai Gogol
Watercolor by Alexander Ivanov (Rome, 1841)

The Sexual Labyrinth
of Nikolai Gogol

Simon Karlinsky

HARVARD UNIVERSITY PRESS

Cambridge, Massachusetts, and London, England   1976

Library of Congress Cataloging in Publication Data

Karlinsky, Simon.
    The sexual labyrinth of Nikolai Gogol.

    Bibliography: p.
    Includes index.
    1. Gogol, Nikolaĭ Vasil'evich, 1809-1852—Relation-
ship with men. I. Title.
    PG3335.K34   891.7'8'309 [B]   76-16486
    ISBN 0-674-80281-0

Contents

Illustrations

Introductory Note

This book is neither a biography of Gogol nor an exhaustive study of his writings. At least seven such works already exist in English (see the Annotated Mini-Bibliography) and there would not have been much point in adding one more critical biography to the list. Instead, this is an examination of a particular neglected area in Gogol's life and work—his sexuality and its manifestations in his literary art. Apart from some digressions on matters of style, subject matter, and form, all of which I believe to be pertinent to my subject, I have tried to limit the book's purview to this one theme, an admittedly one-sided approach. But other aspects of Gogol have been extensively explored; the interested reader can easily fill out the rest of the picture from the studies cited in the text and notes and recommended in the bibliography. A detailed account of changing attitudes toward Gogol in pre-revolutionary Russia and in the Soviet Union was included in order to explain to the reader why so many generations of Russian critics have failed to notice what I see as the source and the cause of Gogol's personal and literary tragedy.

In a recent memoir about the great twentieth-century poet Anna Akhmatova, her friend Lydia Chukovskaya tells us that Akhmatova considered Gogol the most puzzling person who ever lived: "No one can imagine what Gogol was really like. Everything about him is incomprehensible from beginning to end. The individual features refuse to add up to anything." It is the thesis of the present study that an examination of Gogol's homosexual orientation within the context of his biography and writings may provide the missing key to the riddle of his personality. It should be emphasized that, as applied to Gogol in this book, the term "homosexuality" refers to his overpowering emotional attraction to members of his own sex and aversion to physical or emotional contact with women, rather than to any physical sexuality. Much of the evidence for his homosexual

Introductory Note

orientation is circumstantial, and the case for it depends on a multitude of points which may seem less convincing when taken out of their context in the book, but which I believe to be cumulatively valid when considered in their totality.

As the text and notes make clear, the subject of Gogol's homosexuality has been gingerly broached by a number of Western commentators in the past, with results that can at best be described as tentative or inconclusive. Until very recently, this topic was all too often regarded as unsuitable for scholarly examination. One of the finest of Western biographers of Gogol, Vsevolod Setchkarev, had intended to treat this subject in the original German version of his book (published in Berlin in 1953). He decided not to do so when a senior colleague said that he would try to ruin Setchkarev's academic career if his book asserted the fact of Gogol's homosexuality. It is hoped that the passage of time and the change in attitudes have made the subject mentionable and that the factual material included in this book will help to generate a more enlightened view of Gogol's problems.

Gogol's texts and letters are cited in all cases in my own translation from the Russian. As my basic source I have used the USSR Academy of Sciences fourteen-volume edition of his *Complete Collected Works and Letters*, Moscow, 1937-1952. I would like to express my gratitude to two of my colleagues, Hugh McLean and Robert P. Hughes, who encouraged me to explore this topic and who helped me by reading the early drafts and offering their ideas and corrections. I am also grateful to Peter Carleton, who brought to my attention some valuable recent psychological studies in the field of human sexuality, and to Barry Jordan for his help with research, typing, and editorial suggestions. Three Berkeley students who took courses on Gogol with me—Julie Baker, Krista Hanson, and William B. Stephens

Introductory Note

—ended up teaching me things about Gogol that I had not known before and that are reflected in this book. I would like also to mention the impact on my thinking of other American Gogolians. It was the books and articles of Vsevolod Setchkarev, Leon Stilman, Donald Fanger, and, again, Hugh McLean that first showed me the inadequacy of traditional approaches to Gogol and convinced me of the need to examine his life and his work anew.

Simon Karlinsky

Kensington, California
February 1976

THE SEXUAL LABYRINTH
OF NIKOLAI GOGOL

On December 31, 1833, the young Ukrainian writer Nikolai Gogol sat down at the desk in his modest St. Petersburg apartment to ponder the future course he wanted his life to take. He was twenty-four years old and probably the best-known young writer in Russia. His two volumes of stories, published under the general title of *Evenings on a Farm near Dikanka*, Parts I and II, had been received with tremendous acclaim by the reading public throughout the country. Alexander Pushkin, Russia's greatest poet, greeted these stories with a review that mingled delight with amazement. Every literary journal in St. Petersburg wanted Gogol as a contributor, every established writer sought his acquaintance. While on a trip to visit his family in the Ukraine during the previous summer, Gogol had stopped over in Moscow, where he was lionized in literary and theatrical circles. Mikhail Shchepkin, the most famous comic actor of the time, spoke with excitement about appearing in the satirical comedy which Gogol had shown him in draft form and which was to be called *The Medal of St. Vladimir, Third Class*. Early in December of 1833 Gogol had read to Pushkin his new long story "The Tale of How Ivan Ivanovich Quarreled with Ivan Nikiforovich," and Pushkin noted in his journal that the work was "highly original and very funny." By the end of the year Gogol was already at work on the next story of his forthcoming *Mirgorod* cycle, "Old-World Landowners." He could hardly have failed to realize that with these two works the development of his own talent as well as that of Russian narrative prose as a whole was reaching those rarefied regions where the combination of verbal virtuosity and human profundity conspires to produce what is called great literature of permanent significance. In terms of his literary achievement, Gogol's present must have looked auspicious on that New Year's Eve, and his future dazzling.

And yet the young writer was not content. He was dissatisfied with his job, which was to teach history and geography in an exclusive boarding school for the daughters of the higher nobility. What Gogol longed for was to teach history at a major Russian university, either at the one in Kiev (with which he had been carrying on negotiations on this subject for much of 1833) or, preferably, at the one in St. Petersburg. Not that he had any particular training or qualifications for teaching history. But like many nineteenth-century Russians (including Tolstoy), Gogol did not consider writing works of imaginative literature a sufficiently valid calling in life. What he wanted to do was to influence his countrymen, to show them their better moral selves, and to impress them with his brilliance. The position of professor of history seemed to him a better vehicle for achieving those ends than his successfully inaugurated literary career. Besides, at a university Gogol would teach all-male classes and would not need to scale down his grandiose historical conceptions to what, as he put it, "can be grasped by the puny female minds" of his women students at the boarding school (letter to Mikhail Pogodin, February 1, 1833). As it happened, Nikolai Gogol did not particularly like women.

It was not until after he had turned thirty and spent some time living in Rome that Gogol came to have any women friends at all. Throughout his intensely creative St. Petersburg period (1829-1836), there was only one woman with whom Gogol corresponded, his mother. Otherwise, all the hundreds of his personal, literary, and business letters dating from that time were invariably addressed to men. Gogol's personal emotional attachments were likewise directed at males: his younger brother in early childhood, a fellow student at the school he had attended during his adolescence, and eventually the young man

---

"1834"

whom he permitted himself to love openly in Rome in 1839. After he moved to St. Petersburg in 1829, Gogol's personal (as contrasted to literary) contacts were restricted almost entirely to a group of young Ukrainians whom he had known since childhood. They had all attended the same school as he in Nezhin and they had come to the capital at about the same time as he in pursuit of literary, civil-service, and military careers. The most durable of those associations were the ones with Alexander Danilevsky, Nikolai Prokopovich, and Ivan Pashchenko. But for all the warmth of Gogol's affection for these school friends and for all of their pride in his literary achievements, there was an area of their lives that he could not share. They flirted with pretty St. Petersburg girls, they visited brothels where they did "sweaty things behind partitions" (letter to Alexander Danilevsky, December 20, 1832), and eventually they all married and started their own families, moving inexorably out of Gogol's orbit in the process. The unexpectedly desolate final sentences of his otherwise comical story "The Fair at Sorochintsy" (1831) might possibly suggest Gogol's emotional response to these developments: "Is it not thus that the playful friends of our free and stormy youth disperse one by one through the world and finally leave their former brother all alone? How dreary it is for the one who is left behind! His heart is heavy and sad and there is no way of helping him."

These and similar themes must have been on Gogol's mind when he sat down on that New Year's Eve and wrote his remarkable prose poem "1834" (also found in some editions as "Invocation to His Genius"), which is here translated in its entirety.

1834

This is a great, solemn moment. God, how the [succeeding] waves of varied emotions are merged and compressed within it! No, this is no [idle] dream. This is that fatal, irresistible

"1834"

frontier between memory and hope. Memory is no longer here, it is already receding, it is already overtaken by hope. My past rustles at my feet; above me, through the mist, my undeciphered future is dawning. I implore you, life of my life, my guardian, my angel, my Genius. Oh, do not abandon me! Watch over me at this moment and do not stray from me for the rest of this incoming year that begins so enticingly for me. What will you be like, my future? Will you be brilliant, will you be spacious, will you be seething with my great deeds, or . . . Oh, do be brilliant! Be active, be entirely given over to work and serenity. Why are you standing in front of me looking so mysterious, 1834? Why don't you, too, be my angel? Should idleness and indifference dare to touch me even for a while, wake me up! Do not let them take hold of me. Let your numerals, so full of significance, stand before me like an unhushable clock, like one's conscience. Let every one of your numerals strike my ear louder than a tocsin. Let it convulse my entire body like a galvanic rod!

O my mysterious, unfathomable 1834! Where shall I memorialize you with great deeds? Shall it be amidst this heap of houses flung on top of each other, these thundering streets, this seething mercantile activity, this ugly heap of fashions, parades, civil servants, savage northern nights, glitter, and lowly mediocrity? [Shall it be] in my Promised Land—my beautiful, ancient Kiev, crowned with fruit-laden orchards, girdled with my beautiful, wondrous southern skies, with its intoxicating nights, with its mountain strewn with shrubs and harmonious precipices [while] its foot is washed with [the waters of] my pure and swift Dnieper?

Will it be there? O! I do not know what to call you, my Genius, you who used to fly over my cradle with your harmonious songs, who engendered within me such wondrous, intoxicating dreams. Oh, look at me! My handsome one, cast your heavenly eyes down on me. Oh, do not part

---

from me! Dwell with me here on earth as my beautiful brother, if only for two hours every day! I shall achieve . . . I shall achieve. Life is seething within me. My labors shall be inspired. A Divinity inaccessible to earth will hover over them. I shall achieve . . . Oh, kiss me and give me your blessing!

Gogol did not edit this fragment, nor did he intend it for publication. The style shows Gogol at his most bathetic and verges dangerously on self-parody. Some phrases bring to mind the tone of Khlestakov's wooing of the mayor's wife in *The Inspector General*, while others, even more astonishingly, read like an echo of the hero's desperate ravings in the final portion of "Diary of a Madman." But there is no doubt about the reality and earnestness of Gogol's emotions. Written when Gogol was halfway through *Mirgorod*, his most personal cycle of stories, "1834" touches some of the most central strands of Gogol's personal and artistic essence and is certainly one of the most self-revealing texts he ever put down on paper. His awareness of his unique gifts and his overriding ambition are clearly expressed and so is his rather simplistic yearning for the kind of instantly achieved and universally recognized greatness that no amount of literary success, no matter how genuine, could ever gratify. The sudden resurgence of longing for his Ukrainian homeland (from which he was only too glad to escape to St. Petersburg only four years earlier) would find its expression in "Taras Bulba" and "Viy," to be written in the following months—the last works with Ukrainian settings he was ever to write. Equally significant is the picture of St. Petersburg, presented as a mixture of heaps of houses, thundering streets, glitter, and mediocrity. This particular passage shows in embryonic form the entire complex of themes and ideas from which "Nevsky Prospect" and the other stories of Gogol's St. Petersburg cycle would grow, stories that belong at the very pinnacle of his artistic achievement.

Most important of all is the central image of the Genius-brother-lover which dominates the entire fragment. It had been customary in Russian literature since the eighteenth century to personify the writer's inspiration and his talent as a Muse. This practice had become so widespread by Gogol's time that Pushkin was able to give his Muse a concrete role in the principal action of his novel in verse *Eugene Onegin* and to introduce her in person into some of the novel's important scenes. Characteristically and almost instinctively, Gogol replaces the traditional Muse with the much less usual male embodiment of the same principle —his personal Genius. Utilizing the grammatical gender of the three masculine nouns—year, genius, and brother—he then effects a double literary metamorphosis. The year 1834 is transformed into Gogol's talent and inspiration, which is in turn changed into the ultimate object of his innermost desire: a male lover and friend. This desire and the concomitant revulsion against marriage and other forms of sexual involvement with women, toward which the entire weight of tradition and social custom were pushing him, are what can be termed the nerve center of Gogol's biography and of much of his creative achievement. It has been by and large ignored in the vast literature about Gogol, and this is the reason why the present book was written.

To examine Gogol's roots and origins on his father's side of the family is to discern three of the basic, recurrent themes of his life and his writings. His ancestors were provincial Ukrainian clergy—a separate caste in pre-revolutionary Russia—who owned some land and possessed some education, but were lower on the social scale than the local gentry. In the 1760s, the Empress Catherine II, whom posterity knows as the Great, that enlightened German-born monarch who so knowingly discussed human rights and the evil of tyranny in her correspondence with Voltaire and Diderot, decided to turn the previously free Ukrainian peasants into serfs. To this end, she passed a set of edicts making the ownership of land by any class of Ukrainians other than the gentry illegal and extending serfdom as it existed in central Russia to the Ukraine. Gogol's grandfather had to falsify the family records and pass his family off as nobility or face the loss of their land and other property. This he did so successfully that the truth was not discovered until late in the nineteenth century, when the biographers of Gogol decided to take a closer look at the genealogical tables.

Gogol was only two generations removed from these events. The ecclesiastic tradition of his clerical forebears was, however, still strong in the family and it must have contributed to his mysticism and religiosity. The formerly plebeian family had become serf-owning nobles with the aid of Catherine's edicts—and they venerated her memory and worshiped her descendants, the subsequent Romanov rulers. Few of the subjects of the tyrannical, repressive Nicholas I were as steadfastly loyal to this grim ruler as Gogol; the tsar's grandmother Catherine makes gracious appearances in "Christmas Eve," "The Lost Letter" and "The Portrait."

Whether Gogol knew of his family's falsified records or not, the dubious nature of everyone's personal identity is *the* theme to which he returns again and again in one work after another. Impostors mislead small groups of people or even entire

Gogol's Family

communities in *Dead Souls, The Inspector General,* and *The Gamblers.* A man's own nose threatens his sense of self by acquiring a separate identity in "The Nose." On the glittering boulevard in "Nevsky Prospect," a respectable German housewife behaves like a streetwalker, while a prostitute from a brothel assumes the appearance of a Romantic artist's unsullied and disembodied ideal.

It may be superficial to trace specific personal traits to one or the other of a person's parents, but in Gogol's case the temptation to do so is overwhelming. The verbal flair, the wit, the lyricism would seem to come from Gogol's father, a dreamy, sentimental country squire, author of folksy Ukrainian comedies in verse. He died when Gogol was sixteen. The letter the boy wrote to his mother in response to the announcement of his father's death begins with a brief mention of despair and thoughts of suicide and continues for a page with florid rhetoric that hasn't the slightest ring of sincerity about it. Before the letter is finished, Gogol is clearly resigned to the loss ("My sadness soon turned into a light, barely noticeable melancholy"). He then writes of his pleasure at the forthcoming summer vacation and ends the letter with a request for ten rubles he needs in order to buy some books.

The relationship to his mother was far more important in Gogol's emotional development and in his subsequent life. Maria Gogol, née Kosiarowska, was a woman who could have easily stepped off the pages of one of her son's more extravagant literary creations. It is from her that Gogol must have inherited (if such a thing can be inherited) his boundless fantasy, his monstrously fertile imaginative faculty, and, above all, his knack for blurring the real and the imaginary. While Gogol was still alive, his mother had a habit of crediting him not only with his own writings but also with a number of current publications by vari-

Gogol's Family

ous French and Russian authors, including several utterly trashy pulp novels. After his death (she outlived Gogol by fifteen years), she gave interviews in which she claimed that her late son had invented the steam engine and had planned the railroad network that was being constructed all over Russia in the 1850s.

Gogol's letters to his mother make up the lion's share of his surviving correspondence. The forms of address the adult Gogol uses in these letters are either infantile (*Drazhaishaya mamen'ka*, "My Most Precious Mommy") or so grandiloquent as to verge on parody (*Velikodushnaya mater'*, "O Magnanimous Mater!"). But for all the protestations of love and respect, Gogol clearly mistrusts his mother, lies to her continually, and dissembles in major and minor matters for no discernible reason. Vikenty Veresayev justly described Gogol's letters to his mother as the *least* reliable biographical source we have. If one sits down and reads several hundred of these letters at a stretch, the saccharine endearments come to seem a mechanical formula and the impression arises that Gogol must have mistrusted his mother, often been annoyed with her, and secretly held her in contempt.

Maria Kosiarowska was married to Vasily Gogol when she was fourteen. She suffered several miscarriages in the next three years and when she became pregnant in 1808, she made a vow that if she had a son, she would name him after St. Nicholas of Myra, one of the most revered saints in the Russian Orthodox tradition. She prayed for the child's survival to the wonder-working icon of this saint that was known as St. Nicholas of Dikanka. To be on the safe side, however, Vasily Gogol arranged to have the delivery take place at the home of the best-known obstetrician in the Ukraine. Nikolai Gogol, the couple's elder son, was safely born there on March 20, 1809. One year later his brother, Ivan, was born and a year after that, his sister Maria. Some years later, after a few more miscarriages, three

Gogol's Family

more daughters were born who survived. The youngest of them, Olga, was born in 1825 and died in 1907.

Gogol's early childhood was spent at his parents' estate Vasilievka, where the family was comfortably supported by the labor of their two hundred serfs. His closest early attachment was to his brother. All the sources on Gogol's childhood stress that the two boys were inseparable, both at home and later at the elementary school in Poltava, where they were enrolled in the same grade and boarded together at the home of one of their teachers. Ivan's sudden death during the summer vacation in 1819 must have been a shattering blow to the young Gogol. He kept trying to visit his brother's grave, talked only of him to other children, and became morose and depressed. It was partly to dispel this mood that his parents decided to send him to the boarding school for boys in the town of Nezhin. Viewed in conjunction with Gogol's subsequent relationships, his closeness to Ivan seems a kind of *paradis enfantin*, which the writer strove to regain in his later life by his constant search for an equally ideal male friend and companion.

Another formative experience of Gogol's childhood was described by him in a letter he wrote to his mother when he was twenty-four. Advising her on the proper upbringing of his youngest sister, Olga, Gogol wrote:

Talk to her as much as possible of the future life, describe to her in every possible color pleasing to children the joys and pleasures that await the just and what horrible, cruel tortures await the sinners. For God's sake talk to her of such things as often as possible, any time she does something good or bad. You will see the beneficial results this will bring. A strong impression has to be made on a child's sentiments, which will then for a long time retain all that is beautiful. I myself have experienced this—I well remember how I was brought up.

Gogol's Family

I still frequently recall my childhood. You spared no effort to bring me up in the best possible way. Unfortunately, parents rarely do a good job of bringing up their children. You were still young, you had never had any children before, you had never dealt with any, so how could you know what was needed and how to go about it? I remember that I had no strong feelings about anything and considered that everything had been created just for my pleasure. I did not especially love anyone, excepting only you, and even that only because nature herself inspired me with that emotion. I regarded everything with dispassionate eyes and attended church only because I was ordered to or because I was brought there. But while standing there all that I noticed were the vestments, the priest, and the repulsive howling of the sacristans.

But one time—and I recall the occasion as vividly as if it had just happened—I asked you to tell me about the Last Judgment and you talked to the child that I was about the bliss that awaits people as a reward for a virtuous life so beautifully, so understandably, and so touchingly, and you depicted the eternal torment of the sinners in such a vivid and terrifying manner that I was shaken and responded with my entire sensitivity. This implanted and subsequently brought forth some of my loftiest thoughts. (Letter to Maria Gogol, October 2, 1833)

In his book *Gogol's Spiritual Path*, Konstantin Mochulsky writes: "The stress in this account is certainly not on the descriptions of rewards for virtue, but on the portrayal of the sinners' torments. The terrifying picture drawn by the morbid imagination of his mystically gifted mother shocked Gogol. It was a shock he would never forget. His religious consciousness was to grow out of the stern image of Retribution." Several decades later Gogol was to find in Father Matthew Konstantinovsky the preordained instrument of this Retribution, which he awaited with fear and trepidation, on and off, for most of his life.

The School at Nezhin

Gogol entered the boarding school at Nezhin when he was twelve. Except for visits with his family during vacations, this was his home and his world until he was nineteen. It was an all-male world. Despite its location in a small provincial town, the school offered a stimulating intellectual environment. Some of the classes were taught by distinguished scholars who held doctoral degrees. Some of Gogol's fellow students were to make their mark on the literary scene of the times, among them Nestor Kukolnik, the future author of melodramatic and patriotic pageants that were widely performed in Russian theaters during the 1840s and 1850s; Yevgeny Grebenka, author of some of the most popular Ukrainian and Russian songs of the nineteenth century, whose short stories were highly appreciated by Anton Chekhov and are still reprinted; and Vasily Lyubich-Romanovich, who made a name for himself as a historian and a literary translator. The students published a literary journal, the school boasted a symphony orchestra capable of performing works by Mozart, Rossini, and Weber, and the students' dramatic productions enjoyed great popularity in the surrounding area.

It was in the school theatricals that Gogol first gave evidence of his uncommon artistic gifts. The first production of the student's theater was the Neo-Classical and sentimentalist tragedy *Oedipus in Athens* by Ozerov. Gogol appeared in it as the villain, Creon. In Nikolai Khmelnitsky's charming comedy in verse *The Chatterbox*, Gogol starred in the leading role of the garrulous Count Zvonov. But he scored his greatest successes in the roles of comical old women. In Ivan Krylov's *A Lesson to Daughters*, a free adaptation of Molière's *Les Précieuses ridicules*, Gogol was the peasant nanny Vasilisa, who keeps implor-

The School at Nezhin

ing her mannered mistresses to speak, laugh, and cry in Russian and not in French. Gogol's most memorable role was that of the ignorant, authoritarian, and nasty mother of the title character in Denis Fonvizin's great eighteenth-century comedy *The Minor.* Oh, for a time machine that would enable one to go back to Nezhin on that evening in 1827 when the seventeen-year-old Gogol had the earliest triumph of his life playing Mrs. Prostakova! Kukolnik, the future renowned playwright, appeared as Mrs. Prostakova's oafish son Mitrofan; Konstantin Bazili, the future diplomat and author of travel books on the Near East (he was later Gogol's host and guide during his trip to Jerusalem) played the wise old Starodum; and Gogol's future St. Petersburg roommate Alexander Danilevsky was the virtuous heroine Sophie. Danilevsky, by his own admission, did not have much dramatic talent, but because he was the handsomest boy in the school he was invariably called on to play young heroines, such as Sophie, Antigone, and Moina in Ozerov's Ossianic tragedy *Fingal.* His performance was considered pallid, though undeniably decorative; the performances by Kukolnik as Mitrofan and by Gogol as Mrs. Prostakova, however, were remembered for years and are mentioned by all the memoirists who wrote about the Nezhin school.

Many of Gogol's fellow students wrote memoirs or were interviewed by biographers and literary scholars about that period in his life. The consensus of their testimony is that he was not especially popular with other students, despite his accomplishments as an actor. Outwardly he was not a very attractive boy. His long blond hair, elongated face, and abnormally long nose gave him the appearance of a young fox. His neck was covered with messy-looking sores caused by scrofula—a tubercular inflammation of the lymph nodes. Another chronic ailment caused an unpleasant liquid to ooze out of his ears. Kukolnik and Lyubich-

---

Gerasim Vysotsky

Romanovich, neither of whom particularly liked Gogol as an adult, write of his brusque manners and personal untidiness. All memoirists agree on Gogol's satirical turn of mind and caustic wit, which he would exercise at the expense of other students and which could not have endeared him to his victims.

Gogol was not the school's leading scoffer and parodist, however. That honor belonged to Gerasim Vysotsky. Somewhat older than Gogol, Vysotsky suffered from an eye ailment for which the doctors recommended that he carry a parasol. Derided for this by the other boys, Vysotsky replied with razor-sharp repartee, an ability that quickly won Gogol's admiration. When Vysotsky was confined at the infirmary owing to his eye ailment, Gogol spent his time there, too. The older boy's influence on Gogol must have been considerable, for when the first volume of *Evenings on a Farm near Dikanka* was published, many an alumnus of the Nezhin school recognized in it a number of Gerasim Vysotsky's jokes and *bons mots*.

Vysotsky graduated from the Nezhin school two years before Gogol and departed for St. Petersburg, where he obtained a position in the civil service. From the moment of Vysotsky's departure, Gogol began making plans to join him in St. Petersburg. The letters which the eighteen-year-old Gogol wrote to his friend are among the less guarded, more revealing ones that we have. The tone, affectionate at first, eventually becomes amorous and openly erotic. Here is the beginning of the letter of March 19, 1827:

> So you do love me after all, my kind, precious friend. You sacrificed a portion of your valuable time in order to give joy to someone who burns for you with an unfathomable, ardent attachment. Your letter flashed for me like a shooting star of joy. From a remote area of the icy North, where imagination

GerasimVysotsky

warms us up as much as it does here (and where in my dreams my future life has already been realized), I seemed to hear the sounds of a kindred heart that understands me. It was your letter. . . .

Often in the midst of my studies [there comes] the pleasure (it has not entirely abandoned its faithful votary): I make a mental leap to St. Petersburg, I am there with you in your room, we stroll together along the boulevards, admire the Neva and the sea. In a word, I become *you*.   (Gogol's italics)

The conclusion of the long letter which Gogol wrote to Vysotsky on June 26, 1827, reads: "Yours till the grave, unchanging, faithful, eternally loving you, Nikolai Gogol."

It might be tempting to dismiss such lines as adolescent infatuation. But Gogol wrote in this tone to some of his other male friends throughout his life. It might be tempting to qualify these lines as sentimental effusions typical of the Romantic age—it has long been customary to explain away the homosexual sentiments in the sonnets of Shakespeare and Michelangelo as merely a literary device typical of the Renaissance, or the similar sentiments in the poetry of Verlaine and Whitman as simply literary conventions of their age. But in that case, why is it that one never finds this tone and these sentiments in the letters of Zhukovsky (who could be as sentimental as anyone), Pushkin, Odoyevsky, Lermontov, or any other heterosexually oriented Russian writer of Gogol's time?

There is no cause to assume that there was a homosexual love affair between Gogol and Gerasim Vysotsky (in the sense that there was one between Gogol and Iosif Vielhorsky in Rome). But there is every reason for anyone seriously interested in Gogol's work to realize that his erotic imagination was primarily homosexual and that his fear of his homosexual inclinations and his

Gerasim Vysotsky

suppression of them is one of the principal themes of his writings, one of the main causes of his personal tragedy, and a contributing factor to his death. Nineteenth-century Gogol scholarship failed to see this—not only because homosexuality was a taboo subject for most of that century, but also because his admiring countrymen totally misread Gogol's work, assuming that he was an ethnographer, a social critic of the tsarist regime, and the creator of Russian realism. The high (or perhaps low) point of this self-inflicted blindness was probably reached in Semyon Vengerov's turn-of-the-century book *The Citizen-Writer Gogol*. Vengerov, the one-time literature teacher of Osip Mandelstam (who draws an acid vignette of him in *The Noise of Time*), paints a portrait of a Gogol so totally dedicated to the moral betterment of his fellow man that he deliberately suppressed his normal love for women and other earthly pleasures in order to devote himself to serving mankind.

A typical twentieth-century view of Gogol's sexuality can be found in the standard history of Russian literature by D. S. Mirsky (written in England in the 1920s). "The enormous potency of his imagination," writes Mirsky, "stands as a strange contrast (or complement) to his physical sterility. He seems sexually never to have emerged from an infantile (or rather, early adolescent) stage. Woman was for him a terrible, fascinating, but unapproachable obsession, and he is known never to have loved." This is more sophisticated than Vengerov, but it is hardly more perceptive. Like many people of the early post-Freudian age, Mirsky glibly reduces all the less usual forms of sexuality to infantilism and adolescence. The analysis one finds in the two authentically Freudian studies of Gogol's sexuality— Yermakov's and McLean's—moves on much more solid ground, but both of these valuable studies avoid the central issue. Some twentieth-century commentators have speculated about Gogol's

Gerasim Vysotsky

possible impotence or overindulgence in masturbation (for neither of which is there any historical evidence one way or the other) in order to account for the strain of sexual guilt in his life and work in the apparent absence of any sexual activity. One should mention also the reckless and heroic effort by Vasily Rozanov to pinpoint the nature of Gogol's sexuality in his study of Dostoyevsky's "The Legend of the Grand Inquisitor." Sexuality for Rozanov was equated with a man and a woman engaged in an act of procreation and enclosed in a sort of warm (one is tempted to add "and moist") amniotic sac of familial intimacy. Since so much of Gogol's work expresses an aversion to this form of sexuality, Rozanov searched through Gogol's writings for some other variant of erotically depicted woman. He believed he had found his answer in the pages of "Viy." The answer was necrophilia. Rozanov himself found the depiction of the beautiful dead witch in that story so irresistibly erotic that it convinced him that Gogol was sexually attracted to dead women.[1]

Gogol's religious drama, ignored and unnoticed in the nineteenth century, has been given full and sympathetic treatment by such pre-revolutionary writers as Merezhkovsky and in the books by the Russian émigré scholars V. V. Zenkovsky and Konstantin Mochulsky. Perhaps the time has come to give the sexual drama of his life an equally open, unprejudiced treatment.

Gogol's stay at school in Nezhin coincided with what can be seen in retrospect as a very great age in Russian poetry. Vasily

"Ganz Küchelgarten"

Zhukovsky, the older poet who was to be Gogol's close friend and his protector at the tsar's court, had earlier brought to Russian verse a melodiousness and elegance that went beyond anything that even the finest eighteenth-century poets could achieve. He also introduced into Russian poetry the whole range of themes, imagery, and poetic genres of German and English Romanticism. In the early 1820s, the young Alexander Pushkin was dazzling his countrymen with one masterpiece of narrative poetry after another, culminating in his great novel in verse, *Eugene Onegin.* A pleiad of talented and accomplished contemporaries of Pushkin—Baratynsky, Delvig, Yazykov, Küchelbecker, and a number of others—were producing prodigious amounts of poetry the likes of which had never been seen in Russian before. The Romantic prose writers—Bestuzhev-Marlinsky, Pogorelsky, Odoyevsky—were laying the groundwork for the staggering achievements of Russian prose in the second half of the nineteenth century. Although the teachers of literature at the Nezhin school belonged to the old guard and considered Romanticism a heresy and Pushkin a trouble-making whippersnapper, Gogol and his school friends fully realized the importance of the new literary developments. New works by Pushkin are frequently commented upon in Gogol's letters to his parents. Quite early in his school career, he himself composed a sentimental ballad, "Two Little Fishes," in which he expressed his feelings about the death of his beloved brother, Ivan. Other poems and acrostics followed in subsequent years. For the school journal, he submitted a chapter from a historical novel, written in the manner of Sir Walter Scott, then at the height of his international renown and widely translated into all languages. His fellow students did not think much of Gogol's prose efforts and he was advised to stick to poetry. During his last year of school, as Gogol was marking time before graduation so that he could

"Ganz Küchelgarten"

travel to St. Petersburg (where he hoped to share an apartment with Gerasim Vysotsky), he composed a book-length narrative poem about the idyllic life in Romantic Germany. He called it "Ganz [*sic*] Küchelgarten."

Until Vladimir Markov found features of primitivism in this poem and compared it to the work of untutored painters such as Douanier Rousseau, no one had a good word to say of "Ganz Küchelgarten."[2] An imitation partly of some second-rate German models and partly of one of Zhukovsky's ballads ("Theon and Aeschines"), the poem is a Romantic idyll, with the action situated in a sort of enchanted valley near Wismar in Germany. The restless and yearning hero Ganz (it is not clear whether Gogol intended this name to be a transcription of Hans—which would have been "Gans"—or of Heinz; the man's last name is a nonsensical variation on the name of Wilhelm Küchelbecker, a contemporary Russian poet of German extraction) loves the young Luise (her father's name, Wilhelm Bauch, that is, "William Stomach" or "Billy Belly," is another indication of Gogol's tenuous grasp of German realities). Driven by *Wanderlust*, Ganz departs on a tour of Greece and India (there is a chapter describing each of these countries) without telling Luise, who believes herself abandoned. Crazed with grief, she wanders around at night, encountering elves, fairies, ghosts, corpses, and other supernatural creatures dear to the imagination of Romantic poets. Eventually Ganz returns, the lovers are reunited, and the hero ends up by preaching the moral of La Fontaine's fable "The Two Pigeons": if things are good for you, don't wander away but stay put.

The worst thing about "Ganz Küchelgarten" is its versification. Gogol's classmates could not have been more wrong: he simply did not know how to handle verse. In an age when even the third-rate poets could produce marvelously fluent lines,

"*Ganz Küchelgarten*"

Gogol wrote pages and pages of iambic pentameter that continually falls apart. Words are brutally shortened or given extra syllables, endless filler words are thrown in for no reason except the meter, and still most of the time the lines do not scan. Now and then he gives up and writes prose, hopefully trying to disguise it as verse by the addition of ridiculous rhymes that simply refuse to rhyme.

There is no denying that the poem is both derivative and verbally awkward. And yet for a serious student of Gogol it is by no means a total loss. His power of imagination is clearly there, but it is trapped in the wrong medium. One can actually discern three varieties of Gogolian imagination in it. The first, and the least interesting, is the conventional Romantic one: the unreal images of India or the supernatural creatures that Luise observes during her nocturnal wanderings through the forest. But in the midst of that standard *diablerie* of the period, we get a few glimpses of the kind of imagination which in later times came to be called "surrealistic." One such episode, justly admired by Vladimir Nabokov, shows a skeleton which slowly rises from the grave, "wiping its dusty bones with a self-important air" and thereby eliciting the narrator's unexpectedly admiring expletive: "Attaboy!" (*Molodets*). Even stranger is the appearance, among the fairies and ghosts that swirl over Luise, of the huge back of a whale accompanied by a fisherman who "wrapped himself up and went to sleep." One of the surest ways of producing a surrealistic effect is to place something real and prosaic in an otherwise fantastic context. This fisherman seems a creature of twentieth-century imagination, as do so many other things in Gogol. He is a close cousin not only to Gogol's own colonel who walks by as Ivan Shponka is being pulled up the belfry to become a bell (in "Ivan Fyodorovich Shponka and His Aunt"), but also to the passerby in a poem by Velimir Khlebni-

"Ganz Küchelgarten"

kov, who happens to walk by as the continent of Atlantis is collapsing into the ocean. A few of the epithets one finds in "Ganz Küchelgarten" can also be qualified as surrealistic. A herd of cows is referred to as *igrivye*, "frivolous" or "humorous," while thunder is said to be thundering while lost in meditation (*grom v razmyshlenii gremit*).

Most interesting of all are the scenes that in later Gogol would inevitably be termed "realistic." Gogol had never seen Germany at the time he wrote the poem and, as the names of the characters suggest, knew it only from the work of German Romantic poets. But his pictures of German home life—the domestic arrangements of the Bauch family, the building of their home, a dinner party with all the dishes described in loving detail, the dance, the barnyard with all of its animals—are overwhelmingly real and overwhelmingly believable. Yet, apart from a few details that seem to have been suggested by Flemish painting, it all comes out of Gogol's mind. All three kinds of imagination typical of the later Gogol are thus already present in "Ganz Küchelgarten": the romantic, the surrealistic, and the realistic. The last is perhaps the most uncanny of all. It eventually enabled Gogol to visualize Russian provincial life (which he had actually never seen) in *The Inspector General* and in *Dead Souls* with such power that generations of Russians came to believe that he had recorded precise observations of actual reality.

Gogol took the manuscript of "Ganz Küchelgarten" with him when he departed for St. Petersburg a few months before his twentieth birthday. Not that he envisioned a writer's career as his ultimate future. He was carrying letters of recommendation from his mother's influential relatives addressed to important government officials, and he hoped that those recommendations would secure for him a government appointment, preferably within the Ministry of Justice. Even after becoming one of the

St. Petersburg and Germany

most famous writers in Russia, Gogol could never quite reconcile himself to the idea that creative writing was his life's work. What he really seemed to want was to be in a position of power and influence from which he could direct and instruct his fellow men, aspiring to a career first as a government official, later as a university professor, and ultimately as Russia's prophet and moral preceptor. Hence his repeated attempts to escape from the writer's calling, even after success and fame should have convinced him that he had taken the right path.

But Gogol's high hopes were soon dashed. The reunion with Gerasim Vysotsky, for which he had so longed, must have been a total disappointment, for Vysotsky disappears from Gogol's life from that point on. Located by literary scholars at a remote Ukrainian estate some time in the 1870s, the aged Vysotsky was willing to reminisce only about his friendship with Gogol during their school years and had nothing to say about any subsequent encounters. The letters of recommendation brought Gogol some dinner invitations but did not result in the kind of brilliant civil service appointment for which he had hoped. Much of the money he had brought from home was invested in an elegant and fashionable new wardrobe—Gogol's love of fashionable clothes and fabrics and his interest in new clothing styles remained a life-long hobby. He settled in a modest apartment which he shared with his classmate Alexander Danilevsky and accepted a lowly position as a clerk in a government office concerned with property sales registration.

His friendship with the handsome and dashing Danilevsky, whom he occasionally addressed as "my shameless darling" (dushechka-besstydnik) was one of the most enduring relationships in Gogol's life. They shared apartments on several occasions and later they traveled abroad together. Danilevsky was not an especially profound person, but he was good-natured and easy-going and he shared Gogol's interest in clothes and fashions. He also had an abiding interest in women, something that Gogol could never understand. Gogol's advice to Danilevsky on his affairs of the heart is usually couched in tones either of mockery or of ill-concealed distaste. In the early 1840s, after Danilevsky married, Gogol sent him and his wife several sets of instructions on how to conduct their marital affairs that were so peremptory and high-handed that even the affable Danilevsky was offended and temporarily broke off contact with Gogol. Although Gogol quite freely dispensed advice to Danilevsky, he did not always take his friend into his confidence. Thus, Danilevsky was ignorant of Gogol's authorship of "Ganz Küchelgarten" and unaware of its publication, even though it came at the time when the two of them were sharing an apartment.

A few months after arriving in St. Petersburg, Gogol made his first tentative attempt to break into print by publishing a brief poem called "Italy" in one of the literary journals. Partly an imitation of Mignon's song from Goethe's *Wilhelm Meister*, the poem evokes an idealized Italy, where everything is perfection and the population consists entirely of great poets and composers. Encouraged by the poem's favorable reception and discouraged by the failure of his hopes for a brilliant career in the government, Gogol used all his remaining money to publish "Ganz Küchelgarten" in book form. The ensuing tragicomedy has been treated in detail by every single one of Gogol's biographers and there is no need to dwell on it in detail here. Suffice it to say that the volume was overlooked by critics and ignored by readers, including Gogol's friends and acquaintances (who had no way of knowing he was the author, since he hid behind the pseudonym V. Alov). Gogol considered himself disgraced, bought up whatever copies were on sale at bookstores, and burned them—the first of his burnings of his own work. Then, in

St. Petersburg and Germany

desperation, he took the money his mother had sent him to pay off a mortgage and used it to run off to Germany.

To explain his actions to his mother, Gogol wrote her a long, frenzied letter prior to his departure, in which he informed her of a love affair he was having with a woman who was so "lofty and highly placed" that she was totally unattainable. This letter was obviously an exercise in literary style and imagination. By the time Gogol got to Lübeck several weeks later, he had forgotten all about having written it and wrote his mother a second letter of explanation: the reason he had had to go to Germany was to have a cure for a rash on his face and arms. Maria Gogol combined the information contained in the two letters and came to the conclusion that her son had contracted a venereal disease. Gogol's hysterical reply to her accusation deserves to be quoted at length:

With horror I read your letter, mailed on September 6. I could expect everything from you: deserved reproaches, much too kind to me, just indignation and everything else that my ill-considered act could provoke, but *this* I couldn't expect. How could you, dearest mommy, ever think that I had fallen victim to the vilest debauchery, that I find myself on the lowest rung of human degradation! How could you, finally, resolve yourself to ascribe to me a disease, the very thought of which has always made my very thoughts quiver with horror! For the first, and may God grant that it be the last, time in my life, I have received such a terrifying letter. It seemed as if I was hearing a malediction. How could you think that a son of such angelic parents could become a monster in whom not a single virtuous trait was left! No, such things cannot exist in nature. Here is a confession for you: I was carried away only by youthful pride, originating, however, in a pure source, only by an ardent desire to be useful, a desire not tempered by prudence. But I am ready to answer to God that I have not committed even a single depraved exploit; my morality is incomparably more pure than it was at school and at home. As for drunkenness, I never had that habit. At home I used to drink wine, but I do not remember having had any here. But what I cannot understand is how you came to the conclusion that I had that particular disease. It seems I wrote nothing that could indicate that particular disease. I believe I wrote you about the pains in my chest which barely allowed me to breathe and which have now fortunately left me.   (Letter to Maria Gogol of September 24, 1829)

About a decade earlier, the young Alexander Pushkin had contracted gonorrhea. He composed an amusing poem on the subject and wrote jaunty letters about it to his friends, pleased that he was now a real man and hoping to be back in the social whirl in a few weeks, after completing a course of treatment that involved swallowing mercury. About two decades later, the young Lev Tolstoy was to have the same experience. It depressed him and he brooded darkly about getting even with the world by deliberately infecting a few stray streetwalkers. At the end of the nineteenth century, Anton Chekhov wrote an admonishing letter to a woman writer who had sent him a story in which syphilis was equated with vice and depravity. "Syphilis is not a vice," wrote Chekhov, "it is not a product of ill will, but a disease, and the people who have it need warm, human care." None of these other great nineteenth-century writers could have experienced anything like the panicky aversion that throbs in this letter of Gogol, with its obvious equating of sexuality, illness, and total moral perdition.

Gogol's stay in Germany lasted less than a month. The country that he had depicted so idyllically and romantically in "Ganz Küchelgarten" appeared crude, incomprehensible, and alien

St. Petersburg and Germany

when experienced in person. He returned to St. Petersburg bringing with him a collection of German-made trinkets and jewelry which won Danilevsky's admiration, and then made one more determined effort to escape his calling as a writer by deciding to become a professional actor. He arranged to be auditioned by Prince Gagarin, the director of the Imperial Theaters and the husband of the celebrated tragedienne Ekaterina Semyonova, eulogized by many poets, including Pushkin. Gogol appeared for the audition suffering from a toothache and with one cheek bandaged. Asked by Gagarin whether he wanted to try out for comic roles, he answered no: he wanted to play heroic roles in tragedies (the French Neo-Classical drama was still the mainstay of Russian theaters at the time). He read some scenes from Corneille in Russian translation and was told that he had no talent for the stage. In later years, Gogol was a masterly reader of his stories and plays. Posterity has reproached Prince Gagarin for failing to recognize Gogol's histrionic abilities, but in fact he deserves our gratitude. Had he accepted Gogol for the company, the Russian stage might have gained another gifted actor, but the world would have been deprived of a unique writer.

After this defeat, Gogol decided to concentrate on literature. His Ukrainian story, "Bisavryuk," an early version of "Saint John's Eve," appeared in the literary journal *Notes of the Fatherland* in March of 1830; early in 1831 he published two fragments from the novel *The Terrible Boar*, which he later discarded, and a short prose work called "Woman"; and the fall of the same year saw the publication of the first volume of *Evenings on a Farm near Dikanka*. Gogol was already busily mining the native Ukrainian vein in the stories which brought him widespread recognition when he wrote and published "Woman," a piece as highly revealing as it is atypical of his other work. Part story, part parable, it is set in ancient Greece and written in a florid, oratorical style. Plato's disciple Telecles accuses the great philosopher of excessive and unfounded idealization of women. The magnificent, divine Alcinoe, whom Telecles had loved with a sublime, selfless love, had betrayed him with another man. Plato replies that he does not believe it, but even if the accusation were true, a woman's beauty makes her a being so divine, so perfect, and so ideal that no man has the right to pass judgment on her for anything whatsoever. Plato then pronounces a discourse in which he asserts woman's superiority in three areas: in beauty, she is more perfect than man; in the arts, she provides the most elevated subject that any artist may want to depict; and in love, she puts man in contact with his original divine essence. As Plato is finishing his discourse, Alcinoe herself appears in all of her dazzling radiance and Telecles falls at her feet in speechless wonder: "Full of astonishment and adoration, the young man flung himself at the proud beauty's feet and the hot tear of the demigoddess bending over him fell on his flaming cheek."

In his book on Gogol, Vsevolod Setchkarev is quite right in connecting "Woman" with a widespread trend in German idealistic philosophy of the early nineteenth-century. While ostensibly imitating the manner of Platonic dialogues, the piece also elaborates the concept of *das Ewig-Weibliche*, found in the writings of a whole series of German thinkers, from Goethe to Schelling. This is one way of reading "Woman." Another way is to connect it with the letter Gogol wrote to his mother, explaining his sudden departure for Germany by his love for an unidentified highly placed lady. Both the letter and "Woman" seem to be Gogol's attempts to treat a subject that was a favorite of the two contemporary Russian poets he particularly admired, Pushkin and Yazykov. Some of Pushkin's most memorable pages portray beautiful women, depicted with marvelous human sympathy and a matchless power of observation. Yazykov's bac-

_____

"Woman"

chantes and ladies of the night who share university students' revels are always sharply visualized and frankly and openly erotic. Both these poets could draw on their rich lodes of experience in intimate relationships with real women. Gogol had nothing like that to draw on. The totally unreal, ethereal Alcinoe is the earliest of the alabaster goddesses that provide the love interest in some of Gogol's work. Her descendants come in two varieties: the living statues (the Polish girl in "Taras Bulba," Annunziata in "Rome") and the docile, faceless, pretty girls whose very presence is somehow threatening to the hero (the neighbor's sister in "Ivan Fyodorovich Shponka," the governor's daughter in *Dead Souls*). These lovely, often nameless creatures are one extreme of Gogol's collection of unreal female characters, the other being his numerous castrating female manipulators and witches (there are, to be sure, a few more or less *real* female characters in Gogol, who will be discussed at a later point).

There is also a third way of reading Gogol's meaning in "Woman," one that has not been noticed so far in criticism and that can be arrived at by a closer examination of the reasoning that Gogol ascribes to Plato and incorporates into his discourse about the superiority of woman over man. In his argument about the perfection of female beauty, Plato is made to exclaim: "What is woman? She is the language of the gods. We admire the modest, fair countenance of a man, but it is not the image of the gods that we contemplate in him: we see the woman in him, we admire the woman in him, and then only in her do we admire the gods. She is poetry, she is thought, and we are only her incarnation in reality."

This is difficult to translate and even more difficult to interpret, but what Gogol seems to be saying is that woman's beauty represents a sort of absolute yardstick for measuring beauty in general and that therefore the closer a man resembles a woman

"Woman"

the more authentically beautiful he is. In discussing woman's role as a subject for artists, Plato restricts himself to painting and says that as long as the idea for a painting is still in the artist's head it is a woman, but once it is incorporated into an actual physical painting, it becomes a man.

Why then does an artist long with such an unappeased desire to turn his immortal idea into coarse matter and subjugate it to our ordinary senses? Because he is guided by one lofty emotion: to express the divine essence in matter itself, to make even a part of the boundless world of his soul accessible to people, to incorporate woman in man. And should the eyes of a young man who ardently appreciates art fall upon it, what is it they will try to catch in the artist's immortal painting? Do they see matter alone in it? No, it will disappear and before them will open the artist's boundless, illimitable, incorporeal idea. With what animated songs will his spiritual strings then resound! How vividly his irretrievably lost past and his inexorably advancing future will respond, as if to a call of one's native country! How intangibly his soul and the divine soul of the painter will embrace! How the two will merge in an ineffable spiritual kiss!

Thus, on closer examination the paean to woman's beauty turns out to have an underlying layer of additional implications. Woman's beauty provides men with a yardstick necessary for appreciating the beauty of other men, and the depiction of woman in art enables two males (the painter and the spectator, both in the masculine gender throughout) to achieve a spiritual union with unmistakable erotic overtones. Despite the lavish use of such epithets as "disembodied," "intangible," and "innocent," the physical possession of a woman during the love act, which Plato uses as his third and ultimate argument for woman's superiority, is also seen as a vehicle for a divine union of males with other male entities: "When your soul drowns in a woman's ethereal bosom, when it discovers within it its father, the eternal God, its brothers—the feelings and events heretofore inexpressible on earth—what does the soul do then? It then recapitulates the sounds of yore, the former paradisiac life in the bosom of God, projecting it into eternity . . ."

For all of Gogol's determined efforts to compose a hymn in honor of the female principle, male homosexual imagery keeps invading the text of "Woman." The passage just quoted suggests the possible origin of such imagery in Gogol's childhood. Those "brothers" which a man's soul is said to regain through a physical union with a woman may be metaphors (although the words for "feelings and events," *chuvstva i yavleniya,* are both neuter and would not usually suggest a male metaphorical guise). But the image still brings to mind a memoirist's account of the long days Vasily Gogol spent in the fields with his little sons Nikolai and Ivan, reciting poems to them and making them discuss such topics as "the sun" and "heaven."

"Woman" led Gogol into a complex of ideas that were patently alien to him and it left little trace in his later work. In "Bisavryuk," which in a revised form became "Saint John's Eve," one of the four stories in the first volume of *Evenings on a Farm near Dikanka,* Gogol found both the subject matter and the literary manner that made him one of the most highly acclaimed writers in Russia by the time he was twenty-three. Although he did not seem particularly interested in his native Ukrainian heritage as long as he was still at home, during his first year in St. Petersburg he came to realize that the current literary fashions made that heritage a valuable asset. Chateaubriand and Byron had made the remote and exotic cultures of the Moslem Near East popular with the Romantic writers of various countries.

The Romantic Ukraine

The Romantic Scotland of Scott's novels made writers of other countries appreciate the more homely and quaint exoticism of the patriarchal, less cosmopolitan nationalities next door. French writers turned their attention to France's Celtic minorities, while both Russian and Polish writers discovered the Ukraine. By the 1820s, the Ukraine was assuming the same function in the Russian popular imagination that, through Burns and Scott, Scotland had already assumed in the English imagination. Ukrainians spoke a language that was both foreign and comprehensible. Their songs possessed the same degree of quaintness for the Russian ear as the songs of Robert Burns did for the English ear. Ukrainian peasants wore colorful and unfamiliar native costumes, played folk instruments unknown to the Russian peasants, and ate interestingly named native foods (note, for instance, the way Gogol uses Ukrainian dumplings, *halushki,* ubiquitous in his early writings).

A number of Russian writers were capitalizing on this newly found interest in things Ukrainian throughout the 1820s. Vasily Narezhny, a much older writer (1780-1825) than Gogol, published during the last two years of his life the novels *The Seminarian (Bursak)* and *The Two Ivans; or, The Passion for Lawsuits,* which anticipated both the setting and the humor of Gogol's later story about two Ivans and the early portions of "Viy." The pallid Orest Somov and the attractively Hoffmannesque Antony Pogorelsky, both native Ukrainians, enjoyed considerable success with novels depicting the life of provincial Ukrainian gentry and stories of the supernatural derived from Ukrainian legends. Once Gogol became aware of the high esteem in which Ukrainian lore was held by the literary world of the capital, he filled his letters to his mother with requests for information about Ukrainian folk beliefs, customs, dances, foods, proverbs and costumes. The information she supplied from her

The Romantic Ukraine

own knowledge or obtained from her older female relatives and friends he then used to infuse his stories with the fashionable element of local color.

But what, in addition to his own unique blend of humor and fantasy, made the Dikanka stories stand out in comparison with the efforts of Gogol's predecessors was the highly original use to which he put two previously existing theatrical conventions, not normally associated with prose narrative techniques. One tradition was that of the Ukrainian folk comedy, which was largely derived from puppet theater. Ukrainian puppet shows of the eighteenth and the early nineteenth centuries were one-man operations and used two glove-type puppets. The puppets were held over the puppeteer's head and performed folksy skits that involved a certain number of traditional characters that always had to be shown in pairs, since only two puppets could be operated at any one time. Vasily Gippius's book (which is the single most indispensible critical study on Gogol) lists the stock characters of the Ukrainian puppet theater as follows: a comical devil, an evil-tempered peasant's wife, a boastful Pole, a brave Cossack, a sly Gypsy, a simple-minded peasant, and a pompous church deacon. All of these stereotypes are indeed to be found in Gogol's early stories. The technical necessity of showing two characters at a time was carried over from the puppet theater to the Ukrainian folk comedy. Two-character scenes were the rule in the comedies written by Gogol's father (which Gogol asked his mother to send him and from which he took the epigraphs to some of the Dikanka stories). Both the puppet plays and the folk comedies were likely to alternate scenes showing two comical characters with lyrical scenes of two young lovers—just as Gogol's Dikanka stories so often do. It is from this tradition that Gippius correctly derives the structural and comedic elements of these stories.

For plot elements, however, Gogol turned to a tradition that owed little to the Ukrainian or any other Slavic heritage—that of the current Western Romantic opera. "Saint John's Eve," the earliest of these stories and thus seminal to the whole Dikanka cycle, has a rather obvious operatic prototype: Friedrich Kind's libretto for Karl Maria von Weber's *Der Freischütz*, the most popular and representative Romantic opera of that entire age.[3] Like Max in Weber's opera, the hero of "Saint John's Eve" is prevented by parental opposition from uniting with the young woman he loves and is forced to seek supernatural help to win her. Like the hero of the opera, he is put into contact with demonic forces by a mysterious stranger who pretends to be his friend and then lives through a night of horror during which he pledges his soul to Satan. Vsevolod Setchkarev has already compared the nocturnal search for buried treasure in "Saint John's Eve" to the Wolf's Glen Scene in *Der Freischütz*; one might add that the psychedelic lighting effects in that passage were probably suggested to Gogol by the heroine's nocturnal visit to the witch in Antony Pogorelsky's wonderful story "The Poppy Seed Cake Woman of Lafertovo," which is a part of his cycle of stories *The Double; or, My Evenings in the Ukraine*, published in 1825.

The hero and the heroine of "Saint John's Eve" express themselves in extended lyrical soliloquys which sound very much like operatic arias, tinged with imagery and diction derived from the Ukrainian folk song. Operatic elements are in fact quite prominent in four of the other stories found in the two Dikanka volumes and Hugh McLean was quite right to compare these stories to opera and operetta libretti. "Terrible Vengeance," the story that occupies the place analogous to that of "Saint John's Eve" in the second Dikanka volume is, like it, a Romantic opera of Gothic horror in short-story form, while three of the remaining

The Romantic Ukraine

stories, "The Fair at Sorochintsy," "May Night," and "Christmas Eve" are Romantic comic operas. The beginning of "May Night" is a particularly clear example of Gogol's appropriation of operatic conventions for purposes of fictional narrative. One can easily imagine the curtain going up at the beginning of the story to reveal a stageful of colorfully dressed young people performing a choral number during which a Ukrainian hopak is danced. Then the chorus and the ballet withdraw, and the lyric tenor steps forward to sing a serenade to his beloved (Levko's soliloquy). The girl appears, and the two lovers sing a love duet. Later on the village mayor—a comical basso—and his crony—an obvious tenor-buffo role—supply the comic relief. In the second half of the nineteenth century, writers of opera libretti had no trouble converting these stories into popular operas, since they were that to a large extent already, and needed only the music to become full-fledged operas. Rimsky-Korsakov based an opera on "May Night" (but unaccountably failed to utilize the operatic potential of the story's beginning, described above), Moussorgsky did "The Fair at Sorochintsy,"[4] and both Rimsky-Korsakov and Tchaikovsky wrote operas based on "Christmas Eve," the first retaining the original title, the second calling his opera *The Golden Slippers* (*Cherevichki*).

With its use of puppet theater and operatic elements, "Saint John's Eve" pointed the way to the other stories of the Dikanka cycle. But this story is seminal in another, even more important way, because it also inaugurates a basic Gogolian theme that was to become more significant in the works written after the Dikanka stories. Although Gogol follows the plot of *Der Freischütz* more or less faithfully, he rejects the opera's happy ending and introduces into the story a new twist which is bound to result in a tragic dénouement. Max in Weber's opera pledges his soul to the Devil, without involving or endangering anyone else.

Fear of Women and Marriage

At the end of the opera a *deus ex machina* hermit emerges to release him from his pledge, allowing him to save his soul and to marry the heroine. Gogol's Petro, however, has to seal his bargain with the Devil by spilling the blood of an innocent child, and the child offered to him for this purpose is the nice little brother of the girl he loves. Petro finds the treasure and wins the girl, but his victory is purchased at the price of a horrible murder and it obviously cannot bring him happiness. So the marriage turns out to be brief and miserable, Petro perishes by the odd phenomenon of spontaneous combustion, his soul is forfeited to the Devil, and his bride is last seen by the reader as an emaciated nun, frenziedly praying day and night to atone for the grisly crime that she had unwittingly caused.

"Saint John's Eve" is essentially a Romantic horror story and the plot developments outlined above are usual enough for the genre as a whole. Yet it is surely significant that in his very first successful publication Gogol already connected the desire for love and for marriage with punishment, retribution, and loss of life. All that Petro and his beloved Pidorka (the Ukrainian version of Theodora) wanted was to love each other and to be married. Yet this desire delivered them into the power of the Devil and resulted in two deaths and one ruined life. There are no similar instances in the rest of the Dikanka stories (the punishment visited on the father and daughter in "Terrible Vengeance" has other causes), but from *Mirgorod* on, Gogol's male characters who seek love, marriage, or sexual conquest are swiftly and inevitably punished with death, humiliation, and assorted other catastrophes. Andry Bulba is shot by his father; Homa Brut in "Viy" is vanquished by demonic powers; a hopeless infatuation with an unattainable woman drives the hero of "Diary of a Madman" to insanity; Lieutenant Pirogov in "Nevsky Prospect" is humiliated and flogged, his friend Piskaryov loses his life; and

Fear of Women and Marriage

the poor, meek Akaky Akakievich in "The Overcoat," who would not even presume to aspire to love or the possession of another human being, still perishes for daring to desire a substitute wife in the form of a feminine-gender overcoat.

Gogol's idea of a happy ending is actually the very opposite of the traditional one in Western drama and fiction, which usually entails a marriage. A happy ending in a work by Gogol consists, on the contrary, in the male protagonist's escape from the impending marital involvement. Major Kovalyov is triumphant at the end of "The Nose" in having escaped the snares of matrimony (with his nose intact); Podkolyosin in the play *Marriage* has to jump from a second-story window to effect a similar escape; Khlestakov in *The Inspector General* and Chichikov in *Dead Souls* are about to be exposed for the frauds that they are, but in both cases the ominous subject of matrimony is brought up, alerting these worthies to the perils of staying further in the towns they are visiting and precipitating their escapes.

The pattern is too self-evident and too persistent to be accidental. Gogol's correspondence provides us with some further examples. As his younger sisters grew up one by one and found the men they wanted to marry, Gogol's reaction to the announcements of their engagements was invariably negative. He usually asked his mother to reconsider, to withdraw her consent, and if possible to cancel the engagement, even though he knew very little of his sisters' situations and had not met the men involved. When a painter friend brought a bundle of baby clothes to his St. Petersburg apartment and Gogol realized what the bundle contained, he grabbed it and flung it out the window in horror. What could he have been afraid of? Neither in life nor in the literature of his time were marriage or other forms of personal involvement between men and women as closely associated with fear and danger as they seem to have been in Gogol's mind. But what he himself craved was emotional and sexual involvement with other men, and that was indeed a dangerous area, both in terms of social disapproval and, considering Gogol's fundamentalist religious beliefs, in terms of eventual divine retribution. It is perhaps not too far-fetched to postulate a kind of substitution that took place in Gogol's mind and found recurrent expression in his work: since his own emotional and sexual needs could expose him to danger, *all* desire for emotional and sexual involvement, in whatever form, was dangerous and one would do best to avoid it. However, another and far more simple explanation also suggests itself. Since all the men of his age group that he knew were interested in women and were headed for marriage and Gogol wanted no part of either, his recurrent depiction of woman, love, and marriage as dangerous and frightening may have been his way of rationalizing to himself and to the world why he lacked all interest in what everyone else considered desirable and normal.

Several critics (Vasily Gippius more conclusively than anyone, in his excellent second chapter, called "Demonology and Farce") have pointed out that the Dikanka stories are primarily concerned with the intrusion of supernatural forces into an otherwise orderly existence. Except for "Ivan Fyodorovich Shponka and His Aunt," where they are absent, and "The Fair at Sorochintsy," where they have a natural explanation and are the result of a hoax, supernatural forces are indeed rampant in Gogol's Romantic Ukraine. But they are evil and powerful only in the two horror stories, "Saint John's Eve" and "Terrible Vengeance." In "The Lost Letter" and "The Enchanted Spot" they are tamed and mastered with the aid of courage and Christian faith, while in the two "comic opera" stories, "May Night" and "Christmas Eve," the devil and the ghost of the drowned maiden are actually beneficial and aid the young lovers in overcoming the obstacles to their union. Perhaps it is because evil is not all-powerful in some of these stories and is not as firmly connected with sexuality as it would later become in *Mirgorod* that Gogol's treatment of both marriage and sexuality is far more relaxed in *Evenings on a Farm near Dikanka* than it would ever again be in his work.

Three out of the eight stories in the two volumes are actually allowed to end with happy marriages. In "May Night," the most consistently operatic of the stories, the lovers' union is the standard operatic happy ending, and its utter conventionality is redeemed only by the nice surrealistic touch of having the ghost of the drowned maiden draw on her connections in the provincial administrative hierarchy in order to remove the parental objections to the lovers' marriage. The marriages that terminate "The Fair at Sorochintsy" (where the image of mechanically dancing senile hags and the final lament in any case undermine the supposedly joyous finale) and especially "Christmas Eve" are on closer look not quite as conventional as they might appear at first glance. What we get in them are consummations of love triangles between a boy, a girl, and the girl's mirror. The innocent young Paraska in "The Fair at Sorochintsy" may be only an incipient narcissist, yet the thought of her lover immediately leads her to take out her pocket mirror and go into transports of self-admiration. But Oksana in "Christmas Eve" is perhaps the most detailed portrait of a female narcissist anywhere in Russian literature. Oksana's happiest moments are spent trying on her finery in front of her mirror, while reciting adoring speeches in praise of her own beauty. She initially rejects the heroic but rather simple-minded blacksmith who loves her, on the ground that he cannot match her in beauty and would look ludicrous if he tried to wear her ribbons and other adornments. Like the true narcissist she is, Oksana cannot imagine loving anyone but a replica of her own self. So she sets the blacksmith an impossible

Narcissistic Women and Impotent Men

task, which she is sure he cannot carry out, as the price of consenting to marry him, and haughtily dismisses him. But after his disappearance and the rumors of his death she at first feels guilty and then, in a moment of realization that comes in an erotic scene unparalleled anywhere else in Gogol ("tossing about in her bed in all of her bewitching nudity, which the darkness concealed even from her own self"), she comes to understand that the blacksmith's patience and persistence were a form of worship. It is at this point that she falls in love with him. In the brief epilogue to "Christmas Eve" we see Oksana holding a baby and standing in front of the beautifully ornamented house which the blacksmith has built for her. There is every indication that their marriage is a happy one.

Among the mature stories of Gogol's final period (artistically superior to his early Dikanka stories) we find one single instance of a happily married couple—in "The Carriage." The only things we learn about the pretty, blonde, and vapid wife of Chertokutsky in that story is that her relationship with her husband is an amiable one and that she spends hours on end in front of her mirror. Narcissistic women are not at all common in the literature of Gogol's time, and since he had no female friends or close acquaintances during his early years in St. Petersburg, it is not quite clear on what or on whom he could have patterned such narcissistic heroines. Yet the correctness of their psychological portraits is strikingly confirmed if one compares Oksana's motivations and attitudes to the excerpts from the journals of real-life narcissistic women, such as Maria Bashkirtseva and Isadora Duncan, which Simone de Beauvoir quotes in her book *The Second Sex*. Nor is there even a tinge of condemnation in Gogol's depiction of his female narcissists. He finds them amusing, but also congenial and, above all, *safe*. In Gogol's world, where women are often ominous and dangerous, a woman who is infatuated with her own image in the mirror is clearly the least demanding and the least manipulative, and therefore the safest choice for a man if he is foolhardy enough to wish to settle down with one.

Gogol's sympathy for female narcissism becomes even more evident if we examine the sexual symbolism of his nature descriptions in *Evenings on a Farm near Dikanka*. It has long been noted by critics that Gogol frequently sexualizes nature in these stories. While his human lovers express their amorous emotions only in highly lyricized, but on the whole, chaste operatic arias (Oksana alone is allowed her moment of nocturnal auto-eroticism), natural phenomena, such as the earth, the sky, and the rivers, are assigned specific genders (usually, but not always, coinciding with their grammatical genders in Russian) and then permitted to engage in explicit acts of sexual intimacy. However, as Julie Baker has established in her very perceptive unpublished paper on the subject, every time Gogol sets up such a sexual situation in his nature imagery, he is careful to see to it that no actual congress can take place, because the male element is either unable or unwilling to perform, while the female element is too narcissistic or too remote to be able to respond. Thus, in the frequently cited description of a hot summer day in the Ukraine which opens "The Fair at Sorochintsy," an "immeasurable blue ocean" (the sky) is voluptuously bending over the earth and, "bathed in languor," is squeezing her in his "aereal arms." But in the midst of this embrace the sky has fallen asleep and the "amorous earth," serenaded by the song of the lark, adorned by the gold of dry leaves and the emeralds, topazes, and rubies of colorful insects, does not seem to mind the passive inactivity of her celestial consort. This love-making position is reversed in the first section of "May Night," where the sleepy nocturnal pond (masculine gender) tries to make passionate love to the distant

Narcissistic Women and Impotent Men

stars that are reflected on his surface. The outcome is again inconclusive: "like an impotent old man, he held the remote, dark sky in his cold embrace, covering the fiery stars with his icy kisses."

In "The Fair at Sorochintsy," the Ukrainian river Psyol (on the banks of which the young Anton Chekhov was to spend two memorable and productive summers half a century later) is shown personified as a dazzling, self-enamored beauty who narcissistically bares her "silvery bosom" and uses the surrounding landscapes and the plants growing on her banks as her ever-changing wardrobe. The motivations and the reasoning that Gogol ascribes to the Psyol result in a psychological portrait which closely parallels that of Oksana in "Christmas Eve." By contrast, the mighty Dnieper, which plays an important role in "Terrible Vengeance," is shown as a heroic, but petulant and grouchy, male. Unlike the narcissistic Psyol, the Dnieper is at odds with the surrounding landscape and his own banks. For all of Gogol's eulogizing of his beauty, size, and power, the Dnieper is unhappy and depressed: "He does not rebel. He grumbles and complains like an old man, nothing satisfies him, for everything around him has changed. Quietly he feuds with the nearby mountains, forests, and meadows and he carries his complaint against them to the Black Sea."

A sleeping man, an impotent man, and a grouchy old grumbler—this is how Gogol personifies the male element in nature. And contrasted with them are the wide-awake, self-fulfilled, and satisfied female images of the beautiful summer earth and the beautiful river. As so often in Gogol, a powerful sexual imagination is clearly at work here. Both the literary conventions and the social customs of the time would tolerate no sexual expression other than heterosexual, and consequently Gogol has no other choice than to convey his visualization of sexualized na-

---

"Terrible Vengeance"

ture in heterosexual terms. But at the same time he invariably selects the kind of imagery and the form of personification that would effectively preclude the possibility of any sexual consummation.

The two most personal stories in *Evenings on a Farm near Dikanka* and also the most revealing and most prophetic for Gogol's subsequent evolution are "Terrible Vengeance" and "Ivan Fyodorovich Shponka and His Aunt," both in the second volume. While "Saint John's Eve," the horror story of the first volume, draws heavily on the conventions of Romantic opera and on traditional legend formulae, "Terrible Vengeance" is Gogol's authentically original vision of a universe in which humanity is at the mercy of incomprehensible diabolical forces. The plot involves three people: a hot-headed Cossack officer, Danilo, his wife Katerina, and Katerina's father. The father had departed for foreign lands when Katerina was a baby. (He seems to have spent his time in either Turkey or Poland, and it is indicative of Gogol's persistently xenophobic attitude that he refuses to differentiate in this story between the Moslem Turks and the Catholic Poles—both are equally infidels and it does not matter from which of them Katerina's father acquired his heathen ways). He returns when she is a married woman and a mother, and tries to run her life. At first the old man seems merely difficult and cantankerous; then he is gradually revealed to be a necromancer and the murderer of Katerina's mother. Furthermore, he burns with an evil, incestuous passion for his daughter. Danilo and Katerina try to protect themselves and their child against this devil-father, but they are powerless. When the father is locked up in a dungeon from which he cannot escape because its walls were once part of a monastery, Katerina does the one decent, humane thing that anyone ever does in the entire story: she saves her father from burning at the stake so that he can repent

"Terrible Vengeance"

and pray for the salvation of his soul. For that one act of pity, she forfeits the life of her husband, sees her child murdered in its cradle, is driven insane, and is finally stabbed to death. Then comes the father's retribution. In a brilliant hallucinatory sequence that involves distorted perspectives and angles of vision, the villain dashes all over the map of the Ukraine to end up in the Carpathian Mountains, where he is attacked by a group of gigantic corpses.

The scene before the father's end, in which he asks a holy hermit to pray for him, and the hermit receives a divine portent that this particular sinner *must not* be prayed for, is where Gogol reveals the pagan underpinnings of his moral vision in "Terrible Vengeance." In *The Golden Ass* by Apuleius, for example, both sin and misfortune are seen as contagious, and it is considered inadvisable to get involved with anyone sinful or unfortunate, lest one get punished by the gods. But surely there is no instance in the Christian tradition of the Christian God forbidding prayer for a repentant sinner.

The last section of "Terrible Vengeance" is an epilogue which is also a *Vorgeschichte*, an explanation for the horrible events just recounted. The main body of the work shows a world in which there is a Devil but seemingly no God. The epilogue reveals that God was aware of all the torture and carnage and in fact had authorized it all in advance as a form of revenge for a crime committed centuries ago by one of Katerina's ancestors. So both the father and Katerina's family were caught all along in a pre-programed hereditary nightmare, which God had planned in order to punish an ancestor of whom none of them had ever heard. Only Gogol could have dreamed up this merciless God, who inflicts such horrors on several generations because He cares nothing for reason, justice, or mercy, and is interested solely in punishment.

"Ivan Fyodorovich Shponka"

Couched in a hypnotic diction based on folk songs and folk laments, "Terrible Vengeance" is a grim and powerful work. It caught the imaginations of two great Russian writers of a later period. Fyodor Dostoyevsky used it as the basis for his third novel, *The Landlady*. Andrei Bely, in his book *Gogol's Mastery*, gave this story a dazzlingly imaginative, many-layered explication which is one of the most creative and inventive pieces of writing about any work of Gogol's. Only a total blindness to everything that Gogol is and says can account for the Russian tradition, persisting to this day, of considering "Terrible Vengeance" a work for juveniles and suitable for reading by children.

If the grim "Terrible Vengeance" provides us with important clues about Gogol's religious and metaphysical outlook, the whimsical and amusing "Ivan Fyodorovich Shponka and His Aunt" is one of our basic keys to his notions of the relationship between the sexes. Within the narrative framework of the Dikanka cycle, the other seven stories are supposedly told by the village beekeeper Panko[5] and his other rustic cronies. They depict a fairytalelike Ukraine of long ago and their protagonists are all peasants or Cossacks. The story about Shponka, however, is supposedly written by a man of Gogol's own social class, a provincial squire named Stepan Kurochka (that is, Stephen Little-Hen, a possible variation on Nikolai Gogol, which since *gogol'* means "goldeneye duck" may be translated as Nicholas Drake). It is the only story of the Dikanka cycle that is set in the present, portrays provincial Ukrainian gentry, and contains no magical or supernatural elements in any form. The story thus represents an important turning point in the development of Gogol's literary art.

Shponka (his name means "dowel" in Ukrainian) is the earliest of Gogol's meek, put-upon heroes of noble origin. He is not in

"Ivan Fyodorovich Shponka"

desperate straits, as his successors, Poprishchin in "Diary of a Madman" and Akaky Akakievich in "The Overcoat," would be, but he is of their kind—a weak, defenseless man caught in a world run by efficient, powerful, and incomprehensible beings. Like the hero of "The Overcoat," Shponka is also not entirely an adult human being, but rather a combination of a child and a puppet. Both as a schoolboy and as an army officer he is shown to be obedient, dull, self-absorbed, unsociable—and almost devoid of any other human qualities or dimensions. The full extent of dehumanization to which Gogol subjects Shponka becomes evident if one compares him to Ryabovich in Chekhov's "The Kiss"—a very similar personality in some similar situations, but shown by Chekhov as full-blooded, possessing a modicum of sociability and sexuality, and therefore real and quite touching. Gogol's story, for all its ostensible realism, is still very much in the puppet-show tradition, with its sad-sack hero at the mercy of other manipulative puppets, and it is structured largely in the form of duets between the hero and other characters.

The plot, such as it is, shows Shponka resigning his army commission and returning to his family estate, which is being run by his maiden aunt, Vasilisa. The aunt, a powerfully built, energetic matriarchal *and* patriarchal figure, is given to such unladylike pursuits as rowing, shooting game, farming, beating her serfs, and driving a hard bargain in her business transactions. The passive and infantile hero is totally at her mercy, but since the aunt is benevolent and loving, Shponka's situation is at first quite comfortable. A neighboring estate belongs to a heavyset and energetic man named Grigory Storchenko, who runs his household of female relatives with as firm a hand as Shponka's aunt runs hers. Storchenko likes Shponka—and a good thing, too, because there is a land dispute brewing between Storchenko and Shponka's aunt, and our hero would not stand a chance if he

"Ivan Fyodorovich Shponka"

were caught in a clash between these two overwhelming presences.

Then Shponka makes the fatal mistake of saying that he finds Storchenko's blonde sister, Masha, pretty. This gives his aunt the idea of settling the land dispute through the alliance of the two families by marriage. Shponka is a retired army officer, aged thirty-seven, but the possibility of marriage or any other contact with a willing, sexually available female had apparently never occurred to him. While, we are explicitly told, he had on two occasions enjoyed being embraced and kissed by the corpulent Storchenko, "whose fat cheeks felt like soft cushions to his lips," the only sensations he experiences when left alone with Storchenko's pretty sister are bewilderment and acute discomfort. But his preferences are not taken into account, and as the mechanism for arranging the marriage is about to be set in motion, Shponka's panic and sense of claustrophobia climax in an explosively surrealistic dream which suddenly ends the story at a completely unexpected point. The justification for ending the story with this dream—the beekeeper's wife has supposedly used the rest of the text for lining her cookie pan (but the reader is invited to look up Squire Kurochka, who will be glad to tell him how things worked out)—is a typically Romantic device, since the Romantics were fond of fracturing and fragmenting the well-rounded narrative structures they inherited from earlier periods. But the dream itself, totally Freudian and genuinely surrealistic, is a quantum jump of Gogol's imagination into the remote future. The wife in that dream is not the modest, blonde Masha Storchenko, but an incomprehensible invading force which possesses, in Hugh McLean's words, the power of infinite self-reduplication. There are wives in every corner of Shponka's room, a wife in his pocket, and still another one in a piece of cotton that he pulls out of his ear. Later in the dream, "wife" is the

"Ivan Fyodorovich Shponka"

name of a woolen fabric which Shponka is expected to have made into a frock coat and wear. His sense of being totally trapped is vividly spelled out in the passage where his aunt becomes a belfry and he is being hoisted to her top, despite his protestations that he is not a bell. The most surrealistic touch of all is supplied at this point by the colonel of Shponka's old regiment, who just happens to be walking by and who assures Shponka that he is indeed a bell.

The surrealistic portion of the story is a compressed variation on its preceding, relatively realistic sections. The underlying theme of this ostensibly amusing and witty story is deeply serious. On a general level that theme is the helplessness of any one particular person in the face of inexorable forces—not of Fate or the supernatural, as in the other Dikanka stories, but of normal societal processes, possibly beneficial to the majority but deadly for the individual who happens to be different from the rest. It is essentially the theme that was central to two of Russian literature's major masterpieces, Pushkin's "The Bronze Horseman" and Dostoyevsky's *Notes from the Underground*, and it is also one of the main themes of Franz Kafka and of the Theater of the Absurd. In specifically Gogolian terms, however, this theme finds its expression in the recurrent constellation of characters that has been analyzed with admirable insight by Leon Stilman in his essay "Brides, Bridegrooms, and Matchmakers." The constellation consists of a passive and willing young woman, a strong-willed and resourceful older woman, and a frightened, wary male whom the older woman is trying to trap into marriage with the younger woman. We meet this situation again in "The Nose," in *Marriage*, and in a slightly modified form in *The Inspector General*. It would be of course both naive and wrong to equate Gogol with the heroes of these works, but it is also all too clear that he lent these heroes one of his own most persistent

"Ivan Fyodorovich Shponka"

and deep-seated anxieties when he placed them in this particular constellation.

The importance of "Ivan Fyodorovich Shponka and His Aunt" for Gogol's subsequent development can hardly be overestimated. If both his realistic mode and his surrealistic one were discernible in "Ganz Küchelgarten" in embryonic form, it is in this story that he becomes aware of their possibilities and learns how to work with them. With hindsight we can discern in this story the sprouts that would later grow into "The Overcoat," "Diary of a Madman," "The Nose," "The Carriage," and portions of *Dead Souls* (the account of Chichikov's school years). One of the wittiest and most original scenes in *Marriage* is quite obviously a transposition and an expansion of Shponka's tonguetied interview with Masha Storchenko.

The first part of *Evenings on a Farm near Dikanka* was published in September of 1831 and the second in March of 1833. From the typesetters, who reportedly laughed their heads off while working on these books, to Alexander Pushkin, everyone in Russia loved these stories. As Pushkin later described the initial impression made by the two collections: "Everyone was delighted by this lively depiction of a singing and dancing tribe, by this fresh view of the Ukrainian nature, by this merriment that is both artless and sly. How astounded we all were to have a book that forced us to laugh, we who had not laughed since Fonvizin's time." In line with the literary tastes of the time, both critics and readers saw these stories as an entertaining retelling of authentic Ukrainian folk tales and legends (the hard currency *Beriozka*

Literary Success

stores in Moscow and Leningrad today sell lacquered wooden boxes inscribed "Evenings on a Farm near Dikanka," with lids that portray Gogol, looking as he did and dressed as he was in Rome in the 1840s, obediently taking down the story dictated to him by a Cossack beekeeper in the midst of a gaudy pumpkin patch, presumably in the Ukraine). It took about half a century for experts in Ukrainian customs and folklore to show how little Gogol really knew about such things; it took another half century for critics to see the actual roots of these stories in puppet theater and operatic conventions. But for all this, the Dikanka cycle, while by no means first-rate Gogol, remains a colorful and entertaining set of stories. Vladimir Nabokov's blanket dismissal of them (and also of the whole of *Mirgorod*) as so much immature junk has to be considered in the light of his similar dismissal of Molière and Stendhal.

Gogol's new literary success opened many important doors to him. He was able to leave his boring office job and take an appointment as a teacher at the Patriotic Institute, a boarding school for aristocratic young women which enjoyed the patronage of the Empress of Russia ("Her Majesty has commanded me to teach at her school," was the way Gogol announced this change to his mother). Through the intercession of the critic Pyotr Pletnyov, a close friend of Pushkin and the man to whom *Eugene Onegin* was dedicated, Gogol came to meet Pushkin, whom he had venerated since childhood. At that time Pushkin had only six years left to live. He valued Gogol's talent and encouraged him, but contacts between the two writers were too casual to have warranted the legend of personal closeness and intimacy that Gogol created and tried to foster in the years after Pushkin fell in his fateful duel. Of far greater importance and durability was Gogol's friendship with the poet Vasily Zhukovsky. Zhukovsky combined literary pursuits with his position as the tutor and preceptor to the heir to the Russian throne, the future liberator-tsar Alexander II, whose momentous reforms of the 1860s may have had their source in Zhukovsky's humanitarian influence.

The Genius to whom Gogol had addressed his impassioned invocation on that New Year's Eve did not let his prayer go unheeded. The year 1834 was indeed a year of dazzling achievement. The *Mirgorod* cycle was completed, to be followed almost immediately by the first stories of the St. Petersburg cycle. Two comedies were also in the works (*The Medal of Saint Vladimir, Third Class*, and an early version of *Marriage*). But Gogol's ambition was turning more and more in the direction of writing and teaching history. His preparation in this field consisted of nothing more than having taken a history course at Nezhin and having read a few popular German historians of the time whose works were available in Russian translation. Throughout 1833, Gogol made preparation for writing a multivolume history of the Ukraine. A book he wanted to call *The Earth and Its People*, based on his lectures at the Patriotic Institute, is also mentioned in his letters. In February of 1834, his essay "A Plan for Teaching Universal History" appeared in the *Journal of the Ministry of Education*, which was edited by the powerful and arch-reactionary Minister of Education, Sergei Uvarov. This entire trend culminated when Gogol prevailed on Pushkin, Pletnyov, and Zhukovsky to use their influence with Uvarov to get him appointed Professor of World History at St. Petersburg University. The appointment was clearly made on the strength of Gogol's literary reputation, since he lacked anything even remotely resembling academic qualifications or background.

Gogol's stint as a professor is one of the numerous instances in his life and his writings of that peculiarly Gogolian divorce between what is ordinarily perceived as cause and effect, of the

Professor of History

striking incongruity between the ends envisioned and the means suggested for achieving them. Gogol saw in professorship a way of getting a forum for his conception of history and then using this forum for the moral improvement of the finest young minds in Russia. But, as Vasily Gippius has so ably demonstrated in his chapter on Gogol's historical views (Chapter IV, "History"), humanity's past was for Gogol essentially a magical, fairy-tale world. Factual accuracy, written sources, precise information, all these things interested Gogol very little, and in this he is one more link in that grand nineteenth-century tradition of disdain for factual scholarship and exact sciences that stretches from Chateaubriand to Tolstoy. What he wanted to achieve was a brilliant synthesis, ablaze with sparkling rhetoric and as unencumbered by facts as possible. History, as it emerges from the essays and lectures later included in his book *Arabesques*, was for Gogol a wide-screen, technicolor spectacle, with a cast of millions, starring bloody conquerors (Attila the Hun and Genghis Khan held a particular fascination for Gogol) seen as evil magicians who occasionally get their comeuppance at the hands of medieval popes and saints depicted as kindly wizards. Gogol's view of history (and of geography as well, as his essay on teaching geography confirms) is obsessed with giganticism— size, distance, volume, numbers are always spectacular, unbelievable, extreme. Massacres and carnage are emphasized repeatedly and at length—a fact that points to a definite sado-masochistic component in Gogol's imagination, which portions of "Taras Bulba" and "Viy" also bear out. Everything is colorful and swirling and constantly exciting. As for the possible causes or results of all this vividly depicted turmoil, there is no evidence that Gogol thought there might be any, other than Divine Providence.

But Gogol's preoccupation with history was by no means con-

Professor of History

fined to imagination and rhetoric. Behind the verbal pyrotechnics was a solid purpose, which he spelled out clearly in the conclusion of his essay on the teaching of universal history:

> . . . my aim is to educate the hearts of my young auditors, to instill in them that solid sense of experience which history, understood in its true grandeur, opens up for us; to make their principles firm and manly, so that no frivolous fanatic, no passing excitement could make them waver; to turn them into meek, obedient, noble, and indispensable helpers of our Great Tsar; so that in fortune and misfortune, they would never betray their duty, their religion, their noble honor, and their allegiance—to be loyal to the Fatherland and the Tsar.

Just how Gogol's vision of history as a stupefying spectacle of blood and carnage was to effect this particular brainwashing operation is not clear. But it is easy to see why such sentiments must have pleased Uvarov, the coiner of the motto "Orthodoxy, Autocracy, Nationalism," which became the guiding principle for the most reactionary supporters of the tsarist regime for the rest of the nineteenth century, and why they had influenced him to approve Gogol's appointment to the university.

Gogol's actual teaching at the university was another one of those comedies of misunderstanding in which his life abounds. After the three initial lectures (on the Middle Ages, on the migration of the peoples, and on Arab conquests), which impressed the assembled literary luminaries, among them Pushkin and Zhukovsky, and dazzled his students, among them the future novelist Ivan Turgenev, Gogol seems simply to have run out of both the energy and the interest needed to pursue the profession for which he was so ill-suited. For the rest of the school year he either canceled his lectures or resorted to the same stratagem he had used at his audition with Prince Gagarin—he would appear

New Friends

with a bandaged cheek and, claiming toothache as his excuse, restrict his lecture to a few incoherent remarks. Despite the gentle admonitions of his immediate superior, the young vice-president of the Academy of Sciences, Prince Mikhail Dondukov-Korsakov, who received several complaints about Gogol's teaching and was informed of the possibility of a student demonstration against him, this situation dragged on for almost eighteen months before Gogol was asked to resign. Undaunted, he wrote to his Moscow correspondent, the historian Mikhail Pogodin: "The university and I have spat in each other's faces and a month from now I'll be a free Cossack again. Unrecognized, I ascended the podium and unrecognized I now leave it. But during the year and a half—the time of my disgrace, for the general opinion holds that I undertook something that I had no business undertaking—during this year and a half there were many good things that I acquired and there was much that I added to the treasure house of my soul. I am no longer agitated by childish ideas or by the previous narrow scope of my knowledge, but by lofty ideas full of truth and of terrifying grandeur" (letter of December 6, 1835).

Arabesques came out in January of 1835 and *Mirgorod* in March of that year. Gogol's literary position was more secure than ever. But his personal life must have been lonely and frustrating. The important literary contacts which his success brought him were just that. For all the warmth and friendliness of Gogol's correspondence with Zhukovsky and Pushkin, with the Moscow writer Aksakov and the Kievan historian Mikhail Maximovich, none of these people could give him the kind of friendship he longed for. He was in touch with the members of his Ukrainian circle, but they all had their own lives and interests by now. Yet the yearning for intimacy, closeness, and physical touch keeps breaking through in Gogol's letters dating from his

New Friends

St. Petersburg period. These impulses were probably uncon-
scious and they were directed at people who were not at all likely
to be receptive, but they are there, again and again. Writing to
Pyotr Pletnyov from Kursk on his return from a visit with his
mother in the Ukraine, Gogol concludes the letter: "Until then, I
embrace you in my thoughts a 1001 times and remain forever
your Gogol. You cannot possibly imagine how I burn with the
longing to see you. Only a lover flying to a tryst with his beloved can compare with me" (letter of October 9, 1832).

Gogol first met Mikhail Pogodin on June 30, 1832, when he
passed through Moscow on his way to the Ukraine. Primarily a
historian, Pogodin was an important figure in Russian literary
life for much of the nineteenth century. He had wide-ranging literary contacts outside of Russia as well as within it, and he is the
subject of what may well be the most extensive literary biography ever written, Nikolai Barsukov's fascinating *Mikhail Pogodin's Life and Labors*, published in twenty-two volumes between
1888 and 1910. At their first meeting, Gogol and Pogodin discovered a mutual interest in teaching history. But there must
have been more to this meeting for Gogol, for he concluded the
first letter he wrote to Pogodin after resuming his journey as follows: "Farewell my priceless Mikhail Petrovich, brother of my
soul! I clasp your hand. Perhaps this handclasp has reached you
before my letter. You must have felt your hand squeezed by
someone, if only in your sleep. It was squeezed by your Gogol"
(letter of July 8, 1832). Two weeks later, writing to Pogodin
from his parents' estate, Vasilievka, Gogol indulged in a little
daydream: "I long to and can hardly wait to embrace you in person. Do you know, I have been imagining (I have quite a fantasy
for such things) that you might suddenly arrive to visit me at our
estate." The next sentence is disfigured by a censor's cut in all
available editions of Gogol's letters and also in Barsukov's biography of Pogodin. In Russian it reads: *Ya vas* [. . .] *i chem dalee,*

New Friends

tem neveroyatnee. The subject is "I," the direct object is "you" (in the accusative case). The only way to translate this into English is "I [do something to] you and the more [I do it?], the more incredible it becomes." Whatever it was the censors deleted, it surely could not have been more suggestive than the version they left us.

The rest of the passage quoted above goes as follows: "For the time being, I'm still resting. However, I did give birth to two ideas pertaining to our favorite science, which I will show off to you some day. Farewell, Mikhail Petrovich. I kiss you fifty times." Pogodin was at the time seriously considering getting married and was soon forced to make his final choice between the two young women with whom he was involved. Gogol's gushing effusions could not have been particularly welcome and Pogodin must have made Gogol realize this, because his subsequent letters to Pogodin are couched in a much more restrained tone. Their contact continued for the rest of Gogol's life and their relationship had its ups and downs. Gogol thought Pogodin's plan to start publishing a journal in 1839 was ill-advised and wrote a long letter to dissuade him. After citing various literary and practical objections to the venture, Gogol's letter suddenly lapses into an extremely emotional tone: "No, this would be on my conscience. I will beg you on my knees, I will fling myself at your feet. My life, and heart of my heart (*dusha moya*), you know how precious you are to me, as precious as life itself" (letter of November 4, 1839).[6] In one of his letters from Italy, Gogol claimed that the children Pogodin had by his wife were also, in part, his children. But he attacked Pogodin nastily on both personal and literary grounds in *Selected Passages from Correspondence with Friends*; yet this somehow did not prevent Gogol from staying with Pogodin as his house guest during a visit to Moscow a short time after the book was published.

Another striking passage is found in the letter Gogol wrote on

June 27, 1834, to the Kievan folklorist and historian Mikhail
Maximovich, with whom he made plans to settle when he applied for a teaching position in history at Kiev University. Making plans for a joint tour of the Ukraine, Gogol writes: "I would
take you to the banks of the Psyol where we could sunbathe in
the nude and swim . . ." Then, as if feeling that was going too
far, Gogol concludes the sentence with: "and in addition I would
marry you off to a pretty girl, if not to a super-pretty one." (A
similar instance of Gogol's way of betraying attraction for the
male physique and then instantly retracting it occurs in the form
of a salutation used in his brief note to Pushkin's friend, the epi-
grammatist Sergei Sobolevsky, of April 17, 1836: "My tall,
husky, and appetizing for the ladies Sobolevsky!") Most of Gogol's letters to Maximovich about moving to Kiev are not particularly suggestive, however. Instead, they ache with a scarcely
concealed loneliness. For all of his social and literary contacts,
Gogol again and again writes to Maximovich of the simple joy of
getting a little house in Kiev next door to that of Maximovich
and of his wish to have just one close and constant friend.

Anyone who has studied closely the biography of Alexander
Pushkin must be aware that there were prominent and in some
cases highly visible homosexual circles in St. Petersburg at the
time of Gogol's stay there. One such coterie was grouped around
Baron Jacob Theodore van Heeckeren, the Dutch ambassador to
Russia. It included the two principal villains in the complex
drama that cost Pushkin his life: the young Prince Pyotr Dol-
goruky, author of the anonymous letter that set in motion the
events that led to the duel; and the man who killed Pushkin,
Georges D'Anthès, Heeckeren's adopted son and also apparently
his lover before he switched his attentions to Pushkin's wife. At
an earlier stage of his life, Pushkin was a good friend of the
memoirist Philip Vigel (or Wiegel), an important government

St. Petersburg Homosexuals

official who was quite open about his homosexual preferences. During his exile in Bessarabia, Pushkin addressed to Vigel a remarkably tolerant and broad-minded epistle in verse, inviting him for a visit and offering to introduce him to two handsome local brothers who he thought would be responsive to Vigel's advances.

Closer to Gogol's own home ground, his direct supervisor at St. Petersburg University, Prince Mikhail Dondukov-Korsakov, owed his high position in the academic and educational world not to any qualifications, but to his widely known love affair with the Minister of Education, Uvarov, who was a married man and a father. Dondukov-Korsakov's appointment to the position of Vice-President of the Imperial Academy of Sciences was made for such obviously nepotistic reasons that Pushkin was able to ridicule it in a widely circulated epigram which in a punning form revealed Dondukov-Korsakov's *real* qualifications for the job. Thus there was apparently considerable tolerance of homosexual behavior in the very highest social echelon of Gogol's time. Most of the homosexuals we know about, for instance, Vigel, Uvarov, and Dondukov-Korsakov, were also extremely conservative in their political orientation, and this tradition was carried on in the second half of the nineteenth century by the arch-reactionary and openly homosexual writer Vladimir Meshchersky and by the poet Alexei Apukhtin, Peter Tchaikovsky's one-time lover. The tolerance of male homosexuality in high society and the upper governmental sphere is also reported, with revulsion and indignation, by Lev Tolstoy in several significant passages in Book Two of his novel *Resurrection*.

What made Gogol different from such men? For one thing, he did not really belong to the highest social stratum, where Heeckeren's and Uvarov's friends moved. But more important, for all their political conservatism neither Vigel nor Uvarov were noted

St. Petersburg Homosexuals

for the kind of all-pervading religiosity that was so significant in Gogol's life. Being practicing homosexuals thus did not do any violence to their image of themselves. In Gogol's case, the role of religion must have been decisive. A recent study, *Male Homosexuals: Their Problems and Adaptations*, by Martin S. Weinberg and Colin T. Williams (London and Toronto, 1974), contains two chapters which investigate the relationship between religion and homosexuality. Basing their conclusions on statistical studies carried out in three present-day societies (the United States, Holland, and Denmark), which presumably have more permissive attitudes than the society in which Gogol lived, the authors point out that, since most Western religions regard homosexuality as a grave sin, "religious homosexuals may be more likely to experience a conflict between their sexual orientation and their beliefs. Feeling pressure to work out some accommodation between their homosexuality and their religious beliefs, some religious homosexuals may try to suppress their sexual orientation" (p. 252). This must have been what Gogol did during his St. Petersburg period, at least in his private life. The explosive force with which sexual themes push their way to the surface of his consciousness in the four *Mirgorod* stories suggests how desperate this suppression must have been and the violence of the counter-reaction it aroused in his inner self.

Mirgorod means "Peacetown." It was the title Gogol gave to his book that contained four long stories (or perhaps three stories and one short novel): "Old-World Landowners," "Taras Bulba," "Viy," and "The Tale of How Ivan Ivanovich Quarreled

Sexuality in Mirgorod

with Ivan Nikiforovich" (the last will be referred to hereafter as "The Two Ivans" for the sake of convenience). Where the Dikanka stories, except for "Ivan Fyodorovich Shponka and His Aunt," were set in a fairy-tale-like Ukraine of the eighteenth and early nineteenth centuries, *Mirgorod* moves into new territory historically and geographically, as well as socially. Two of the stories—"Old-World Landowners" and "The Two Ivans"—are about members of the Ukrainian gentry of Gogol's own time. "Taras Bulba" is a historical novel, set apparently in several centuries all at once and with action ranging over vast territories. "Viy" is situated in the city of Kiev and in a nearby village; its action seems to be in the eighteenth century.

But while the arrangement of the respective stories into groups of four was somewhat arbitrary and mechanical in the two parts of the Dikanka cycle (each part consisted of one horror story, one comic opera in story form, one puppet play in story form, and one story about the village deacon's dashing Cossack grandfather), the stories in *Mirgorod,* for all their apparent heterogeneity, possess a thematic unity that truly makes them a cycle. All four are basically variations on the same central theme: the orderly, adjusted existence of one man, two men, or a group of men is catastrophically disrupted by a sudden, forced confrontation with sexuality in one form or another.

The significance of sexual themes, images, and symbols in *Mirgorod* and the importance of that entire cycle for our understanding of Gogol's sexual attitudes was not generally perceived until the American scholar Hugh McLean read his paper "Gogol's Retreat from Love: Toward an Interpretation of *Mirgorod*" at the Fourth International Congress of Slavicists, held in Moscow in 1958. Considering the location of the congress, the paper was provocative in two major ways: it offered a totally new interpretation of Gogol which diverged from the views of him

Sexuality *in* Mirgorod

that were held by nineteenth-century Russian utilitarian critics and that are the only acceptable views of Gogol in the Soviet Union, and it used a Freudian approach to arrive at its conclusions. As it happens, a Freudian analysis of Gogol's life and work had already been attempted by the Soviet psychiatrist Dr. Ivan Yermakov, whose book was brought out by the State Publishing House in 1924, at a time when the Soviet government had not yet banned all scholarship that sought to explain reality in any terms other than Marxist-Leninist. Yermakov's study contains a number of highly interesting observations, particularly in his examination of "The Two Ivans," but like many Freudians (or Marxists, or Structuralists, or any other scholars who draw on a theory developed in a nonliterary field to explain a work of literature), he is primarily interested in using Gogol to demonstrate and assert the principles of his chosen doctrine. McLean's paper belongs to the opposite and far more rare and valuable variety. He uses Freudian insights to explain and illuminate the content of the four *Mirgorod* stories from an entirely new and wholly convincing angle.

The reaction of the official Soviet literary-critical establishment to McLean's paper was one of disbelief and outrage. Hadn't the great revolutionary-democratic critics of the nineteenth century and the Soviet critics from the 1930s on established once and for all that "Old-World Landowners" and "The Two Ivans" were pointed, socially progressive satires on the idle and parasitic Ukrainian gentry, that "Taras Bulba" was a great patriotic epic celebrating the Ukrainian people's fight for their independence, and that "Viy" was a reworking of a folk legend into an allegory about an upper-class exploiter-witch who rides on the back of the young student representing the Ukrainian people?[7] Now McLean comes along, claiming that "Old-World Landowners" is a portrayal of infantile regression to an oral-gratification

Sexuality in Mirgorod

stage, and that "The Two Ivans" depicts an unsuccessful search for escape from sexual and emotional commitment into a chaste friendship with a member of the same sex, while "Taras Bulba" and "Viy" are death wish re-enactments, in the first case with obvious Oedipal overtones. Furthermore, McLean convincingly connected the Freudian elements in the four stories to Gogol's own repeatedly expressed aversion to heterosexual emotional and sexual involvement. The shock of the Soviet critical establishment and the denunciations of McLean's paper in Soviet journals[8] are understandable. Less easy to understand is the ignoring of this ground-breaking study by various Western scholars who have written about Gogol since 1958.

The examination of the four *Mirgorod* stories that follows owes to McLean's paper its central insight about their sexual content, but it will proceed along non-Freudian lines. A reader interested in a Freudian examination of Gogol's sexuality is referred to that paper, which is far more complex and perceptive than the brief summary of it above can indicate. Also, to forestall the possible accusation that the author of this book is obsessed with sexual themes to the exclusion of everything else, let it be admitted at the outset that the four *Mirgorod* stories are not exclusively or even primarily concerned with sex. They are indeed what they are traditionally considered to be: "Old-World Landowners" is an idyllic depiction of Ukrainian rural life, "Taras Bulba" is a military romance that oddly manages to blend devices borrowed from Homer's *Iliad* with those of Scott's novels, "Viy" is a Gothic horror story that continues the line of "Saint John's Eve" and "Terrible Vengeance," and "The Two Ivans" is a satirical, comic story about two useless, idle people in a provincial town. But, in addition to all these self-evident dimensions, each of the four stories contains a central sexual theme, and these themes and their relationship to similar themes

---

"Old-World Landowners"

in the other stories of the cycle form a very definite pattern that gives us a key to much of what Gogol is about.

"Old-World Landowners" and "The Two Ivans" were written before the other two stories; furthermore, Gogol left them as they appeared in the original edition of *Mirgorod*, whereas "Viy" and especially "Taras Bulba" underwent considerable later revisions. It is therefore more convenient, both chronologically and thematically, to begin with these two stories, rather than follow the order in which Gogol himself arranged them in the book. Vasily Gippius has ingeniously called "Old-World Landowners" Gogol's middle idyll or middle utopia—the first one being the bucolic valley in which the action of "Ganz Küchelgarten" takes place, and the last one the oligarchic, slave-owning utopia described in certain portions of Gogol's last book, *Selected Passages from Correspondence with Friends*. The story is an idealized transposition of the Philemon and Baucis myth from Ovid's *Metamorphoses* into a patriarchal landed estate in the rural Ukraine. The "Old-World" of the title designates manor and serf owners, who belonged to old-fashioned society (no opposition between the Old World and New World is implied in the original Russian title). In the first few pages, Gogol's narrator explains that he is fond of the old, noble Ukrainian families, whose money and property have been in the family for generations, and contrasts them with contemptuously described Ukrainian *nouveaux riches* of more recent vintage. Being as conservative socially as he was politically, Gogol expresses here his unequivocal preference for the old gentry and his distaste for the new gentry of plebeian origin, not realizing, obviously, what light this cast on his own family's record.

Like their prototypes in Ovid, Gogol's modern Philemon and Baucis, who are named Afanasy Ivanovich and Pulcheria Ivanovna, lead a touchingly simple and gracious life on their remote

"Old-World Landowners"

estate, which, as Alexei Remizov has perceptively observed, is also the Garden of Eden before the Fall. Theirs is the only truly meaningful and happy marriage that we find anywhere in Gogol. The couple is very different indeed from the cardboard operatic lovers or the female narcissists and their male worshippers of the Dikanka stories and from the grotesque couples that populate the landed estates of Great Russia in *Dead Souls*. Pulcheria is perhaps Gogol's most attractively presented, safest, and least threatening female character. Her marriage to Afanasy is solidly built on mutual respect, companionship, and touching concern for each other's welfare. There is only one thing missing from this otherwise perfect marriage: any kind of sexual involvement. Afanasy is sixty and Pulcheria is fifty-five. Gogol expects his readers to assume that at that age they are too senile to have any interest in such things. But just in case anyone does not get this point, we are explicitly told that they have separate bedrooms and that all romantic aspects of their relationship belonged only to the very earliest stage of their marriage, when they eloped together many years ago. At the time the reader meets them, their relationship is purely fraternal. If we were not told that they were husband and wife, we might assume that they were a brother and a sister living under the same roof, a point that is further emphasized by their having the same patronymic, which would normally imply that they had the same father.

This chaste and innocent old couple is placed by Gogol in an environment whose two main qualities could not coexist in the natural order of things: a lavish fertility and a total absence of all sexuality. The surrounding land is bountiful, the plants and animals ceaselessly breed and proliferate. The housemaids who work for the couple continually become pregnant, but we are assured by the narrator that no men were involved in all these pregnancies, since the only male member of the household apart from Afanasy is a little serving boy who is too young to be sexually active. The main sensual outlet for all—the masters (who share one huge festive meal a day and about ten minor ones, including several snacks during the night), the housemaids, the housekeeper, and even the pigs and the geese—is constant overeating. Not surprisingly, frequent stomach aches are a normal part of everyone's lives.

There is a curious reversal of the expected roles in running the household in "Old-World Landowners." Afanasy, the husband, leads a dronelike existence of almost total inactivity. Apart from an occasional outing to the fields, where he watches the mowers, he plays almost no part in running the estate. His only other function is chasing the geese away from the front porch and preventing them from entering the house, which he does every day, after having had his morning coffee. We know from reading about the goose-faced wives in Ivan Shponka's dream and from the role of geese and ganders in "The Two Ivans" that these domestic fowl had a symbolic association with sex for Gogol. Afanasy's quotidian repulsion of their invasion might therefore suggest that it was he rather than his wife who was the keeper and preserver of chastity in the family.

Pulcheria is the more active and imaginative of the spouses. It is she who does whatever management of the estate and the house gets done—a situation unthinkable in any of Tolstoy's novels (especially *Family Happiness*), but one that had its prototypes both in Gogol's fiction ("Ivan Fyodorovich Shponka and His Aunt") and in his life. As the elder son of an estate-owning family, he would naturally have been expected to take over the management of the family estate after his graduation from school. Gogol, however, left those matters to his mother and his sisters throughout his adult life, so it must have been natural for him to imagine estates run by women, a situation that was not all that usual in Russian or Ukrainian life in his time. Pulcheria inspects the property and the forests, deals with the bailiff, stores up endless supplies of jams, preserves, and liqueurs. Fortunately, a bountiful nature supplies Afanasy, Pulcheria, and their retainers with plenty of food and other necessities—fortunately, because she is not a very effective manager and all those around the couple, not only their bailiff and servants, but even the guests of their own class whom they receive so graciously, constantly steal them blind. Simply by virtue of their innocently patriarchal ways and their love for each other, Afanasy and Pulcheria live in prosperity and plenty. When their nephew, who inherits their estate, tries to run it in a more normal and rational manner, he somehow manages to ruin it within a year.

Only the most tendentious reader or one blinded by the standard sociological presuppositions of traditional Russian criticism could read "Old-World Landowners" and see in it an indictment of any social class or way of life. Gogol may poke gentle fun at the elderly couple's naiveté, their gluttony, their limited horizon, but he also clearly loves them, admires them, and is charmed by them. They are the very personification of that comfortable life devoid of all change for which Gogol shows such high regard in his essays in *Arabesques* and *Selected Passages*. Not only are they touching in his view, but they have also solved the problem of how to live in closeness and affection with another human being while escaping from the menace of either distasteful and terrifying heterosexual sex or forbidden homosexual sex. And indeed, Afanasy and Pulcheria are the only people anywhere in Gogol who have truly solved it.

Can anything threaten this secluded, idyllic, settled life? Yes, of course: old age and death. So death does appear on the scene, but in a guise that would make little sense anywhere but in a work by Gogol. It comes in the form of a confrontation with the sexual urge and the realization of its pervasive power. The agent of this confrontation is Pulcheria's pet gray cat, the third principal character in the story and another one of Gogol's animals that function as sexual symbols. This demure and shy little feline is the animal-world counterpart of Ovid's Baucis (whose name means "over-modest") and of Pulcheria herself. But, being an animal, the cat is not very good at suppressing her sexual urge. Unlike the self-impregnating housemaids, she brings the entire subject into the open.

The little gray cat is seduced by some feral tomcats who live in the woods ("the way a foolish peasant girl is seduced by a platoon of soldiers") and leaves the house to join them. She returns briefly later, bedraggled and starving, but as soon as she is fed, she flees to the woods again. The message that the cat brings to her mistress is that a life of anarchic freedom and sexual fulfillment is preferable to the sedate, comfortable, but sexless existence of Afanasy and Pulcheria. This is, of course, a message that Pulcheria cannot accept or even confront. But its impact is so devastating that she chooses to see in the cat's return a portent of her own death. With touching concern, she arranges for her husband-brother (or, perhaps, husband-child) to be taken care of and looked after and then, in a scene that turned out to be uncannily prophetic of the circumstances of Gogol's own death, stops eating, lies down, and dies.

The reading of the sexual emancipation of the cat as an agent of death might have seemed far-fetched if "Old-World Landowners" were not a part of a cycle in which this same message is spelled out in every single one of the stories in one form or another. This interpretation is, moreover, also supported by the account of the origin of "Old-World Landowners." According to the famous folklorist Alexander Afanasiev, the actor Mikhail

"Old-World Landowners"

Shchepkin told Gogol that his grandmother took the return of her missing cat for a death portent. This was supposedly the genesis of "Old-World Landowners." When Shchepkin saw Gogol shortly after the publication of *Mirgorod*, he jokingly exclaimed: "Why, that was *my* little cat!" "Yes, but the tomcats are mine," Gogol replied, confirming the importance of the sexual theme for the basic conception of the story.

"Old-World Landowners" belongs among Gogol's very finest achievements—a nearly flawless piece of writing. With almost no story to tell, Gogol lets his style and tone hold everything together and it works. The story's reputation as one of the fountainheads of Russian realism is, however, both exaggerated and undeserved. It is too idyllic and at the same time too hyperbolic to be any kind of slice of Ukrainian rural life. Ukrainian land may be fertile, but it does not possess the kind of lush, tropical fecundity Gogol depicts. No estate could be subjected to pilfering on such a huge scale and go on functioning. With all that constant overeating, everyone in the story should be enormously obese—and yet no one is. With the field flowers and grasses invading a traveler's carriage and the doors singing and speaking in the Tovstogub home, surrealistic fantasy gently raises its head here and there. As is so often the case in Gogol, just when the surface texture of the life he is describing seems most vivid and believable, a closer look reveals his imagination and fantasy steadily working underneath.

Whereas "Old-World Landowners" is a patriarchal idyll, the *Mirgorod* story Gogol wrote just before it, "The Two Ivans," is a

"The Two Ivans"

broad farce with overtones of social satire. The fictitious first-person narrator in "Old-World Landowners" was a cultivated, self-effacing person, a friend and guest of Afanasy and Pulcheria. The fictitious narrator in "The Two Ivans" is quite different. He is an inveterate gossip, an irrepressibly good-natured chatterbox, eager to tell the reader everything he knows. He is also a bit dull-witted and something of a Pollyanna, not realizing that many of the things he finds so delightful and admirable are actually quite unattractive or unpleasant. This obtrusive, gushing busybody introduces the reader to the two protagonists of the story, whom he considers wonderful, lovely people, but who, as is quickly revealed, are anything but that: the tall, thin, prudish, and prissy Ivan Ivanovich, an absurd pedant, with his dated and labeled melon seeds, whose unfeeling cruelty is revealed during his conversation with a starving peasant woman he meets at church; and the short and fat Ivan Nikiforovich, a slob and a glutton, who leads a life of almost total immobility.

The two Ivans are friends and neighbors. Both are noblemen who reside in the small town of Mirgorod (which supplies the title for the entire cycle of stories), supported by the produce of the farms they own in the outlying area. One is a widower, the other an old bachelor. They have sex lives of sorts, which the prudish narrator gradually reveals to the reader, seemingly without realizing the full import of what he is saying. The more resourceful and better organized Ivan Ivanovich has a convenient arrangement with his serf girl Gapka (a colloquial and contemptuous Ukrainian version of Agatha), by whom he has children he cannot officially acknowledge as his own, but who call him "Daddy" nonetheless. The obese and inactive Ivan Nikiforovich has a part-time mistress, a rather horrifying noblewoman who visits him periodically and at such times takes him and his entire household into her hands (the narrator, after outlining the situa-

---

"The Two Ivans"

tion, pretends to be totally puzzled by the causes of her influence). Not only do the two protagonists have the same first name, but so do the women in their lives. Ivan Nikiforovich's mistress is named Agafya (the Russian and Church Slavic version of Agatha) Fedoseyevna and she is as castrating a female as one is likely to meet anywhere in literature.

Gogol might almost have deliberately created Agafya Fedoseyevna to fit the needs of his future Freudian exegetes. Her *modus operandi* throughout the story is to grab men by some protruding part in order to dominate and subjugate them. She is casually and briefly introduced in the very first paragraph as "the very same Agafya Fedoseyevna who bit off the tax assessor's ear." Once she arrives at Ivan Nikiforovich's house, she grabs him by his plum-shaped nose (both literally and figuratively) and forces him to change his mode of life for the rest of her stay. Outwardly she is as grotesque and unpleasant a woman as Gogol could get away with depicting without offending his readers with his misogyny: "Agafya Fedoseyevna wore a bonnet on her head, three warts on her nose, and a coffee-colored dressing gown with a yellow flower pattern. Her body was shaped like a tub and because of this it would be as hard to locate her waist as to see your own nose without a mirror. Her legs were short and shaped like two plump pillows. She gossiped and ate boiled beets for breakfast and was very good at scolding; and throughout these varied pursuits, her face never for a moment changed its expression, something that usually only women can manage." (The boiled beets for breakfast and the three warts listed among the wearing apparel are typical of the stretching of logic and other forms of surrealistic humor in which Gogol indulges throughout this story.)

It is surely not accidental that this distillate of everything that frightened and repelled Gogol about women should appear in the one story that under its comic veneer postulates at least a possibility of homosexual attachment between men. In general, the relationships between the two Ivans and their respective Agathas are highly instructive. The more subtle and more active Ivan Ivanovich simply uses the woman, who is his personal property, as a convenience. Situations in which men employ women for procreative purposes and as mere vehicles for sexual release, while remaining in full control, do not particularly alarm Gogol, as can be seen from the relationships between Taras Bulba and his wife, between Major Kovalyov in "The Nose" and the lower-class women with whom he flirts, and between Homa Brut in "Viy" and the market women to whom he occasionally rents his sexual services in exchange for food, lodging, and money. It is when the woman is treated as an equal, when she is allowed to get the upper hand, or when the man's love or desire for her make him lose control that things become unpleasant, unmanageable, and eventually lethal.

While Ivan Ivanovich uses his Agatha, Ivan Nikiforovich is used by his. This harridan is a noblewoman, his social equal, far more active and forceful than he, and he is simply stuck with her. But things are not really tragic for Ivan Nikiforovich, merely inconvenient. Agafya Fedoseyevna moves in with him only now and then, staying at her own home in another town most of the time. During her absences, he is only too happy to console himself with the close and affectionate friendship that unites him to his neighbor Ivan Ivanovich. There is no trace of affection or emotional involvement in the two men's respective relationships with the women in their lives. Instead, the two direct whatever emotion or affection they are capable of at each other. For all the amusing non sequiturs that the narrator piles up to describe their friendship, there is no mistaking the depth of their commitment to each other and of their mutual need. Their involvement with

"The Two Ivans"

each other is, in fact, the only likable thing about either of them. Indeed, if we accept the sexless relationship between the two old people in "Old-World Landowners" as a true heterosexual marriage, the closeness between the two men that Gogol describes at the beginning of "The Two Ivans" is something suspiciously like a sexless homosexual marriage. Except for sharing the same house, all the components of the bond that unites Afanasy and Pulcheria in "Old-World Landowners" are present: companionship, mutual respect, concern for the other's comfort, and even occasional gentle joshing of the kind that spouses are likely to indulge in. They are so inseparable that one of their fellow townsmen comments that the devil himself must have tied them together with a string.

These two dissimilar but mutually compatible men go on living in friendship and harmony in the small town where everyone for some unfathomable reason respects and admires them until they are separated by the violent quarrel that begins in the second chapter of the story. The provocation for the quarrel seems so minor and the circumstances that aggravate and intensify it so patently insignificant that traditional Russian criticism chose to read this part of the story as social satire plain and simple: supposedly Gogol's only aim in showing us these two silly, narrow-minded people who quarrel on a trifling or nonexistent pretext is to expose the pettiness and uselessness of the landowning gentry as a class. But if one reads the description of the quarrel closely and with attention to detail (which, in any case, is the only way of reading Gogol), one will see that it all adds up to a complicated symbolic charade on sexual themes.

The gross and crude Ivan Nikiforovich, it turns out, owns an elegant hunting rifle which he does not use or need. His more subtle and delicate friend Ivan Ivanovich feels that *he* would be a more fitting owner of that rifle. When his friend refuses to give it to him, Ivan Ivanovich offers a trade: he will give a pig and two bags of oats in exchange for the rifle. The Freudian Dr. Yermakov, who hunted diligently for phallic symbols throughout Gogol's work, must have felt that he had really hit pay dirt with "The Two Ivans." And indeed it would be hard to think of another work of literature as satisfying in this respect, what with the radish-shaped heads of the two heroes, the assessor's bitten-off ear, Ivan Nikiforovich's plum-shaped nose, which is constantly being grabbed by Agafya Fedoseyevna, and the discussion of whether or not he has a tail. However, Yermakov does seem to be onto something with his phallic interpretation of the nature of the proposed exchange. The rifle is an elegant, precise, and functional object which Ivan Ivanovich feels must correspond to his own sexuality rather than to that of his friend. His offer of an exchange may thus be interpreted on the symbolic level as: "You now have the symbol for my kind of stylish and functional sexuality. I want it, and in exchange I will give you your own kind of crude and sluggish sexuality in the form of a pig and two bags of oats."[9] Gogol himself would of course have reacted with horror and indignation to such an interpretation of the story, but if the symbolism is taken into consideration, the offer does indeed look like a veiled homosexual proposition.

Ivan Nikiforovich rejects the offer with considerable violence and, to top things off, insults Ivan Ivanovich by calling him a gander, that is, the male of goose. This is not normally an insulting word in either Russian or Ukrainian—it is absurd and inappropriate, rather than offensive. The fury of Ivan Ivanovich's reaction to this appellation becomes clearer if we again go along with Yermakov and agree that the gander, like the rifle and the pig, is a phallic symbol, and that by calling his friend a gander Ivan Nikiforovich exposes the sexual nature of the proposed exchange. There are precedents elsewhere in Gogol that confirm

"The Two Ivans"

the sexual interpretation of the three symbols. In "Old-World Landowners," Pulcheria asserts that her sixty-year-old husband cannot possibly leave her and go off to war because "his firearms had become rusty from disuse." As mentioned previously, geese in "Old-World Landowners" make unsuccessful attempts to enter the house from the front porch and have to be routed by Afanasy. Pigs in Gogol's work make a regular habit of forcible and violent entry into human dwellings. In a climactic scene in "The Fair at Sorochintsy," a pig breaks a window and shoves its snout through it, terrifying a roomful of people. In "The Overcoat," a "normal young pig" rushes out of a private residence in St. Petersburg and knocks a policeman off his feet. In a later chapter of "The Two Ivans" and in "Viy," pigs likewise break through manmade partitions and barge into enclosed areas occupied by human beings, actions strongly suggesting that they are associated with both sexuality and violence in Gogol's mind.

Despite the insult and its unthinkable implications, the fondness of the two men for each other and their mutual need are so self-evident that the narrator is quite sure that they will make up on the very next day. But at this crucial moment Agafya Fedoseyevna chooses to make one of her unwelcome appearances at Ivan Nikiforovich's. Hearing of the quarrel, she resolves to do everything in her power to aggravate it. Her role at this point illustrates as clearly as anything could the essential thematic and conceptual unity of the four *Mirgorod* stories. Each one of them contains one female character whose function it is to break up good relationships between men (or, in "Old-World Landowners," the relationship between a man and his sister-mother-friend). These characters are certainly an odd assortment: an ugly provincial battle-ax, a dazzling Polish beauty, an evil Ukrainian witch, and a demure gray cat. But all of them are outside of the male characters' control, all are sexually active and

"*The Two Ivans*"

available and therefore, as so often in Gogol, dangerous and destructive to male companionship.

Agafya Fedoseyevna's machinations are so successful that even the narrator, who until this point found everyone and everything delightful, loses his composure and feels compelled to curse her. A war is declared between the two households that involves even the servants and the animals. The children of Ivan Ivanovich and the dogs of Ivan Nikiforovich—these two groups are curiously equated with each other throughout the story, except that the dogs seem to be slightly more intelligent—are brutally assaulted if they venture into enemy territory. The crowning insult comes when Ivan Nikiforovich reiterates his verbal accusation in visual form by constructing a goose pen on the edge of his former friend's property. In a wonderfully mock-poetic, mock-melodramatic scene, Ivan Ivanovich takes his revenge by stealing up at night to saw off the posts that hold up the goose pen. There is a strong erotic tinge to the imagery with which Gogol parodies the pseudo-poetic Romantic clichés: the moonlight, the fragrant flowers, the lovesick bellringer climbing over a fence, and the amorous bare-breasted city girl tossing on her lonely bed and dreaming of a hussar's moustache and spurs. Ivan Ivanovich is frenziedly sawing away at the pen's oakwood posts when: "All of a sudden he uttered a cry and went numb all over: he thought he saw a corpse; but he soon came to his senses, seeing that it was a goose that stretched its neck toward him through a partition (*prosunuvshii k nemu svoyu sheyu*)." Even at this parodistic moment, the connection between sexuality and death, so central to all of *Mirgorod*, is quietly made.

There follows a series of mutual denunciations to the legal authorities. Each of the two Ivans insists that the other is a criminal who should be manacled and condemned to hard labor after being divested of his status as a nobleman. The penalties pro-

"The Two Ivans"

posed make no sense on any logical or realistic level, but if the story's symbolic sexual underpinnings are perceived, Ivan Niki-forovich's charges of bestiality (*skotopodobnye i poritsaniya dostoinye postupki*) and sacrilege can be seen as not quite so meaningless after all. The legal comedy, with its quotations from official documents couched in a jargon that progressively makes less and less sense (English translators of Gogol invariably doctor these passages so that they make some kind of sense, thereby undermining the effect of Gogol's original text), builds up to a crescendo of absurdity, at which point Ivan Ivanovich's pig, the one which was offered in exchange for the rifle, decides to take matters into its own hands, or rather into its snout. It violently forces its way into the municipal courthouse and steals the original copy of Ivan Nikiforovich's complaint against its master—a unique case where a sexual symbol emancipates itself from the logic of the situation and of the narrative context and defends itself in the only way it can, that is, by performing a symbolic act of sexual assault. For this outrage, it is condemned to die and be made into hams and sausages.

The pig's intervention magnifies the feud to the point where the situation becomes disturbing and annoying to the entire municipal administration of Mirgorod. A concerted effort is made by everyone in the city to effect a reconciliation. During one of Agafya Fedoseyevna's periodic absences, a festive dinner party is given by the mayor at which the two former friends are brought together. The attempt comes tantalizingly close to success, but Ivan Nikiforovich cannot refrain from mentioning in public that he did in fact call Ivan Ivanovich a gander. "Had Ivan Nikiforovich acted differently, had he said *bird* and not *gander*, the situation could still have been saved. But now, everything was over." The accusation had been made for the third time and this time before witnesses. The entire city realizes that

"The Two Ivans"

no reconciliation is possible. The two former friends are now doomed to live out their lives in mutual hatred and detestation and to spend all their money on pointless, interminable lawsuits, while they become progressively ever more lonely, poor, and bitter.

In the last three pages of "The Two Ivans," the bouncy chatterbox who has been narrating the story suddenly bows out and the first-person narrative is taken over by an entirely different voice: an introspective, subdued, and compassionate narrator, very similar to the one in "Old-World Landowners." The strong element of social satire that pervades the story up to this point also disappears. In elegiac, dirgelike tones, further underscored by the mournful imagery of autumn and rain, this new narrator tells us of the bitterness and pain with which the two heroes now have to live. An affectionate relationship between the two males has been broken up, and Gogol cannot maintain the satirical manner of the rest of the story while commenting on what for him is clearly a heartbreakingly sad situation: "Here once lived in touching friendship those two unique men, two unique friends."

So the narrator leaves rain-drenched Mirgorod, uttering the concluding sentence of the story, one of Gogol's most frequently quoted phrases: *Skuchno na ètom svete, gospoda,* usually translated as "It's a dreary world, gentlemen." A somewhat closer rendition would perhaps be: "How dreary it is to live in this world, ladies and gentlemen." The adverb *skuchno,* which can be variously interpreted to mean "boring," "dreary" (as in Chekhov's "A Dreary Story"), or "tedious," and the entire tenor of the ending strongly bring to mind the ending of "The Fair at Sorochintsy." The causes for the boring or dreary mood are spelled out more explicitly in "The Fair at Sorochintsy" (see p. 3), but they are identical in the two stories. Life will find some way of breaking up a close and loving attachment between man and man and this is what makes this world such a heartbreaking and dreary place for Gogol.

All four *Mirgorod* stories begin happily and all have unhappy endings. In "Old-World Landowners," the happy situation at the outset unites a man and a woman who have managed to ban all sexuality from their lives. In "The Two Ivans," two men live near each other in contentment and harmony until the possibility of sexual contact between them is raised, if only on the subliminal level. The other two stories, "Taras Bulba" and "Viy," begin with depictions of happy all-male brotherhoods that are shattered when one of their members falls under the spell of a woman.

"Taras Bulba," Gogol's impassioned hymn in praise of war, violence, and death, is probably his best-known work. Almost everybody seems to like it. Russian governments—from that of Nicholas I to the present-day Soviet one—value it for its insistence on the eternal unity of the Russian and Ukrainian people under Russian rule and its implicit opposition to any Ukrainian separatist tendencies. But the Ukrainian nationalists also love "Taras Bulba," since for them it is an evocation of past Ukrainian military glory. Non-Russian readers who may feel uncomfortable in the real-unreal atmosphere of Gogol's other writings love this work because in it they find themselves on more familiar territory, comparable to the historical novels and military romances of other literatures. The two big-budget films that were based on it, the French one that starred Danielle Darrieux

"Taras Bulba"

and Jean Pierre Aumont in the 1930s and the American one of the 1950s with Yul Brynner, turned "Taras Bulba" into a colorful historical pageant of a decidedly conventional kind. Leoš Janáček, however, did look deeper into the core of Gogol's conception, as the titles of the three sections of his orchestral rhapsody *Taras Bulba* (1914-1918) testify. They are: (I) "Andry's Death," (II) "Ostap's Death," and (III) "Prophecy and Death of Taras Bulba."

Gogol lived in what Donald Davie has termed the Heyday of Sir Walter Scott. According to Gogol's one-time secretary, Pavel Annenkov, Scott was not only Gogol's favorite foreign writer, but also the one whose work he knew better than that of any other. The historical novel in the manner of Scott was the dominant literary genre of the age, but Gogol was also strongly attracted to the deliberately shocking, blood-and-guts novels of the French *école frénétique*, as exemplified by such writers as Jules Janin and Eugène Sue. From the very beginning of his writing career, he repeatedly attempted to wed these two fashionable modes of writing in a work on a subject taken from Ukrainian history. His earlier efforts in this direction (one of which was so gory and sadistic that the censor banned its publication) did not satisfy him and were abandoned. The version of "Taras Bulba" printed in the 1835 edition of *Mirgorod*, which is a kind of skeletal sketching out of the work as we now know it, came closer to the mark. But it is in the revised 1842 version that Gogol finally learned how to write a successful historical novel. As twentieth-century Gogolian criticism has discovered in recent decades, the essential ingredient that enabled him to graft a subject from Ukrainian history onto a hybrid of Scott and Janin was Homer, of all people. Stylistic mannerisms and formulae from the *Iliad*, not noticed by Gogol's contemporaries and first pointed out by Valery Bryusov in 1909, have been repeatedly documented in

"Taras Bulba"

"Taras Bulba" by various American and German scholars. All these imported ingredients were amalgamated by Gogol into one of the most ultra-nationalistic works in all literature, and they are also the reason why many foreign readers feel more at home with "Taras Bulba" than with any of his other works.

The subject to which Gogol applied the lessons he had learned from his admired foreign models was one that he himself obviously found vastly congenial. The free-booting, all-male Cossack republic of Zaporozhskaya Sech (The Trans-Cataract Stronghold) was, historically, at the height of its power in the sixteenth century. These Dnieper Cossacks, like other Cossacks elsewhere in Russia, were originally peasants who had fled to outlying regions to escape serfdom. But while residence in the frontier area put them out of reach of the tsar's police, it also exposed them to attack by neighboring foreigners. To deal with this contingency, the Dnieper Cossacks of the Ukraine banded together into a military unit that had its headquarters on an island upstream from the cataracts of the Dnieper. Their military might soon enabled them to branch out into raiding and marauding, which they directed against all neighboring populations: Poles, Russians, Turks, and Crimean Tatars. Gogol portrays these Cossacks as staunch defenders of Orthodoxy and passionate Russian patriots. Historically, this interpretation is utterly untenable, for the Cossacks were just as likely to ally themselves with the Poles or the Turks *against* Russia as they were on other occasions to support it. One of their most renowned leaders in the sixteenth century, Hetman Pyotr Sahaidachny, was an ally of Poland and a consistent supporter of Polish policies. The only loyalty the Cossacks knew was to their own military republic, not to the country of their ancestors' origin. Their wives and families, if they had any, might live in any of the neighboring countries, as Gogol himself well knew. In his story "Christmas

Eve," when the Cossacks from the Sech are introduced to Catherine the Great and are asked by her about their family arrangements, they reply: "There are some of us who have wives in Poland, some who have wives in the Ukraine, and some who have wives even in Turkey."

The brief outline of the Cossacks' situation in "Christmas Eve" is based on far more solid historical grounds than the picture of pro-Russian patriotic fervor we find throughout "Taras Bulba." But then, as we know from Gogol's historical essays, facts and dates were of little import to him. He points out throughout the story that "Taras Bulba" takes place in the fifteenth century. But the military operations of the Sech against Poland and the siege of the fortress of Dubno, which form the main action, did not take place until the sixteenth century. The Kievan Academy in which the two sons of Taras study was not founded until the seventeenth century. All this was not the crux of the matter for Gogol. What he saw in the Cossacks of the Sech was an association of beautiful, virile males, united in their love for one another and their distaste and contempt for everyone else. "There are no bonds more sacred than the love of comrades!" Taras Bulba exclaims in his impassioned paean to male friendship in Chapter IX. "Only man can be akin in soul, though not in blood. There have been comrades in other lands, too, but such comrades as in Russia there have never been." That speech, too long to be quoted in toto, with its remarkable assertion that men loving other men is something exclusively Russian, deserves a careful examination that goes beyond its patriotic rhetoric, for it is a key to much of Gogol's basic outlook.

The military camaraderie of their camp fulfills and satisfies all of the Cossacks' emotional needs. "Lovers of the military life, lovers of gold goblets and rich brocades, lovers of money could always find their work here. Only those devoted to women could find nothing here, for not one woman dared to appear even on the outskirts of the Sech." The one thing these men love even more than they love each other is the art of war. Like his model Scott, Gogol found the spectacle of grown-up men slugging and pummeling each other, as in "Viy," or slashing, shooting and decapitating each other, as in "Taras Bulba," edifying and exhilarating. There is no intermediary, fictional narrator in "Taras Bulba" as there was in "Old-World Landowners" and "The Two Ivans," and therefore we must take the poetic idealization of warfare to represent Gogol's actual views. "Andry became totally immersed in the enchanting music of bullets and swords. He did not know what it meant to plan or to calculate, to take stock of his own or the enemy's strength. A battle was for him a savage kind of voluptuousness and intoxication; there was something festive for him in those moments when a man's head is aflame, when everything flickers and grows confused before his eyes, when heads are lopped off, when horses crash thunderously to the ground, while he rushes as though drunk through the whistling of bullets and the glitter of sabers, dealing blows on all sides and not feeling the ones dealt him."

This kind of battle imagery, dear to the hearts of Romantic writers, is vastly popular even in our own day, as many a wide-screen technicolor film will easily confirm. Gogol, however, connects the love of battle not only with patriotism, but also with the teachings of the Christian religion. Angels appear in one battle scene, acting as male Valkyries, and carry the souls of slain Cossacks to a Valhalla-like paradise presided over by a Cossack-loving Christ. Anyone who is not a Cossack and does not belong to the Orthodox Church is an infidel, and, as Taras Bulba puts it, "both God and the Holy Writ command us to kill infidels." The way to deal with the infidels is either to convert them or to wipe them off the face of the earth. "Let us drink, comrades," Taras toasts his companions, "let us drink first of all to our holy Orthodox faith; may the time come at last when our faith will spread throughout the world and be the only holy faith everywhere and all the infidels, whoever they may be, will become Christian!"

Taras Bulba himself is such a hallowed and revered figure in the Russian and Ukrainian literary tradition that it would probably strike many as nothing short of sacrilege to take a cold, hard look at him. The Romantic Age admired such characters, as it admired the Byronic brawlers and duel-seekers of Lermontov and Bestuzhev-Marlinsky. But different ages have different ways of looking at certain personality types. Taras Bulba's present-day counterpart would be a leader of an armed motorcycle gang or a *capo di famiglia* in the Mafia. For all his talk about comradely love and religion, his principal aim in life is to seek out and provoke violence. Violence is the necessary way of proving one's manliness to oneself and to others: "it does not matter where one fights as long as one fights, because it is indecent for a gentleman not to be engaged in warfare." For some incomprehensible reason, Taras insists that his two sons complete a course of studies at the Kievan Academy, where they are taught humanities, Latin classics, and theology. This education is all the more incongruous because they are clearly expected to forget everything they have learned the moment they leave Kiev and devote themselves entirely to martial pursuits.

Both Gogol and Taras Bulba keep insisting throughout that the Cossacks wage war only to defend their church and religion. This sits very badly with the commentators who annotate the Soviet editions of Gogol; they invariably maintain that Taras and his Cossacks were really fighting to preserve Ukrainian national independence. When Taras brings his sons to the Sech, there happens to be no war on. The old man immediately sets out to create one. He tries to organize a raid against Turkey, even though there is a peace treaty with the Sultan. The elected leaders of the Sech refuse to violate this treaty: the Cossacks have sworn to keep it by their church and their religion. But Taras needs and wants to see his sons kill people, so he engineers the political takeover of the Sech by a faction willing to go along with his plans. It turns out not to have been necessary: some Cossacks arrive with the inflammatory rumor that Orthodox churches in Polish-occupied territories are being desecrated by Catholic priests and handed over to the Jews. This gives the Cossacks a handy pretext for a pogrom against the local Jews; then off they march against Poland. The fortress of Dubno is besieged and its population is starved into submission. When we are allowed to see the fortress from the inside, it is seen to be an entirely Polish city, and the only church found in it is an impressively beautiful Catholic one. The pretext for the entire campaign seems to have been totally spurious, but it does give the Cossacks plenty of opportunity to pillage, maraud, impale babies on spears, cut off women's breasts, and remove the skin of their prisoners' legs prior to releasing them—all in the name of the Church and Christ (or, *mutatis mutandis*, of preserving national independence).

Taras Bulba's son Ostap is a chip off the old block. All he lives and breathes is war and fighting. He forces himself to get good grades at the academy, which he detests, because his father will not allow him to kill any people unless he graduates. He picks a fight with his own father the moment he appears in the story and he never stops fighting until he is tortured to death in the main square of Warsaw. He has no other wishes and no other dimensions, and for Gogol he is a totally beautiful and fulfilled young man. Taras Bulba's other son, Andry, at first seems to have been cast in the same mold. But Andry has a serious flaw: he is inter-

"Taras Bulba"

ested in women and he becomes emotionally involved with one.

In the world of "Taras Bulba," women have a definite place. They are a disposable commodity, useful primarily for bringing new Cossacks into the world. Taras Bulba can be sentimental and shed an occasional tear when he thinks of his comrades who are no longer with him. But his pipe (feminine gender in Russian), in defense of which he loses his life, clearly means more to him than his wife does. Gogol manages a remarkably sympathetic portrayal of Taras Bulba's wife and he outlines her lack of rights and her subjugated position with a feeling that almost borders on compassion. And yet we are not even told her name —we know her, like the two other principal female characters of "Taras Bulba," the Polish beauty and the Tatar maidservant, only by her function: the wife of Taras and the mother of Ostap and Andry. This stands in significant contrast to the full names of dozens of incidental male characters cited in the story. The wife is visited by Taras only very rarely, she keeps his house and prepares his food, but apart from that she simply does not count. Her wishes do not matter, no one cares whether she is hurt or unhappy, and Taras silently ignores her desperate pleas to let her spend one more day with the sons she has not seen for many months before they are marched off to war, where they will both lose their lives. When she was young and pretty, Taras used her as a conveyance to acquire sons; now that the sons are grown, she is allowed to remain as a housekeeper and unpaid servant. It is as simple as that.

Ostap would presumably have repeated this pattern with a young Cossack girl if he had not managed to get himself killed. But Andry does something unprecedented. Not only does he become involved with an aristocratic Polish beauty, but he places himself in her power. This is a double betrayal. He betrays the Cossacks and the Orthodox faith, and even more

---

"*Taras Bulba*"

important within the framework of *Mirgorod*, he betrays the all-male comradeship of the Sech. For this he is condemned to death and shot by his own father. Andry submits meekly and allows himself to be shot, for the message he gets is the same one that Pulcheria got from her cat in "Old-World Landowners" and that Homa Brut will get in the demon-infested church in "Viy": *the wages of sex is death.* Taras has an explicit sado-masochistic fantasy about mutilating and eviscerating the seductress who has led his son into temptation, but since he cannot get his hands on her, he has to content himself with torturing and killing several other attractive Polish women whom he manages to capture and with murdering the young, handsome brother of Andry's Polish beauty when he briefly appears at the end of the story.

In contrast to the vitality of the colorful Cossack characters, the Polish beauty is one of Gogol's idealized alabaster females, a replay of Alcinoe from "Woman." Her one big speech is couched in the diction of a folk song or folk lament, which is wildly out of character for this supposedly aristocratic, worldly, and well-traveled young woman. Her love scenes with Andry revert to the operatic love duets of the Dikanka stories and are perhaps even less convincing. The description of the embrace and kiss that seal her confession of love must have been embarrassing for Gogol to write, for it contains what is surely his single most awkward lapse: her lips are pressed against Andry's cheek while he is kissing her mouth, which is said to respond to his kiss—a feat that clearly requires three pairs of lips to accomplish. No such awkwardness occurs in Chapter VIII, where crowds of Cossack men kiss and hold hands with each other prior to splitting their army into two units and separating for a long time.

Almost all the commentaries on "Taras Bulba," whether Russian or foreign, speak of its hero as generous, dashing, brave, and loyal. Even in this story, his most derivative work since

"Taras Bulba"

"Saint John's Eve," Gogol's verbal magic is so potent that it has forced generations of readers to overlook his hero's brutality, sadism, placid chauvinism and hatred of all other nationalities, his cold-blooded murder of his own son (with its famous smug self-justification: "I begat you and I shall kill you!"), and even the remarkable stupidity he displays when he starts arguing about the Cossack cause with the jail warden in Warsaw and thus misses his chance of seeing Ostap for the last time after expending enormous effort to effect the meeting. Taras Bulba is as easily mistaken for a portrait of a good, natural man as is that other *mafioso* of Russian literature, Tolstoy's Hajji Murad. But a careful, attentive reading of the story by a reader who does not accept Gogol's ideology of religious and nationalistic conquest (the final vision of the dying Taras is one of the whole world united under the rule of the Russian tsar) will show "Taras Bulba" to be a glorification of national and religious intolerance and of *machismo* at its most brutal and cruel. Ultimately, as Janáček's rhapsody points out, the central core of the work is an apotheosis of death. "Taras Bulba" supplies us with an essential clue for understanding an important aspect of Gogol's mentality. Its traditional reception teaches us a serious lesson about Russian culture in general.

The exact time when the first version of "Taras Bulba" was written is not known. Since "Viy" was written shortly before the publication of *Mirgorod*, one might assume that it was the last story of the cycle to be written. This would make sense, because it is in this story that the sexual themes treated in the other three

"Viy"

come into their sharpest focus. In no other work did Gogol confront sexuality so openly and in so many of its aspects. The personal and unconventional elements are so numerous that he must have thought it best to cover his tracks with a footnote that reads: "*Viy* is a colossal creation of the popular imagination. This is the name the Ukrainians use for the ruler of the gnomes, whose eyelids reach down to the ground. The entire story is a folk legend. I did not want to alter it in any respect and am setting it down in the simple form in which I heard it." Actually, apart from some very general motifs about witchcraft and possession by witches, there is very little folklore in "Viy." The gnomes, as Leon Stilman, among others, has pointed out, do not occur in Ukrainian or any other Slavic mythology. They are Germanic and were made popular in the Romantic Age by the fairy tales of the Brothers Grimm. The early portion of the story is quite realistic, while its last portion has a clear literary model and antecedent: Robert Southey's ballad "The Old Woman of Berkeley," which Gogol knew in a fine Russian adaptation by Zhukovsky. The mythology of "Viy" is not that of the Ukrainian people, but that of Nikolai Gogol's subconscious.

Like much of "Taras Bulba," the beginning of "Viy" is a reflection of Gogol's nostalgia for the happy male camaraderie of the boarding school at Nezhin. The six years that elapsed between the time of his departure from the school and the time he wrote *Mirgorod* covered that period with a patina which concealed the occasional rejections and unpopularity that he suffered in Nezhin. What remained in his memory was the warm and affectionate circle of male friends, which he came to miss badly in St. Petersburg and which he recreated in an altered and slightly disguised form in "Taras Bulba" and in the opening pages of "Viy." The all-male world of "Viy" is that of a religious seminary in Kiev. With humor and gentle irony Gogol evokes

"Viy"

the seminarians' day-to-day existence: their lusty ways, their convivial outings in the country, their school theatricals, and their genial pleasure in sharing each other's company. Corporal punishment at school is part of the normal routine. Fist fights, either on a one-to-one basis or in two opposing groups, are one of the accepted modes of entertainment.

The boys are divided into four categories in accordance with their age and the degree of advancement in their studies. The youngest are called grammarians, then come the rhetoricians, the still older philosophers, and, finally, the almost entirely adult theologians. The division is comparable to the classification of American college students into freshmen, sophomores, juniors, and seniors, a point that is missed in such English translations of "Viy" as the one found in the Constance Garnett-Leonard J. Kent volume, where these appellations are assumed to refer to the students' majors or preferred subjects. After an overall panorama of student life, Gogol zeroes in on three particular seminarians who become lost in the fields during an outing in the country. The eldest bears the inelegant name of Halyava (meaning "top part of a boot"; the Ukrainian idiomatic saying "to jump higher than the top of your boots" means to get into bad trouble). The other two have pseudo-Roman names, Latin being traditionally associated with divinity schools: Homa Brut ("Thomas Brutus") and Tibery Horobets ("Tiberius Sparrow"). Homa Brut, the hero of "Viy," might well be the most full-blooded, sensible, and psychologically healthy of Gogol's protagonists. A lazy southerner, he manages to be pragmatic, resourceful, and courageous without any false heroics while he is being stalked by assorted monsters. Homa is on occasion naively opportunistic, he loves drink and women, and he is not above a little petty larceny or selling his sexual favors to affluent market women or bakers' wives—an altogether likable young man, in short, and far better company than Taras Bulba's compulsive, murderous sons.

F. C. Driessen has perceptively observed that the action in "Viy" alternates regularly between day and night, the daylight scenes being cheerful, sociable, and logical and the nocturnal ones terrifying and irrational. As night falls around the three students lost in the fields, the faint, distant howling of a wolf is heard—this howling recurs periodically in the story, gradually increasing in volume. Its significance is finally revealed when it ushers in the appearance of Viy himself at the end. Eventually, the students make their way to a secluded farm and talk the innocuous-seeming old woman they find there into allowing them to spend the night. The woman lets them in, but on the condition that they sleep in separate places, that is, she does what women do in all the other stories in *Mirgorod:* she separates the men from their male companions. Her rationale is quite explicit: "my heart will not be at peace, if all of you are lying together" (*u menya ne budet spokoino na serdtse, kogda budete lezhat' vmeste*). The usual English translation of this phrase, "my mind won't be at rest if you are all together," misses an important point.

Separated from his friends, Homa Brut is offered a sheep sty as his place of lodging. Sheep, like horses and dogs, are among Gogol's safe and friendly animals, not tainted with any dreaded sexual associations. As Homa is getting settled for the night, however, an inquisitive pig pokes its head in from a neighboring sty. Homa, who has not read Gogol, sees nothing ominous in this. He kicks the pig in the snout and turns over on his other side to go to sleep. But a reader who is familiar with "The Fair at Sorochintsy" and "The Two Ivans" knows that the pig's appearance indicates that sex and violence cannot be far away. And indeed, the door opens, the old woman comes in, and ap-

"Viy"

proaches Homa with outspread arms. He instantly perceives her intentions to be sexual:

> "So that's it," thought the philosopher. "But no, my sweet. You're too old!" He moved away slightly, but the old woman unceremoniously approached him again.
> "Listen, granny," said the philosopher. "It is a fast time now and I am the kind of person who would not break a fast for a thousand gold pieces."
> But the woman opened her arms and tried to catch him without saying a word.

The old woman turns out to be a powerful witch. Her burning glance deprives Homa of his voice and of the ability to move. With the swiftness of a cat (another by now familiar Gogolian animal—in "Saint John's Eve" and "May Night" cats were associated with witchcraft and evil, and in "Old-World Landowners" a cat acted as a herald of death), she mounts him and forces him to gallop all over the steppe with her on his back. The erotic nature of this nocturnal ride is conveyed by Gogol in unmistakable terms.[10] In the magnificently poetic moonlit summer night (which had seemed dark and terrifying only a short while earlier to the three students), Homa feels "a languid, unpleasant, and at the same time voluptuous sensation that assailed his heart." His mounting erotic frenzy needs an object at which to direct its release. Since the old crone on his back is unsuitable for that purpose, Homa conjures up a vision of an upside-down world reflected under his feet (the motif of upside-down reflected worlds was also used in "May Night" and "Terrible Vengeance"). It is a world in which "some different sun" shines instead of our moon and bluebell flowers become actual ringing bells. Out of this psychedelically reversed reality, there rises a nude water nymph, "all glitter and quiver." The description of the nymph, as dazzling a verbal *tour de force* as Gogol's famous passage about Plyushkin's garden in *Dead Souls*, is the verbal equivalent of a Renoir nude, but one that is iridescent with all the colors of the rainbow (and hopelessly untranslatable—the available English versions do not even begin to do it justice). For once, Gogol manages an entirely convincing depiction of a beautiful (and nude) woman. With the appearance of the nymph, Homa experiences what seems to be an orgasm: "But what was that? Is it wind or music? It rings and rings and writhes and comes closer and stabs your soul like some kind of an unbearable trill. [. . .] He felt a diabolically sweet sensation, a kind of agonizingly terrifying pleasure."

Sobered by his sexual release, Homa comes to his senses and begins reciting prayers and incantations against evil spirits. This loosens the witch's grip. But as soon as he is freed from her power, Homa jumps on her back in his turn and beats her brutally with a wooden log as she rapidly gallops under him. She collapses and then reveals her true identity: instead of being an ugly old witch, she is really a lovely young woman. As she lies on the ground, bruised and wounded, Homa flees. He returns to Kiev and his former easygoing ways and starts a liaison with a young widow who keeps him in money and liquor, helping him forget his strange nocturnal adventure. With this, the first, shorter section of "Viy" ends.

In this first section, the witch's powers work only during the night. As the second section begins, we realize that they can invade the diurnal regions as well. The witch who disguised herself as an old peasant woman was actually the beautiful young daughter of an aristocratic, wealthy, and influential military officer. Like all desirable and dangerous young women in Gogol, she has no name of her own—she is called "old woman" in the first section of the story; *pannochka*, that is, "young noblewoman," "young mistress," for most of the second section; and "corpse" toward the end of the story. Not only does this lack of a name connect her with the similarly nameless Polish beauty in "Taras Bulba," but the term *pannochka*, by which these two seemingly different young women are referred to, also underscores the similarity of their function in the two stories. The Polish beauty meant no harm and probably she truly loved Andry, while the Ukrainian *pannochka* first rapes Homa and then seeks to deprive him of his life. But this is a Gogolian world where women's conscious intentions count for little, since the result of the two involvements is the same for the two young men involved—death and destruction.

Homa Brut is careless enough to reveal his name and his school to the old woman when he asks her for a night's lodging. This delivers him into the witch's hands. First from her death bed, then from beyond the grave she commands the diurnal powers—her father, the rector of the divinity school, and even the friendly Cossack guards with whom Homa is quick to establish an understanding—to bring Homa to her. Under protest and against his will he is taken to her father's village, where he is forced to read prayers over her coffin for three nights (this aspect of the story comes from Zhukovsky's version of Southey's "The Old Woman of Berkeley," in which a dying witch bids her son, a monk, to protect her from the Devil by praying over her body for three nights). With his remarkable pluck, Homa Brut might have survived his three nights of horror in the haunted church, had these nights not alternated with his almost equally unsettling experiences on the days that precede them. The daytime revelations deliver him to his enemy more surely than the demons she can conjure at night.

Before going off to his first vigil, Homa hears the story of his predecessor, one of the witch's earlier victims, the kennel hand

Mikita. The witch rode Mikita as she had Homa and she drove him to his death by spontaneous combustion (it was widely believed in countries around the Mediterranean basin that sinful persons can catch fire from within and be reduced to ashes; death by this means also occurs in "Saint John's Eve"). But in her dealings with Mikita she showed herself to him as her true and attractive self. Why did she have to disguise herself as an old woman during her initial encounter with Homa? Obviously, in order to make her task more interesting by setting a handicap for herself. Slowly, an important fact about Gogolian seductresses must dawn upon the reader and perhaps on Homa. Sex is only a means for them; their ultimate aim is power and domination. It is with this realization that Homa goes to the church on the first night.

Just before going to church on the second night, Homa observes a curious little scene which an unwary reader may easily overlook, but which seems to be a key to the final dénouement of "Viy." The Cossacks and domestic servants who had brought him from Kiev and had been keeping him company play a game of ninepins. The game is said to be very enjoyable for both the participants and the spectators, because the winners are rewarded with a ride on the loser's backs. "Homa vainly tried to force himself to join this game; but some obscure thought was stuck in his head like a doornail." What can this thought have been? Homa was undergoing his terrifying ordeal because he had allowed a woman to ride on his back and he rode on hers, experiencing intense sexual pleasure, for which he was now presumably being punished. But here were men using each other in the same manner and doing so with impunity. The implications of all this may or may not have occurred to the happily adjusted heterosexual that Homa Brut clearly was, but the possibilities of the situation could hardly have been lost on Homa's creator.

After his second night in the haunted church, during which

"Viy"

half of his hair turns gray from the ordeal, Homa resolves to make his escape. But the witch's father adamantly refuses to release him. When Homa runs away, the previously friendly Cossacks catch him and forcibly return him to the village. If on the first day the story of Mikita spelled out the deeper causes of woman's power over man, on the third day Homa realizes that escape into male solidarity is now cut off. Men will also betray their fellow males to the omnipotent female principle. In desperation, Homa gets drunk and dances a trepak in the middle of the courtyard—a gesture of hopeless defiance, rather than of any kind of joy or pleasure.

The progression of events in the church on the three nights on which Homa reads the prayers over the witch's coffin is quite similar to the daytime progression. On the first night, the dead witch arises from her coffin, tries to grab Homa, and causes her coffin to fly about the church. But Homa is prepared: he makes a magical circle around himself and recites powerful incantations which make him invisible to the witch. On the second night she calls for help and the church fills with animal-like monsters who are, however, neuter (*chudovishcha, strashilishcha*). They frighten Homa badly, but, being neuter and presumably sexless, they cannot get at him. On the third night, the dead witch plays her trump card by enlisting male help.

"Bring Viy! Go fetch Viy!" he heard the corpse say. And suddenly a stillness fell upon the church; the howling of wolves was heard in the distance and soon heavy footsteps resounded throughout the church. With a sidelong glance he saw that a stocky, powerfully built, ungainly man was being brought in. He was covered all over with black earth. His arms and legs, strewn with earth, protruded like strong, sinewy roots. He trod heavily, stumbling with every step. His long eyelids hung down to the very ground. Homa noticed with horror that his face was of iron. He was supported under the arms and brought directly in front of the spot where Homa was standing.

"Lift my eyelids: I cannot see!" said Viy in a subterranean voice, and the entire gathering rushed to lift his eyelids.

"Do not look!" an inner voice whispered to the philosopher. He could not restrain himself and looked.

"There he is!" shouted Viy and pointed an iron finger at him.

Nowhere else in Gogol do we find such a potent concentration of his worst fears and nightmares as in this scene. The "obscure thought" that had prevented Homa from joining the Cossacks in their game of ninepins is here brutally brought into the open. A man who yields to homosexuality would perhaps be free from the witch's power—a literally "unthinkable" escape in the ninepin episode, but an escape nonetheless. Now a mighty male earth spirit enters, his maleness emphasized by his ultra-phallic anatomy—few things could be as phallic as eyelids that hang to the ground.[11] He causes others to lift these eyelids for him in what seems to be an unmistakable erection, a double one, which with the pointing iron finger becomes a triple one—a triple whammy, as Al Capp would have put it. All three are directed at another male, Homa, graphically spelling out the possibility of one man's sexual desire for another. That is horror number one. Horror number two is that this desire, so long suppressed and now so forcefully exposed, is used only as an instrument to betray its object to a vengeful female. And the ultimate horror is that it all takes place in a church, which, if one is right in assuming that it was religion that kept Gogol from acting out his homosexual impulses, lends the entire scene a tinge of deliberate blasphemy.

"Homa is betrayed by his own glance," writes Leon Stilman in his wonderfully perceptive essay "The All-Seeing Eye in Gogol." "Here, not to look means to remain invisible. One mustn't look at what is horrible. The temptation is great but it should be resisted. Once you glance at what is horrible, you yourself will be seen and then there is no saving you." The finale of "Viy" is Gogol's terrified glance into himself and the only answer he can give to what he sees there is the same one he comes up with throughout *Mirgorod:* death. The monsters which hurl themselves upon Homa when he is pointed out to them by Viy are not fast enough: Homa dies of sheer terror before they manage to get to him. In the brief epilogue which Gogol added for the 1842 edition, Homa's erstwhile friends Halyava and Tiberius Sparrow discuss how he could have escaped the powers of the witch. Tiberius, who has now advanced to the grade of philosopher in his studies and has the same status that Homa Brut had at the beginning of the story, says that the only way to deal with witches is not to be afraid of them. But he also realizes that they are everywhere: "After all, all the women who sit at the market stalls in Kiev are all witches." If Tiberius learned any kind of lesson from the fate of his friend Homa, he will now stay away from all women, including the ones at the market. The lesson of "Viy" lends a final touch of symmetry to the *Mirgorod* cycle as a whole. "Old-World Landowners" and "Taras Bulba" contemplated heterosexuality, "The Two Ivans" turned to homosexuality, and "Viy" takes in both and adds a touch of sado-masochism to boot. It does not matter what form of sexuality one opts for— pain, danger, and death are invariably the final outcome.

"Viy" and Undine

The demon whose entire appearance takes up less than one page of "Viy" but after whom the entire story is so appropriately named—and it might well be the finest horror story in the Russian language—has haunted the imagination of many Russian writers and poets, among them Mayakovsky (in whose "War and the World" the poet is possessed by Viy) and Mandelstam (in whose very last poem Viy is mentioned). But, apart from being a personification of Gogol's own sexual terrors, just who or what is Viy? Folklorists have looked long and hard for him for more than a century and found nothing. Leon Stilman derives his name from the Ukrainian word for eyelash, *viya*. Gogol apparently twisted this feminine noun so that it acquired an unexpected masculine gender. Considering the long-known connection of "Viy" with Zhukovsky's translation of Southey's ballad, it is odd that Russian scholars have failed until now to perceive the obvious connection of Viy's name, his appearance, and a number of other features of the story with one of Zhukovsky's other best-known translations, his version in unrhymed hexameter of Friedrich de Lamotte-Fouqué's German prose romance *Undine*.

Lamotte-Fouqué, a German Romantic writer of French Huguenot descent, found the ingredients for his story of the star-crossed marriage between a water sprite and a mortal in the writings of Paracelsus. Published in 1811, his *Undine* immediately became a minor classic of the German Romantic tradition, and it has fascinated an impressive array of creative minds ever since. Heinrich Heine, who had little patience with the excesses of the Romantics, considered *Undine* a "wondrous, lovely poem," the very distillate of the best aspects of Romantic sensi-

---

"Viy" and Undine

bility. Albert Lortzing turned *Undine* into an opera (1845) that is still occasionally revived in German provincial theaters. Richard Wagner is known to have read *Undine* out loud to his family on the eve of his death and to have concluded his reading by playing and singing the contextually appropriate final lament of the Rhine maidens that concludes *Das Rheingold:* "Traulich und treu ist's nur in der Tiefe: falsch und feig ist was dort oben sich freut!" This was the last time Wagner played the piano in his life. *Undine* was one of the primary myths that dominated the childhood of the poet Marina Tsvetaeva; writing her essay "On Germany" in 1919, Tsvetaeva cited the heroine of *Undine* as the supreme example of good faith and reliability, thus, unbeknownst to herself, agreeing with Wagner on the work's central idea. Jean Giraudoux based his play *Ondine* on Lamotte-Fouqué's tale. It was presented in Paris by Louis Jouvet in 1939 with fantastically beautiful sets and costumes by Pavel Tchelitchew, and in the 1950s it provided Audrey Hepburn with a memorable starring vehicle on Broadway.

Vasily Zhukovsky first read *Undine* in 1816. He immediately resolved to do a Russian translation, but for a number of years he could not decide whether to render it in prose, rhymed verse, or blank verse. He finally settled on Russian hexameter—the irregular meter which Russian poets had devised for translating Greek and Latin epics—as being most suitable for his purpose. Zhukovsky began his translation of *Undine* in the summer of 1831, at a time when Gogol was spending several weeks in Tsarskoye Selo, where he saw Zhukovsky almost daily. The first three chapters of Zhukovsky's version were published in a literary journal late in 1835 ("Viy" is assumed to have been written at the end of 1834). The complete work was published in 1837. Gogol read it in Baden-Baden and wrote to one of his correspondents that he found it "miraculously lovely" (letter to Var-

"*Viy*" *and* Undine

vara Balabina of July 16, 1837). Considering the friendly relations between Gogol and Zhukovsky, it is not unreasonable to
assume that Gogol might have been shown the early portions of
Zhukovsky's translation prior to its publication.

In the fourth chapter of *Undine*, the Knight Huldbrand describes to Undine his adventures in the enchanted forest he has
had to cross in order to reach the fisherman's hut where he first
meets her. His first encounter is with the ruler of the gnomes:
"Suddenly I see a little man / Standing next to my horse, a disgusting, dirty hunchback / With a face the color of earth and
such an enormous nose that it seemed / To be the same length as
the rest of the monster's body." The knight has to bribe the head
gnome to let him continue his journey. He throws him some gold
pieces, whereupon the gnome causes the earth under him to
become transparent: "And at that moment / It appeared to me
that the earth's insides were suffused with light; / The grass
became like transparent emerald; my eye / Could freely pierce it
to the depths; and then the subterranean / Region of the gnomes
was opened to me." This particular portion of *Undine* might well
be the source not only for Homa Brut's visions of the transparent
earth during his nocturnal ride on the witch, but, considering
Wagner's fondness for *Undine*, for certain details of Wotan and
Loge's descent into the Nibelheim in *Das Rheingold*. The ruler of
the gnomes throws the coins the knight gives him to his underground subjects, but they reject the gold as counterfeit. They
crawl upward, pointing at the knight with their long fingers
strewn with metallic dust. A nameless terror overcomes him and
he escapes by galloping off on his horse.

The prancing and leering ruler of the gnomes of Lamotte-
Fouqué and Zhukovsky has a personality that is, of course,
vastly different from that of Gogol's slowly stumbling Viy; but
there are enough details common to both works to rule out mere

"*Viy*" *and* Undine

coincidence. The "face the color of earth" of the German head gnome brings to mind both Viy's earth-strewn body and limbs and his iron face; the nose as long as the creature's body may well have suggested Viy's floor-length eyelids; and the long, accusing, metal-covered fingers of the gnome's subordinates are certainly very much like Viy's accusing iron finger that causes Homa to die of sheer terror. The relevant wording is in all cases that of Zhukovsky, rather than of Lamotte-Fouqué. The ruler of the gnomes is "brown-yellow" all over in the German original, which made no reference to his face or the earth; the earth spirits are called "kobolds" in Lamotte-Fouqué, but "gnomes" in Zhukovsky; and their fingers in the original are merely dirty. All this, in conjunction with the acquisition of X-ray vision by both Homa Brut and the Knight Huldbrand, enabling them to look into the earth's interior, would seem to indicate that the fourth chapter of *Undine* must have been very much on Gogol's mind when he was writing "Viy."

Once the connection between the two works is recognized, the derivation of Viy's name from that of a character in Zhukovsky's version of *Undine* may also be postulated. Prior to his encounter with the ruler of the gnomes in the fourth chapter, the Knight Huldbrand has his life saved by the heroine's uncle, the powerful ruler of the water spirits, called in the German original Oheim Kühleborn ("Uncle Cool-spring" or "Uncle Cool-well"). To render "Kühleborn" into Russian, Zhukovsky altered the normally feminine noun *struya*, "jet of water," so that it assumed the masculine gender; that is, he applied to it exactly the same procedure that Gogol used, according to Leon Stilman, to obtain Viy from *viya*. Both derivations seem highly appropriate, since Undine's uncle is as obviously associated with jets of water as the earth spirit Viy, because of his abnormal eyelids, is connected with eyelashes. But Zhukovsky's coinage Dyadya Struy,

"Viy" and Undine

"Uncle Jet," in addition to being a derivation from *struya*, also happens to be a rather complex pun on traditional Slavic terms for family relationships.

Modern Russian and Ukrainian both use the word *dyadya* for "uncle." The word was introduced in post-medieval times, replacing the previously used Common Slavic terms that distinguished between paternal and maternal uncles. Like modern languages of the West and South Slavic groups (compare modern Polish *stryj* and *wuj*), medieval Russian had *stryi*, "paternal uncle," and *vuy* or *uy*, "maternal uncle." The replacement of these terms with *dyadya* (which originally meant "older male relative" or "male tutor") may well have occurred partly because *uy* sounded uncomfortably close in its pronunciation to one of the most unprintable words in the Russian language and the one most frequently seen in Soviet grafitti: *khuy*, which *The Oxford Russian-English Dictionary* translates as "prick" or "tool." Even after their disappearance from literary and colloquial Russian, *stryi* and *uy* survived into modern times in certain regional dialects and in folk poetry. Most literate Ukrainians understand these words to this day, even though they may regard them as rather pretentious Polonisms when used by a Ukrainian.

Zhukovsky may or may not have been aware of the full punning possibilities of his coinage Dyadya Struy, which begins with a jet of water and then ends up as "Uncle Uncle-Uncle" (*Struy* being a hybrid of *stryi* and *vuy*). But Gogol, with his Ukrainian background and his reading knowledge of Polish (he is known to have read a number of books in Polish in the course of his investigations into Ukrainian folksongs in the early 1830s), could not have missed the point and its verbal and phonetic possibilities. Now, there is obviously no way of getting inside Gogol's mind or of tracing his mental processes (even if

"*Viy*" *and* Undine

Henri Troyat, in his biography of Gogol, repeatedly pretends that he can). But if we keep all the *Undine*-related points outlined on the last pages firmly in mind, the following equation of spoonerisms clearly seems to suggest itself:

$$\frac{\text{STRUY (water spirit)}}{\text{STRYI (paternal uncle)}} = \frac{\text{VUY (maternal uncle and, possibly, phallus)}}{\text{VIY (earth spirit and, possibly, phallus)}}$$

The only hitch, of course, is that to yield a perfect spoonerism, the resultant form for the earth spirit would have to have a non-palatalized *v* and the name of the monster would thus be Vyi. The word *vyi* means "howling" in Ukrainian, which would have been appropriate contextually because of the wolves' howling that announces Viy's appearance. But this meaning would have been lost on most Russian readers, since the Russian word for "howling" is *voy*. Despite the slight phonetic discrepancy between Viy and *vyi*, the present hypothesis (and it is certainly no more than a hypothesis) would seem to come closer to explaining the title of "Viy" and the origin of some of that story's imagery than most previous efforts. The derivation, if true, could not be more ironic. In *Undine*, love between a man and a woman and their physical union are represented as the most fulfilling goal imaginable on earth and also as the path toward profound spiritual enrichment. Conjugal love and its consummation are what endow the previously soulless water sprite Undine with an immortal human soul and a heroic moral stature. The demon whom Gogol may have derived from this poem represents perhaps the most violent and impassioned rejection of human sexuality in all its forms that literature has ever known. That Gogol himself apparently did not fully realize the enormity of the chasm that separated his artistic vision from that of Pushkin

After Mirgorod

or Zhukovsky only confirms the justice of Hermann Hesse's observation that "no great poet has the power fully to interpret his own vision."

Writing *Mirgorod* and particularly "Viy" must have been a tremendous catharsis for Gogol. Even before the cycle was published, his development as a writer took new turns on several levels simultaneously, turns that can most plausibly be credited to the temporary exorcism of Gogol's inner sexual demons that was effected by the writing and publishing of *Mirgorod*. "Gogol's Retreat from Love," which Hugh McLean so ably discerned in *Mirgorod*, could now be halted, and it was—in the stories of the St. Petersburg cycle on which he had embarked while still working on *Mirgorod*. To be sure, woman is still the source of danger and ruin in the St. Petersburg stories and love and marriage are still to be avoided, but this constant Gogolian theme now appears in conjunction with new and different themes and is mostly subordinated to them. The retreat from love was not totally discontinued in Gogol's work after *Mirgorod*, however, because it was gathering new momentum and covering a new kind of trajectory in the series of plays which Gogol was writing more or less simultaneously with the stories of the St. Petersburg cycle.

Another major effect of *Mirgorod* was to cut Gogol's umbilical cord to the Ukraine. Up to "Viy" everything he wrote took place in the Ukraine; after it, nothing did. From that point on, everything he wrote was set either in St. Petersburg or in some nebulously obscure town in the central Russian provinces

After Mirgorod

("Rome" was the only exception to this rule). And, since "Viy" was such a powerful confrontation with the supernatural, it also marked the end of the Romantically demonic element in Gogol's work and, with the sole exception of "The Portrait," the end of any kind of supernatural element. Not that the Devil or the assorted lesser demons vanished from Gogol's work after *Mirgorod*. Dmitry Merezhkovsky in his book *Gogol and the Devil* showed most convincingly that they are still there, not only in personified form, as in the case of the allegorical demon who lights the lanterns at the end of "Nevsky Prospect," but also as the internalized and cryptic diabolical forces, familiar from Gogol's later correspondence, that pull the strings behind the scenes in such works as *Dead Souls* and "The Overcoat." Still, from "Viy" on Gogol's thematic preoccupations and the very atmosphere of his work change, suddenly and totally, in such a manner as to make the water nymphs, witches, and ghosts of *Evenings on a Farm near Dikanka* and *Mirgorod* neither needed nor possible any more. All in all, it would be hard to overestimate the importance of *Mirgorod* as a watershed separating Gogol's early manner from his later one.

The first three stories of the St. Petersburg cycle were completed during Gogol's ill-fated stint as a history professor, and they were published early in 1835 in a two-volume miscellany of his writings called *Arabesques*. In its composition *Arabesques* was even more of a hodgepodge than the somewhat similar later book, *Selected Passages from Correspondence with Friends*. Besides the three stories (which are the reason the book is still remembered), *Arabesques* contained Gogol's lectures on history, separate chapters from the two historical novels he began prior to writing "Taras Bulba" and then abandoned, some literary criticism, and a few essays on assorted other subjects. No one but literary scholars specializing in the study of Gogol ever bothers

Essays in Arabesques

to read any of his nonfictional writings. Only the most complete academic editions of his work in Russian are likely to include them. Foreign translations are all but nonexistent. And indeed, nonfictional Gogol is hard going: verbose, rhetorical, convoluted, and all too often beside the point. But just the same, his essays help us understand in greater depth his mentality, his aesthetic outlook, and his moral and political views.

The devil's dozen of essays found in the two volumes of *Arabesques* can be divided, to put it bluntly, into the ones in which Gogol writes of things he understands and loves (such as literature, painting, and, up to a certain point, music) and the ones on topics that Gogol grasps only in the realm of his imagination. Those that belong in the first group, like the analogous essays in *Selected Passages*, are critical contributions of permanent value. Such are "A Few Words on Pushkin," "On Ukrainian Folksongs," and "Sculpture, Painting, and Music," with its concluding sentence, "But should music ever abandon us, what will become of our world?" which became a motto of Russian Symbolists like Blok, who, to be sure, interpreted it in their own, post-Nietzschean way when they quoted it. Like all the other major Russian writers of the nineteenth century, Gogol understood literary processes more deeply and could write of them with greater perception than that epoch's much-vaunted literary critics.

The essays of the second group, however, are the ones that demonstrate Gogol's one-of-a-kind perception of the world in all of its glaring uniqueness. Here we find such flights of fancy as his overblown lectures on his own brand of ahistorical history (see p. 51), his ostensibly practical suggestions on how to teach geography ("Thoughts on Geography"), and his proposal for improving modern architecture ("On Contemporary Architecture"). A geography teacher, Gogol maintains, would do best to avoid all textbooks, which will only inhibit the students' imagination. Detailed maps showing national borders and all those curved shorelines are also confusing. Instead there should be simplified, crude outlines of each continent in black and white accompanied by imaginative, poetic verbal characterizations of that continent. Thus the student should be told that Asia is a place "where everything is so great and far-flung; where people are so pompous, so cold in appearance, and then are suddenly inflamed with indomitable passions; where they have childlike minds and yet are convinced that they are more intelligent than anyone; where everything is either pride or slavery," and so forth and so on. In Africa there are "lions, tigers, coconuts, palm trees, and people who differ but little in their appearance and sensual inclinations from the great apes who migrate in hordes all over the continent." The main thing is to make the students *visualize* what is described to them. Moving Asian tigers into Africa and covering that entire continent with hordes of roving King Kongs is clearly preferable to factual information, since it stands a better chance of capturing the students' imagination. Some of Gogol's imagery in "Thoughts on Geography" is oddly reminiscent of "Kubla Khan," with the difference that Coleridge would never have thought of using his poem as a geography lesson.

In architecture, Gogol particularly admired the Gothic cathedrals of the Middle Ages, especially those in Cologne and Milan. These buildings, like those of ancient Egypt and India, fulfilled what Gogol considered to be the aim of architecture: to awe the masses into unthinking submission to the laws of church and state. With the Renaissance and the Baroque, architecture deteriorated. It lost its spiritual qualities and its impressive massive and gigantic forms. To restore to architecture its former spirituality and sense of awe, Gogol proposes to construct what sound very much like skyscrapers—some half a century before Louis Sullivan:

> Towers, gigantic, colossal towers, are indispensable in a city, to say nothing of the importance of their use as Christian churches. Besides affording a view and being ornamental, they are needed to give the city a distinct profile, to serve as lighthouses, showing all people the way, preventing them from losing their way. In national capitals, they are needed even more for keeping the suburbs under surveillance. In our cities, the height of the buildings is usually limited to affording a view only of the city itself. But actually, it is essential for the capital to have a clear view for at least 150 versts in all directions; to this end, perhaps only one or two more stories could be added—and everything is changed. The radius of vision increases with height in an extraordinary progression. The capital thus gains tangible advantages, being able to oversee the provinces and to foresee everything in advance. The building, by becoming slightly higher than usual, gains in majesty. The artist gains from the inspiration to which the immensity of the building disposes him and experiences a greater tension.

As Leon Stilman points out in his commentary to this passage in "The All-Seeing Eye in Gogol," here Gogol is already the visionary preacher of *Selected Passages,* insistently offering advice that no one could possibly follow even if he wanted to. "What is typical here," writes Stilman, "is the concern for the interests of the state. The capital city here obviously stands for the state authorities, the tsar's government, which is located in the capital. It is this government that needs that immense watchtower in order to keep the suburbs under surveillance and thereby to foresee everything in advance—an odd idea, incidentally, which somehow confuses remoteness in space with remoteness in future time." Gogol's astigmatism in the perception of reality was a chronic condition, and it contributed to his ability to create a uniquely distorted vision of the world, just as the physical astigmatism from which El Greco suffered enabled him to conceive the distorted figures we so admire in his canvases.

The essays on history, geography, and architecture, when carefully read, spell out Gogol's political views, which remained unchanged from his adolescence to the time of his death. Victor Erlich has characterized these views as "tame, conformist, and officious" and pointed out that the supreme political concept for Gogol, one which took precedence over everything else, was the state, the government (and, one might add, its human embodiment, the tsar), rather than the country, the people, or mankind. Gogol never claimed to hold any other political views, and had his essays in *Arabesques* been read with attention when they were first published, he would have been spared endless accusations of self-betrayal and apostasy after the publication of *Selected Passages*. Even such a generally fair-minded and unprejudiced observer as Ivan Turgenev refused to take seriously Gogol's reading of excerpts from the *Arabesques* essays to him shortly before Gogol's death as proof that his political convictions had remained constant. "And this was said by the author of *The Inspector General*, one of the most subversive comedies that ever appeared on the stage," Turgenev commented incredulously.

While the nonfictional portions of *Arabesques* were either skimmed through or entirely ignored, the three new works of fiction which the book contained were recognized as a major literary event. These were "Nevsky Prospect," "Diary of a Madman," and the first version of "The Portrait." Together with "The Nose," first published in 1836 by Pushkin in his literary journal *The Contemporary*, and "The Overcoat," completed in

1841 and first published, together with the stories just enumerated, in the third volume of Gogol's collected prose in 1842, these stories constitute what is called the St. Petersburg cycle. Gogol himself recognized that these stories belonged together by including them in the third volume of the definitive edition of his writings for which he drastically reworked "Taras Bulba" and "The Portrait." In addition to the St. Petersburg cycle, the 1842 volume also contained two other pieces of prose fiction which for thematic and stylistic reasons are not a part of the cycle— "The Carriage" and "Rome."

The five St. Petersburg stories form a cycle not only because their action is situated within a certain clearly designated neighborhood in the center of that city, carefully and precisely identified by specifically mentioned landmarks (some of which are still extant in present-day Leningrad), but also because, like the *Mirgorod* cycle, the St. Petersburg stories are a set of variations on the same basic theme. They are all about the loneliness and helplessness of their male protagonists, each of whom has to undergo some unprecedented ordeal in the midst of an indifferent and impersonal big city. The term "alienation" was not to be coined by Karl Marx for at least another decade, and Gogol could not have been familiar with that concept, but that is in essence what his St. Petersburg stories are all about, in one way or another. Gogol discovered this theme and this particular formulation of it at a time when, as Donald Fanger has persuasively shown in his book *Dostoevsky and Romantic Realism*, Balzac in France and Dickens in England were also inaugurating the great central myth of the nineteenth-century realistic novel: the solitary ambitious or underprivileged hero face to face with the corrupt and impersonal metropolis. As Fanger pointed out, Fyodor Dostoyevsky inherited and synthesized the three variants of this theme that Gogol, Balzac, and Dickens pioneered more or less simul-

The St. Petersburg Stories

taneously and independently of each other. *Crime and Punishment* was the result.

Within the Russian literary tradition, Gogol's St. Petersburg stories follow the somewhat earlier precedent of Pushkin's "The Bronze Horseman" and "The Queen of Spades" in originating the image of a ghostly, fantastic St. Petersburg, the most beautiful, but also the most unreal city in Russia. It is curious indeed that Gogol, who was able to describe the central Russian provinces (which he had seen only fleetingly during his travels) with such believable palpability in "The Carriage," *The Inspector General*, and *Dead Souls*, turned the city in which he had lived and worked for six years into a vision of phantasmagoric unreality. It is this unreal St. Petersburg that we find later on in Dostoyevsky's *The Double* and "White Nights," in Bely's *Petersburg*, and in so many fine poems by Blok, Akhmatova, and Mandelstam.

At the center of attention in Gogol's St. Petersburg cycle are six utterly solitary male figures ("Nevsky Prospect" has two protagonists): two professional painters, two lowly civil servants, one junior army officer, and one mid-echelon civil servant trying to pass as an army officer. All six were born into the Russian gentry, but none of them occupies a position of any importance. These men range in age from the painter Chartkov in "The Portrait," who is twenty-two at the beginning of the story, to the painter Piskaryov and Lieutenant Pirogov in "Nevsky Prospect," who are in their mid-twenties, to Major Kovalyov in "The Nose," who is thirty-seven, to Poprishchin in "Diary of a Madman," in his early forties, and Akaky Akakievich in "The Overcoat," who is over fifty. Some of them, such as Kovalyov and Pirogov, are gregarious by nature, while others, such as Piskaryov and Akaky Akakievich, are of solitary disposition. But none of the six has any family or real friends, and when each is

The St. Petersburg Stories

overtaken by his particular unexpected crisis—and this is what happens eventually to each and every one of them—there is simply no one to turn to and nowhere to go for help. Poprish-chin, Kovalyov, and Chartkov have live-in servants, who could have been confidants or at least listeners. But unlike Khlesta-kov's resourceful and helpful servant in *The Inspector General,* these domestics are simply a part of the faceless multitude that surrounds the protagonists in the metropolis.

Whatever devilry, tragedy, or mischief may have stalked Go-golian characters in the Ukrainian settings of Dikanka or Mir-gorod, they all lived in warmly integrated communities and had their families and loved ones to turn to in times of crisis. The social environment of the protagonists of the St. Petersburg tales could not be more different. There is only one instance of a spontaneous and friendly contact between two men in the entire cycle: the conversation between Piskaryov and Pirogov when we first observe them in "Nevsky Prospect." But the two men part immediately after that one conversation, and although Piro-gov is said to be Piskaryov's close friend, he cannot even find time to attend his supposed friend's funeral at the end of the story. The loneliness and isolation of all these men in the St. Petersburg cycle are so total and their vulnerability to fate is so taken for granted—even the police and the authorities to whom Kovalyov and Akaky Akakievich vainly appeal can offer no help or protection—that one cannot help wondering what Go-gol's own experiences in St. Petersburg must have been like. His correspondence and other biographical records tell us that his years in St. Petersburg were a time of hectic social and literary activity, a time of splendid artistic achievement. Could it have been that the self-discipline he had to exercise to suppress his need for warm human contact of the only kind he was capable of experiencing was already taking its psychological toll in inner loneliness, frustration, and alienation, as it clearly was in the last decade of his life? Such a supposition would go a long way toward explaining both the desolate situation of single males in the St. Petersburg stories and Gogol's later decision to settle in Rome.

When catastrophes do overtake the men in the St. Petersburg stories, women (real ones or surrogates) are indirectly responsible in four cases out of six. The women are not witches or manipulators, they mean no harm, they are not even interested in the men whose ruin they cause, and in one instance the "woman" is an inanimate object. In the St. Petersburg cycle, the mere presence of a woman in a man's life seems enough to spell death, insanity, or physical punishment. The hero of "The Nose" does escape, inexplicably and illogically, even though a manipulative woman tries to maneuver him into marriage and there is some talk of her resorting to witchcraft to attain her aim. In this particular case, Kovalyov's unexpected escape may be seen as just another of the absurdist incongruities in which "The Nose" abounds. Chartkov in "The Portrait" is the only one of the six to shun all sexual or even symbolic contact with women. His only dealings with women are social and professional and his punishment at the end of the story comes for the betrayal of his artistic calling. It is the only punishment that makes sense in the entire cycle and the only deserved one.

"The Portrait" is the most conventional story of the cycle and also the least satisfactory artistically. It was attacked by the critics when first published in *Arabesques*, and Gogol thoroughly reworked it in Rome for the 1842 edition. With its enchanted portrait of an evil moneylender who comes out of the portrait's frame to exercise a nefarious influence on the life and career of a promising young painter, the story is in some ways rather standard Romantic fare, reminiscent of both Poe and E. T. A. Hoffmann. But within this familiar configuration, Gogol offers a serious treatment of an important social problem: society's pressure on the creative artist to sell his talent for material advantages. The problem is still very much present, of course, and it is endemic in every known form of modern society. The highest rewards and greatest honors still go not to those who produce the best art of the age but to those whose art pleases the ruling class and the people in a position to foot the bill. The situation of Gogol's Chartkov can in fact be most instructively compared to the situation of painters in the Soviet Union under Stalin, as outlined by Ilya Ehrenburg (not nearly so important an artist as Gogol, but an astute social observer when he allowed himself to be) in his post-Stalinist novel *The Thaw*. The inescapable conclusion of such a comparison is that in the 1830s Chartkov had the freedom to choose whether to betray his artistic integrity or not; for Ehrenburg's painters in the 1930s, the choice is between selling out or giving up art altogether.

As Vladimir Nabokov has observed, Gogol had a way of planning his works and devising their central ideas *after* writing them. *The Inspector General* and *Dead Souls* were provided with rationales and explanations some time after they were published. "The Portrait," however, follows the precedent of "Terrible Vengeance" and has a built-in elucidation in the form of an explanatory epilogue. The explanation in the 1842 version is totally different from the one offered in the 1835 edition. The earlier version of the epilogue blamed Chartkov's involvement with the haunted portrait and his artistic downfall on the intrusion of the Antichrist into the world; in the later one, the conflict is between the demon of materialism and the spiritual values that art embodies. Neither epilogue really works. One particular artist's sellout is too slender a theme to support the great mystical concept of the Antichrist all by itself. The epilogue of the

"The Portrait"

1842 version is both better written and somewhat more convincing in terms of the story's central idea. But the only stronghold Gogol can think of opposing to the overwhelming forces of evil and materialism is the one we have already encountered as the ultimate answer in "Saint John's Eve" and "Terrible Vengeance": the walls of a monastery. Since the diabolical forces use money to corrupt art, this is the only place where a creative artist can be safe. The eerie scene in which Chartkov keeps awakening from oppressive nightmares only to find that he has awakened into still another dream was obviously very much in Dostoyevsky's mind when he was describing Svidrigailov's delirium in *Crime and Punishment*.

"Nevsky Prospect" is, like "The Portrait," quintessentially Romantic in its conception, but it is a far more satisfactory and influential piece of writing. The urban theme is predominant and the thoroughfare that gives the story its name almost becomes a principal character in its own right. In a firework-like display of verbal flair and visual imagination, Gogol makes the reader follow the comings and goings of the various types of people on Nevsky Prospect (that is, Avenue), making wide use of synecdoche, a special form of metonymy in which a part represents the whole. People on Nevsky Prospect are reduced to a bonnet, a pair of bouffant sleeves, a moustache, a pair of eyes, or a smile, bringing to mind the drawings of Gogol's near-contemporary Gerard Grandville (1803-1847), who portrayed a theater audience as eye-headed people and otherwise replaced the head or the body with some other anatomical feature. Gogol's imagina-

"Nevsky Prospect"

tion was prodigious enough to enable him to anticipate methods of visualization that we associate with the art of considerably later periods: Impressionism (Plyushkin's garden in *Dead Souls* and the water nymph episode in "Viy"); Cubism and Italian Futurism (the opening pages of "The Carriage"); Surrealism (everywhere, but particularly in "The Nose"); and, here, in "Nevsky Prospect," Expressionism: "The sidewalk rushed under him, carriages with their galloping horses seemed immobile, the bridge stretched out and broke at its arch, a house stood with its roof downward, a sentry box was falling toward him, and the sentry's halberd and the gilded letters of a shop's sign with scissors painted on it seemed to be glittering on his very eyelashes."

Against the background of the kaleidoscopically mutating street, the drama of man's search for woman and love is acted out in the two principal episodes of the story, one tragic, the other farcical. The smug, self-satisfied vulgarian Lieutenant Pirogov and his painter friend Piskaryov each espy the women of their dreams. At first they think they are talking of the same woman, but then they realize that the painter was drawn to an ideally beautiful dark girl wearing a flowing cape, while the officer was taken with a cute and winsome little blonde. Like the attractive and potentially available young women in other works by Gogol, these two have no names. The brunette walks rapidly along the street in her elegant attire, without looking right or left, while the blonde stops at every shop window and constantly ogles the passers-by. Each of them seems to be suitable for the young man whose eye she has caught. The idealistic painter wants a woman attuned to his artistic aspirations, while the prosaic lieutenant has only a bit of amorous dalliance in mind. But, as Gogol warns at the end of the story, appearances are deceptive on Nevsky Prospect. The poetic dark woman turns out to be a prostitute from a brothel, while the coquettish blonde

is a German housewife of unassailable virtue. The painter tries
to become involved with the prostitute and to rescue her from her
way of life. She does not want to be rescued, and the painter,
crushed by the collapse of his ideals in the face of crass reality,
withdraws into a world of dreams, takes opium, and eventually
commits suicide by slashing his throat while under the influence
of the drug. The lecherous lieutenant gets off easier: he merely
gets flogged by the German lady's jealous husband and his cronies, an affront that his flighty nature enables him to survive and
even to forget after consuming some pastry and attending a
dance.

In the Piskaryov portion of "Nevsky Prospect," Gogol inaugurates still another major theme of Russian nineteenth-century
literature to which many of his successors were to turn: the encounter of a sensitive intellectual man with a prostitute and her
resistance to his efforts to reform her. In 1862 Apollon Grigoriev
gave this theme one of the finest treatments it has ever received
in his impressive autobiographical narrative poem "Upstream on
the Volga." Two years later, Nikolai Chernyshevsky offered his
own simplistic solution to this problem in his atrociously written but influential novel *What Is To Be Done?* For Chernyshevsky, all one needed to do was to give the prostitute a sewing
machine: in no time at all, she would become a productive member of society and an intellectual in her own right. Dostoyevsky
savagely lampooned this notion in *Notes from the Underground*,
written the same year as Chernyshevsky's novel. Later, in *Crime
and Punishment* and *The Idiot*, Dostoyevsky very effectively
stood the subject on its head, as Alexander Blok was also to do
in his own way in his play *The Incognita* (1906). Tolstoy's version of the situation is found in *Anna Karenina* (the subplot that
involves Nikolai Levin and his ex-prostitute mistress). One of
the most level-headed and, at the same time, sensitive treatments

of the subject appeared at the end of the century in Chekhov's story "An Attack of Nerves" (1889). All in all, this is a progeny of which Gogol would have had every right to feel proud, had he but lived long enough to see it.[12]

The remaining three stories of the St. Petersburg cycle, "Diary of a Madman," "The Nose," and "The Overcoat," stand at the pinnacle of Gogol's achievement as a prose writer. Their amazing originality, their translator-defying verbal precision and inventiveness, and their universal significance give them a permanent place in the front ranks of Russian and European literature and a special luster that no later achievement of Russian prose, be it that of Tolstoy, Chekhov, Bely, Babel, or Nabokov, has been able to dim. In some miraculous way, the sensibility embodied in these three stories transcends both Romanticism and nascent nineteenth-century realism and has a way of speaking directly to the twentieth-century imagination. Written less than a decade after the deaths of Beethoven and Goethe, they read like the work of a contemporary of Franz Kafka, Raymond Queneau, or Tommaso Landolfi.

The hero of "Diary of a Madman"[13] is the most articulate and most fully human of Gogol's trio of meek, put-upon little men. Unlike his predecessor Shponka and his successor Akaky Akakievich, Aksenty Poprishchin (the name is derived from *poprishche*, "profession" or "chosen field of work") takes an active interest in the world around him. Where Shponka sits in his room, cleaning his buttons and setting mousetraps, and Akaky Akakievich reduces his spare-time interests to copying the same

"Diary of a Madman"

documents he has to copy for a living, Poprishchin reads poetry (awful doggerel, admittedly, but he does read it), goes to the theater (choosing the worst and most obvious farces, but he does go), reads newspapers, takes an interest in current politics, and feels attracted to a pretty actress he hears singing a song in a vaudeville. Even apart from his hopeless passion for his boss's daughter, this madman has a whole array of desires, reactions, and responses to life that make him incomparably more full-blooded and "normal" than the supposedly perfectly sane Shponka and Akaky Akakievich. What puts him in the same class with them is that he is, like them, a very small being caught up in a world controlled by mysterious and all-powerful personalities.

A dimension that makes Poprishchin unique in Gogol's work is his strong, desperate, and frequently asserted sense of class pride. Socially, he is reduced to the level of lackeys and flunkeys; his absurd menial duties at his superior's—sharpening goose quills—bring him down to the level of servants, despite his minimally respectable position within the civil service hierarchy. Yet, again and again, Poprishchin harps on his noble origins. This kind of class pride may be more feudal and more primitive than the more modern kind of rank-and-position-based social snobbery practiced by Major Kovalyov in "The Nose," but it is this pride that gives Poprishchin the minimal self-respect that Shponka and Akaky Akakievich so obviously lack. This class pride is also consonant with Poprishchin's particular form of insanity, megalomania. By imagining himself to be the king of Spain, he simply restores to himself the social importance that his serf-owning ancestors once had.

In the nineteenth century, "Diary of a Madman" was frequently read as a clinical case study. Medical specialists wrote and published articles certifying that the story contained a classical outline of the onset of paranoia, a fully believable account of how a normal and sane man retreats into a world of daydreams and loses his mind under the pressure of his unbearably humiliating and lowly position in life and his disappointments in love. Such an interpretation could only arise from the widespread nineteenth-century delusion that Gogol was a photographic realist, recording Russian life with objective precision. In the very first entry of the madman's diary Poprishchin overhears a conversation between two dogs, Madgie and Fidèle, and discovers that they are carrying on a correspondence. The idea of the man's initial sanity is thus undermined by Gogol at the very beginning: the distance in logic from the talking and corresponding dogs to believing oneself the king of Spain is not great enough to provide room for development of an incipient insanity.

Poprishchin's reaction to his discovery of the canine correspondence (Gogol got this idea from Cervantes via a story by Hoffmann) is typical: it offends his sense of caste. "I have never in my life yet heard of a dog that was able to write. No one but a nobleman by birth can write correctly. To be sure, some merchant-bookkeepers and even a few serfs may write a little now and then, but their writing is for the most part mechanical: no commas, no periods, no style." Such peculiar equating of domestic animals with enserfed peasants and sometimes with children appears in a few other works by Gogol: the parallel functions of Ivan Ivanovich's serf children and Ivan Nikiforovich's dogs; the similar treatment accorded their children and horses by the well-born strollers of "Nevsky Prospect," who inquire equally about the health of both (the strangeness of this conjunction is further driven home by the narrator, who hastens to assure the reader that the children deserved to be inquired about along with the horses because "they displayed great talents"); and in *Dead Souls* the equating of Chichikov's horses with his

servants, which Gogol accomplishes by assigning the horses colloquial, peasantlike speech mannerisms that place these animals
on the mental and social level of serfs.

Our view of Poprishchin's world is binocular: it is shown alternately through his diary and through excerpts from the correspondence of the dogs, which he intercepts (this last device, of
course, utterly precludes all possibility of interpreting the story
on a conventionally realistic plane). The observations of the little lapdog Madgie are in all cases more level-headed and more
informed than those of the madman himself. It is through Madgie's eyes that we get to see and to know the object of Poprishchin's hopeless infatuation, his superior's daughter Sophie. Poprishchin can see Sophie only the way Telecles saw Alcinoe,
Andry Bulba saw his Polish beauty, and Piskaryov saw the
lovely prostitute: as a disembodied angelic being, an ethereal
vision of purity and beauty. To Poprishchin's credit, however,
this exalted view does not prevent him from dreaming of entering Sophie's bedroom and joining her there, which Telecles or
Piskaryov would never have presumed. But, as seen by her lapdog, Sophie is a vain, frivolous upper-class girl who cares only
about balls, parties, and dresses and is very conventionally in
love with a dark-haired young courtier.

Alone among Gogol's desirable young women, Sophie has a
name and a personality of her own. This is partly because this
wealthy young woman from the highest social stratum is totally
and hopelessly unavailable to the lowly pen-pusher Poprishchin.
No sexual contact between them is even remotely possible, and
Gogol can for once forego the panic that invariably overtakes
him when an attractive young woman enters his narrative. In
addition, Sophie is observed at close quarters not by a potential
lover, but by a very special reporter: her dog, a young female
herself, who often sounds like Sophie's close friend and social

equal. Poprishchin's idealization and Madgie's ironic but affectionate gossiping combine to portray one of Gogol's very few fully real and fully alive female characters. Sophie is neither deep nor especially admirable, but she is a character who exists as a person in her own right, and as such she is a welcome change from the idealized statues, witches, and castrators who pass for women in so much of Gogol's work.

From the dog's letters, Poprishchin learns that Sophie is in love with her court chamberlain and is about to become engaged to him. His desperate *cri de coeur* at this discovery ("Everything that is best in this world is taken by the court chamberlains or the generals. You find yourself your own poor man's treasure, you think it is within your reach, but a court chamberlain or a general will snatch it away") was eagerly seized upon by nineteenth-century critics as evidence of Gogol's social consciousness and his philanthropic attitudes. But of course Sophie, who sees Poprishchin as a "turtle in a sack" and who cannot refrain from laughter at the sight of him, never was his in any sense and could not be "taken away" from him. Gogol rather cruelly inverts the standard literary ploy of an old and ugly rich man trying to win the love of a young and pretty woman who is poor by portraying instead an unprepossessing and aging poor man hankering after an unattainable, wealthy young beauty. Poprishchin's love for Sophie, as touching as it might appear, is simply further evidence of his insanity, of the divorce of his thinking from actual reality.

The news of Sophie's impending marriage pushes Poprishchin over the brink, and he takes refuge in the delusion that he is the king of Spain. The insane asylum to which he is taken and the tortures that were inflicted on the inmates of such institutions in the nineteenth century under the guise of treatment are described in all their starkness. This portion of the story is another of those

"Diary of a Madman"

uncanny prophecies of his own last days that we find here and there in Gogol's writings. The tortures to which reputable physicians subjected Gogol himself just before his death are little different from what Poprishchin had to endure. The final entry in the diary crowns the story with a shattering emotional climax. Poprishchin's pain and despair become as real for the reader as they are for the character. Freedom and release are momentarily gained through an imaginary escape in an airborne troika flying over a landscape that might have been painted by Marc Chagall. Then a sudden comical grimace of pure insanity—the announcement about the wart under the nose of the Dey of Algiers— terminates the story on a highly poignant note.

"Diary of a Madman" is an amazing performance, a work that manages to be simultaneously Gogol's most touching tragedy and his funniest comedy. The delicious mini-parodies, scattered throughout the story, can be perceived only on repeated readings: the parody of police investigation novels ("I need to have a talk with your little dog"); of the literary critics who demand a human-interest angle at all costs ("Give me a human being! I want to see a human being, I require spiritual nourishment that would sustain and delight my soul," Poprishchin exclaims, disgusted at having to read about Madgie's canine love affairs); and of the editorial style of commenting on current political affairs ("England will not tolerate such and such, France has such and such interests to consider, etc."). Not the least remarkable thing about "Diary of a Madman" is that this tale, told by a madman and a dog, contains some of Gogol's most believable and real human beings, including the dogs.

Surrealism: "The Nose"

The world inhabited by the protagonists of the St. Petersburg stories is a threatening world of sudden reversals, deceptive appearances, and unimagined danger emerging from unsuspected quarters. In "The Portrait" this state of affairs is attributed to the mystically corrupting power of money and to the machinations of the Antichrist; in "Nevsky Prospect" to the demon of deception who lights the lanterns so that they show everything in a false light; in "Diary of a Madman" to the insanity of the narrator. When Gogol began writing "The Nose," he intended to motivate the absurdities, incongruities, and deliberate illogicality of this story by presenting it as a bad dream of the hero's. The Russian title of the original draft was *Son* ("Dream"). In the final version, the dream framework was omitted, and the original title was changed to read backward, producing *Nos* ("Nose"). Reading the title backward is an essentially surrealistic procedure, one of many that we find in "The Nose," the most authentically surrealistic of Gogol's works, the one where we find this variety of imagination, which in more diluted form is to be found in so much of Gogol's other writings, at its most dense and concentrated.

Much has been written about the Gogolian imagination and several theories have been devised to explain it. Wolfgang Kayser in Germany, Yuri Mann in the Soviet Union, and Victor Erlich in the United States have all advocated the concept of the grotesque in literature as the key to understanding the Gogolian form of fantasy.[14] Much of what they have to say is interesting and, up to a point, persuasive, but their definition of the grotesque, which places Gogol in the company of Swift, Hoffmann,

Poe, Kafka, Pirandello, and Mayakovsky in literature and suggests Hieronymus Bosch, Goya, and Dali as his parallels in the visual arts, is much too broad. It ignores the specifics of Gogol's particular artistic method. The narrower concept, Surrealism, which can be subsumed within the grotesque as one of its varieties, would seem to be much more to the point. The term "Surrealism" was not devised until the 1920s, but the notion that a heightened sense of reality can be achieved by the juxtaposition of familiar and even prosaic elements in an incongruous or unexpected context was known and exploited by certain nineteenth-century writers and painters. Lautréamont's famous encounter between a sewing machine and an umbrella on a dissecting table results from precisely the same kind of imagination that is involved in Gogol's having the ghost of the drowned maiden arrange for a letter of recommendation from the provincial administrative headquarters in "May Night," or in his naming a horse Assessor (*Zasedatel'*), a dog Patroness of Charity (*Popechitel'-nitsa*), and a serf Gregory Go-Right-Up-To-It-But-You-Won't-Get-There (Grigory Doezzhai-Ne-Doedesh') in *Dead Souls*. Lautréamont is not likely to have known Gogol, but his *Les Chants de Maldoror* contains an episode about a man who meets a familiar-looking person in a brothel and discovers that person to be one of his own hairs which has acquired a separate identity. Together with Lewis Carroll, both Gogol and Lautréamont belong in the select company of authentic nineteenth-century surrealists in literature; their counterparts in the visual arts are not Bosch and Goya, but some of their own contemporaries: Grandville, Tenniel, possibly Fuseli, and most certainly the recently rediscovered Richard Dadd (1817-1886). Ignored and confined in a mental institution for most of his lifetime, Dadd is a painter whose canvases are a far closer visual counterpart to "Diary of a

Surrealism: "The Nose"

Madman" and "The Nose" than the numerous illustrations Gogol's own countrymen have provided for those stories.[15]

The text of "The Nose" was written in three successive versions, each succeeding one more dead-pan and impossibly unreal than the last. In February of 1835, Gogol offered the first version of the story to the journal *Moscow Observer*. Despite Gogol's reputation and the wide popularity of his work, the journal turned the story down for being supposedly too "trivial" and "filthy." One year later, Pushkin, who found that "The Nose" contained "much that is unexpected, fantastic, merry, and original," published the first revised version in his journal *The Contemporary*. The final version, which added some of the most important episodes to the story, was done by Gogol for the 1842 edition of his collected prose. It is by far the most complete and satisfactory one.

The tale of the nose begins in a perfectly prosaic manner, with exact information about the date, the time, and the place of the events to be described. The barber and his wife to whom we are then introduced are actually the standard simple-minded peasant and his shrewish wife of the Ukrainian puppet theater tradition, whom Gogol had already described in their native surroundings in "The Fair at Sorochintsy." Transferred to the unfamiliar milieu of St. Petersburg, this couple may be hard to recognize for what they are, but their dialogue is very much true to type. When a human nose is discovered in one of the loaves of bread that the wife has just baked, she instantly blames it all on her husband. In Gogol's most explicit pre-Freudian vein, she scornfully points out that while he can still hone his razor on a leather strap, he is approaching a state where he will not be able to perform his conjugal duties. To top off this sexual non sequitur, she calls her husband *potaskushka*, that is, a strumpet or a (female)

Surrealism: "The Nose"

streetwalker (English translations, by rendering the word as "gadabout," once again sabotage Gogol's meaning). (This is not the only instance of an angry character in Gogol reaching for an insult that could only be applied to a person of the opposite sex. Mr. Omelet in *Marriage*, feeling that the bride had cheated him, asks the matchmaker to tell her she is *podlets*, that is, a male scoundrel.)

The principal character of "The Nose" and the original owner of that missing appendage is a civil servant named Kovalyov. He has attained the rank of collegiate assessor and come to St. Petersburg from the Caucasus to find a suitable appointment. To make himself appear more dashing, Kovalyov prefers to be known by the military equivalent of his civil service rank and calls himself Major Kovalyov. After explaining rather delicately that the man has no business appropriating a military rank, Gogol pointedly refers to him as Major Kovalyov for a whole long paragraph, spelling the rank and the name out repeatedly even where the pronoun "he" would have been expected. The man is clearly a snob, a poseur, and something of a fraud, a cheerful, easygoing vulgarian and a close cousin of Lieutenant Pirogov from "Nevsky Prospect." He is also much given to pursuing women of the lower class. When he wakes up one morning to find his nose missing, he correctly perceives his loss as a threat to both his chances of finding a new appointment and his social life, to say nothing of his chances for sexual conquests.

Kovalyov's reactions to his predicament are understandable enough, but the course of action on which he embarks can only be described as Gogolian. He considers his vanished nose a piece of missing property, and he seeks to have it restored by appealing, in this order, to the police, to the press, and to medical science (the last, in the natural order of things, would of course have been his first resort). In describing Kovalyov's encounters with the men representing these three spheres, Gogol sets up several traps for readers who may be expecting familiar situations and logical motivations. Kovalyov's visit to the police official's apartment may easily enough be taken for a satire directed against corrupt and bribable policemen. They were indeed a frequent target of Russian satirical writers throughout the nineteenth century. But what looks like satire actually resembles a painting by René Magritte more than it does any kind of pointed social commentary, for the policeman in question has a mania about loaves of sugar: "In his home, the antechamber, which also served as the dining room, was piled high with sugar loaves supplied to him by merchants out of pure friendship."

The scene in the newspaper office, with its classified advertisements of serf girls for sale, offered alongside a spirited young horse "only seventeen years old" and some turnip and radish seeds received directly from London, may likewise strike a modern reader as an indictment of the moral squalor of Russian life at the time. But those realia represent for Gogol simply the humdrum details of everyday life; he needs them as the background for the concealed central joke of that passage, which is an advertisement extending an invitation to amateurs of old shoe soles to come and haggle over them daily from eight to three in the morning (not believing her eyes, Constance Garnett changed the time to three in the afternoon). The young doctor to whom Kovalyov takes his problem next is described as a tall man who had "pitch-black sideburns, a fresh-faced, healthy doctor's wife, ate fresh apples every morning, and kept his mouth extraordinarily clean, gargling every morning for three quarters of an hour and polishing his teeth with five different sorts of brushes." The rich, profuse, and incongruous details by which this doctor is described refuse so stubbornly to add up to any kind of coherent impression that some Russian commentators at the turn of the

---

Surrealism: "The Nose"

century, when it became fashionable to look for devils in every line of Gogol, decided that this faceless outline of a doctor must be the Devil incarnate.

Unable to effect the return of his nose with the aid of temporal powers, Kovalyov decides to attribute its disappearance to the machinations of a certain lady of his acquaintance. With this Mme Alexandra Podtochina (her name comes from the perfective verb *podtochit'*, "to undermine"), widow of a staff officer, we at last find ourselves on familiar Gogolian territory. She has been trying to lure Kovalyov into marriage with her daughter; he has successfully evaded her wiles and now he thinks she has removed his nose with the aid of witchcraft as a stratagem to force him to comply. Typically, we are told the mother's first name, patronymic, last name, and her late husband's rank, while the daughter, who is matrimonially available, has no name at all. But Mme Podtochina, while refusing to give up her matchmaking plans, pleads innocent to the charge of witchcraft, and her reply seems to convince Kovalyov, although a veteran reader of Gogol is more likely to return the verdict of "charge not proven."

Before the nose gets restored to Kovalyov's face, it is (1) baked in a loaf of bread; (2) dropped by the barber into the river; (3) transformed into an important government official, who attends church services at the Cathedral of Our Lady of Kazan and refuses to hobnob with its former owner, the latter being far too beneath him (or it) in social position; (4) exposed as the leader of a band of criminals, who is arrested as he tries to flee the country; (5) brought back wrapped in a handkerchief by a policeman; and (6) found not amenable to being restored to its former place by the doctor, who advises Kovalyov to pickle it in alcohol and sell it to the highest bidder. The barber who found the nose in the bread and threw it into the river was also supposedly the

nose's confederate in the criminal gang that the police uncov-
ered; at the end of the story, he is amiably shaving Kovalyov
again. The mystery of the missing nose is solved by an almost
totally blind policeman, who not only manages to retain his
position on the force despite this handicap, but claims that he
inherited the condition from his mother-in-law. The only justification the author can offer for all this is: "No matter what anyone may say, such things do happen in this world—rarely, but
they do happen."

The most logic-defying piece of writing in Russian literature to
this day, "The Nose" is narrated in a consistently matter-of-fact
manner of poker-faced seriousness. From Gogol's time to our
own, there has always been a group of critics in Russia (their
political orientation changes every few decades, but their basic
outlook has remained constant regardless of how far to the right
or to the left their politics may veer) who are primarily concerned with whether a given work of literature teaches the reader
a valuable lesson and what sort of example it will set for young
people. Mindful of how irritating "The Nose" was sure to prove
for such a mentality, Gogol incorporated into his story's penul-
timate paragraph a prepackaged response from this particular
critical camp. "But what is most strange, most incomprehensible
of all is that authors can choose such subjects. I must confess
that this is altogether unfathomable, it certainly is . . . No, no, I
cannot understand it at all. In the first place, it is of no use to the
Fatherland, and in the second place . . . but no, in the second
place there is no use either. I simply have no idea what this is
about." This little disclaimer served to forestall the expected
kind of criticism—a clever stratagem that produced exactly the
results Gogol intended.

Like the work of the French and Spanish surrealists of the
1920s (André Breton, Luis Buñuel, the early Salvador Dali),

Surrealism: "The Nose"

who sought to incorporate in their art the discoveries of Sigmund Freud, combined with those of Karl Marx, "The Nose" is an obvious sitting duck for Freudian and Marxist interpretations. As could have been expected, Dr. Yermakov had a field day with this story, seeing phallic symbolism not only in the major's missing nose and the barber's loaf of bread, but also in the nose's entry into the cathedral, which takes place on March 25, the Feast of the Annunciation. In most Soviet criticism, however, the nose has traditionally been seen as an allegory for Kovalyov's sense of class and its loss as his real or imagined loss of social position. But the beautiful consistency with which the runaway nose remains both a person and an object throughout makes mincemeat of any such reductionist interpretation of the story. Like all works of authentically surrealistic art, "The Nose" stubbornly resists paraphrase or conversion into an allegory. As either a sexual joke or a social satire it is very small potatoes. As a vision of the surreal within the ordinary, as a revelation of metaphysical absurdity, as the piece of magnificently inspired nonsense it really is, it is beyond compare.

Then he suddenly dreamed that his wife was not a human being but some sort of woolen fabric and that in the city of Mogilyov he went to see a merchant in his shop. "What sort of fabric would you like?" said the merchant. "Why don't you take some wife, it's the most fashionable fabric! It wears so well! Everyone is having frock coats made from it these days." The merchant measured off a length of wife and cut it. Ivan Fyodorovich put it under his arm and went to the Jewish tai-

Non-Human Wives: "The Carriage"

lor. "No," said the Jew, "this is a poor fabric. No one has frock coats made from it."

This episode from the hero's dream in "Ivan Fyodorovich Shponka and His Aunt" marks the first appearance of the theme of substitute or surrogate wives, which becomes very important in Gogol's later work. As his literary art matured and deepened, Gogol was apparently no longer willing or able to portray conventional heterosexual love relationships, which he had never experienced in person, which he disliked and knew only from literature. As a perceptive literary artist, he must have realized how unconvincing his efforts in this direction, from "Woman" to the love scenes in "Taras Bulba," had been. He got away with expressing his fear and loathing of heterosexuality in a whole series of remarkable works, among them "Ivan Fyodorovich Shponka and His Aunt," "Viy," and "Nevsky Prospect." In two of his plays, *The Inspector General* and *Marriage*, he discovered ways of parodying and ridiculing the entire notion of love and marriage between men and women. In Chapters VIII and IX of "Taras Bulba" he went as far as he dared in proclaiming his attraction for and devotion to warm emotional bonds between men. But in the writings of his last and possibly most important period, Gogol was seriously handicapped by a predicament that in effect barred him from describing any sort of responsive emotional involvement with which he himself could empathize. The result was that emotional sterility and sense of emotional impotence of which so many commentators have complained in Gogol's work, without, however, trying to discover the underlying causes.

When Marcel Proust found himself faced with the same problem, he resorted to the stratagem of disguising certain of his originally male characters as females, so that his hero could be in-

Non-Human Wives: "The Carriage"

volved emotionally not with Gilbert, but with Gilberte, not with
a heterosexual man named Albert, but with a lesbian named
Albertine. No such notion was likely to have occurred to Gogol.
What we find instead in his later work is the frequent situation
where the male protagonist is involved emotionally with a character who has a woman's name or is of feminine gender, but who
is neither a woman nor, for that matter, a human being. Suggested initially in the episode from Ivan Shponka's dream quoted
above, the device surfaced next in "The Carriage" (also translated as "The Coach" and as "The Calash"). This story, a dazzling bit of Gogolian *jeu d'esprit*, usually leaves most non-Russian
readers cold, even though Tolstoy considered it the very peak of
perfection among Gogol's works. It was after reading "The Carriage" that Anton Chekhov, who in the spring of 1889 had re-
read Turgenev and Goncharov, as well as most of Gogol's work,
wrote to his friend Alexei Suvorin: "But how spontaneous, how
powerful Gogol is in comparison! What an artist he is! His 'Carriage' alone is worth two hundred thousand rubles. Sheer delight, nothing more or less. He is the greatest Russian writer."

What so delighted Tolstoy, Chekhov, and innumerable other
Russian readers about "The Carriage" is the prodigious stylistic
inventiveness which Gogol lavishes on this seemingly unpreten-
tious little anecdote. This aspect of Gogol usually makes the
translators of his work into English acutely uncomfortable, and
they have traditionally done their best to flatten his writing manner by rendering it in the most neutral English they can muster.
Those who read in English the opening pages of "The Carriage,"
describing the arrival of a military garrison in a dusty little provincial town, have no way of knowing what a marvel of innovative technique they are. Using the synecdochal method that was
so effective in "Nevsky Prospect," Gogol causes the military men
to materialize on the scene gradually, bit by bit, one moustache

---

Non-Human Wives: "The Carriage"

or cap or scrap of conversation at a time, with a technique that partakes both of cubistic painting and of cinematographic montage.

In its few brief pages, "The Carriage" outlines a confrontation between the all-male society of the garrison officers (all of them apparently bachelors) and a local married landowner with a somewhat shady military past. The landowner, who is the principal character in the story, bears the totally impossible name of Pifagor Chertokutsky ("Pythagoras from the Devil's Nook," from *chert*, "devil," and *kút*, "corner" or "nook"; this is a more likely etymology than "Dock-tailed Devil," which is sometimes offered for this name). He attends a drunken stag party given by the general of the brigade, which is also graced by the presence of a "robust southern beauty" named Agrafena Ivanovna. In a story by Bestuzhev-Marlinsky or a poem by Yazykov such a female presence at military men's revels would of course be an uninhibited local courtesan; but Gogol pulls a fast switch— Agrafena Ivanovna, despite her Christian first name and patronymic, is the general's beautiful mare. The general brags of her beauty and the other men admire her physique in terms that might almost suggest she was the general's mistress. To hold his own in the company of these bachelors he likes and envies, Chertokutsky changes the subject of the conversation from horses to carriages, in order to be able to boast of the marvelous Viennese-built conveyance he owns. Carried away by the conviviality (in Gogol's original text there was detailed specification of the degree to which the various guests at the party unbuttoned their clothes; this was deleted by the tsarist censorship as supposedly disrespectful to the military authorities and reinstated in the Soviet editions), Chertokutsky invites the officers to his home for lunch the next day, so that they may inspect and admire his carriage. The carriage (*kolyaska*, feminine gender) is clearly Chertokutsky's equivalent of and answer to the general's Agrafena Ivanovna. His pretty blonde wife, whom one would have expected to assume this function, is mentioned only as an afterthought, after the invitation has been extended, discussed, and accepted: "There, your excellency, you will also make the acquaintance of the lady of the house."

Chertokutsky gets drunk, oversleeps, forgets about the invitation, and makes no preparations for receiving his guests. His wife, with whom he has that rare thing in Gogol, a close and affectionate relationship, and who is referred to throughout the story only as "the blonde" and as "the pretty one" (compare the full name and patronymic of the general's mare), is of no help. Being a likable Gogolian narcissist, she spends the entire morning admiring her own beauty before the mirror and trying on a new white blouse that "draped around her body like flowing water." The officers arrive, riding in their own elegant carriages (some of them sitting on each other's laps) or on horseback. Unable to face his guests, Chertokutsky seeks refuge in the very carriage he had invited them to inspect. When the general asks to see the carriage, the hero is discovered and disgraced.

Considered by itself, "The Carriage," for all the filigreed mastery of its technical execution, may appear no more than a bit of amusing literary fluff. But examined against the background of the sexual symbolism that pervades Gogol's other work, this story of the humiliation of a happily married heterosexual at the hands of a circle of mutually committed and mutually adjusted bachelor officers is not quite as inconsequential as it might first appear. The device of replacing human female characters with animals or inanimate objects—in this case a horse and a carriage —develops the suggestion already found in Ivan Shponka's dream, and it is a device that was to reappear in some of Gogol's most important later work. Both Andrei Bely and Vladimir Na-

Alienation and Love: "The Overcoat"

bokov, neither of whom was aware of Gogol's homosexual inclinations, have asserted in their respective books on Gogol that
the traveling case of Chichikov in *Dead Souls* was actually his
wife (this case is referred to on occasion by the masculine gender
word *larchik*, but at critical points in the novel, a feminine gender word, *shkatulka*, is used). The "heroine" of the play *The
Gamblers* is a deck of cards named Adelaida Ivanovna. The
most important and the most consistent application of this ob-
ject-as-woman device (self-evident in Russian, since all the feminine-gender objects have to be referred to as "she") occurs in
Gogol's supreme masterpiece, "The Overcoat."

The single most famous short story in the whole of Russian
literature, "The Overcoat" is also the most widely misunderstood. Russian critics of the nineteenth century enveloped it in a
thick fog of sentimentalization. It was credited with being the
beginning of the philanthropic trend in Russian literature, the
first depiction of the "insulted and injured" little man, the first
realistic depiction of poverty and any number of other literary
firsts, to which historically it did not have the slightest claim.
The celebrated and oft-quoted maxim "We all emerged from
under Gogol's overcoat," long incorrectly attributed to Dostoyevsky and ultimately traced to the turn-of-the-century French
critic Melchior de Vogüé, implied that Russian realism in its totality grew out of this one story. Such a view remains widespread to this day, despite the availability of the epoch-making
studies of this story by Boris Eichenbaum and Dmitry
Čiževsky,[16] who conclusively proved decades ago just how
wrong and historically unfounded the traditional reputation of
"The Overcoat" is.

Humanitarian concerns, philanthropic sympathy for the
downtrodden, and concern for the "little people" had been a part
of Russian literature since the Sentimentalist tales Nikolai Ka-

Alienation and Love: "The Overcoat"

ramzin wrote in the 1790s; oppressed and exploited peasants were featured in comic operas with texts by Nikolev and Kniazhnin that Catherine the Great herself warmly applauded back in the 1770s. A poor, insignificant mail carrier, depicted with great sympathy and compassion, was the protagonist of Pogorelsky's "The Poppy Seed Cake Woman of Lafertovo" (1825); realistically portrayed poor and humble government clerks are found in Pushkin's "The Bronze Horseman" (1833), in Lermontov's unfinished novel *Princess Ligovskaya* (1836), and in a host of works by their lesser contemporaries. Even the arch-reactionary government flunky and spy Faddei Bulgarin published in the late 1820s a story about a poor and virtuous cab driver. By 1841, when "The Overcoat" was completed, there was absolutely nothing left to pioneer along these lines—Gogol was simply offering his own treatment of one of the most wide-spread themes and situations in the literature of his time.

Sociologically, what is remarkable about "The Overcoat" is not its portrayal of poverty, which was ordinary enough at the time, but its description of urban alienation. It is this aspect of the story that firmly places it within the context of the other stories of the St. Petersburg cycle, written some five years before it. But while the heroes of the other St. Petersburg stories chafe under the burden of loneliness and alienation, the hero of "The Overcoat" seems to have chosen them of his own free will as his natural mode of existence. The real literary triumph of "The Overcoat" is neither the rather obvious sentimentalist episode of the young man who taunts Akaky Akakievich and then realizes with dismay that he has been hurting a fellow human being nor the moving little requiem that Gogol sings after his protagonist's death, but the sympathy the story arouses in the reader for the least human and least prepossessing character in all literature, a

Alienation and Love: "The Overcoat"

man whom the author, furthermore, systematically undercuts and ridicules.

The very name Akaky Akakievich Bashmachkin[17] is calculated to invite contempt and derision. The original Greek name Acacius (it occurs in Voltaire as Akakiah) means "immaculate" or "without blemish," but its Russian version sounds in pronunciation suspiciously as if it might be derived from _okakat'_ or _obkakat'_, "to beshit," "to cover with excrement." Russian adults, who have been familiar with "The Overcoat" and its hero for most of their lives, fail to perceive the connection, but Russian children who hear the name Akaky Akakievich for the first time usually giggle and look embarrassed. With his hemorrhoidal complexion, his untidy clothes always bespattered with garbage, with watermelon rinds and melon peelings clinging to his hat, and the flies in his soup he eats without noticing them, to say nothing of his excremental name, Akaky Akakievich is a character who would hardly seem calculated to arouse the reader's sympathy or to be appealing.

Gogol downgrades the man's mentality and his personal character with equal ruthlessness. An incoherent, almost mindless loner, on the verge of muteness and mental retardation, Akaky Akakievich speaks "for the most part in prepositions, adverbs, and, finally, such particles as have absolutely no meaning." He has no interest in the surrounding world, of which he takes notice only as much as is necessary to insure his bare survival. Compared to him, even the withdrawn Ivan Shponka is a model of awareness and involvement. His life is reduced to copying documents, which he does for a living at work and for his own amusement at home—a copying machine in human form that is unaware of the contents of the documents and is concerned solely with the written characters it copies. There are no other dimensions to Akaky Akakievich's character and no other interests in his life. Poprishchin in "Diary of a Madman" suffers from being at the bottom of the social and administrative ladder; Akaky Akakievich remains there by choice, stubbornly resisting all efforts to promote him to a higher rung and deliberately excluding himself from all human contact and all sociability, because this is the only way he is able to exist. In this manner he survives to the age of fifty, although his withdrawn mode of existence resembles that of a clam or an oyster more than that of a human being. All this needs to be said not in order to belittle Akaky Akakievich, which would be inhuman, but to point out, in view of the story's stubborn reputation as a paragon of compassionate humanitarianism, just who this person in the center of the story is and just what Gogol does to him and with him.

Several accounts of the origin of "The Overcoat" are cited in the literature about Gogol. The most frequently quoted version stems from the memoirs of Pavel Annenkov, not always the most reliable source, despite its author's one-time close association with Gogol. According to Annenkov, the story evolved from an anecdote Gogol heard about a poor civil servant who coveted a hunting rifle, got one by scraping and saving, and lost it by dropping it into the water the very first time he went duck shooting. Far more likely is the derivation of this story from a literary source, "The Demon" (1839) by Nikolai Pavlov, a prose writer whose work Gogol vastly admired and publicly championed on several recorded occasions. The connection between these two works, first pointed out by the nineteenth-century critics Stepan Shevyryov (in 1846) and Apollon Grigoryev (in 1859), has recently been conclusively demonstrated by Elizabeth C. Shepard.[18] What unites the two stories is not only the several close textual parallels cited by Shepard in her essay, but

Alienation and Love: "The Overcoat"

also the basic love triangle between the poor and humble elderly government clerk, the haughty and pompous high official who is the clerk's superior, and the clerk's pretty young wife. Gogol's device of replacing the human wife with a feminine-gender object, while typical of him in general, became a highly original stroke when it was introduced into the situation borrowed from Pavlov's story. In order to make his point, Gogol had to reject the usual Russian word for overcoat, which is neuter, and name his story after a special model with a cape and fur collar, *shinel'* (this style was called a "carrick" in English, according to the findings of Vladimir Nabokov) that is feminine in gender. The textual references to the overcoat as Akaky Akakievich's "life's companion" and "the radiant guest" who shares his earthly existence are also all in the feminine gender in Russian (this very essential dimension of the story is lost in the English translations). The Soviet film based on "The Overcoat," which starred Roland Bykov and was shown on American television, drove this point home still further by having Akaky Akakievich hold a lighted candle and place another next to the overcoat that is spread on his bed—a clear reference to the Orthodox wedding ceremony.

"The Overcoat" is thus in essence a love story, the most genuine, touching, and honest one in Gogol's entire *oeuvre*. This fact, although not noticed by Gogol scholars until Dmitry Či-ževsky demonstrated it in 1937, had been intuitively understood by two of Gogol's important younger contemporaries who wrote what were meant as ripostes and correctives to "The Overcoat." Dostoyevsky's first novel, *Poor Folk*, written in 1845 (four years after the publication of Gogol's story) and Ivan Turgenev's play *The Bachelor* (1849) both depicted elderly, poor, and lonely government clerks living in situations similar to that of Akaky Akakievich. However, instead of becoming senti-

Alienation and Love: "The Overcoat"

mentally attached to an overcoat, Dostoyevsky's and Turgenev's characters become involved with real young women and
find fulfillment in helping these women cope with the problems
and difficulties they face. Dostoyevsky's protagonist (who reads
"The Overcoat" in the course of the novel and protests vehemently that it distorts reality and slanders people like himself)
loses the companionship of the young woman he befriends as
heartbreakingly as Akaky Akakievich loses his overcoat. But
Turgenev's kindly and resourceful elderly clerk (it was a role
Turgenev wrote especially for Gogol's actor-friend Shchepkin) is
actually preferred by the young woman to the superficial and
heartless young man with whom she is involved at the beginning
of the play. The desire on Dostoyevsky's and Turgenev's part to
correct the Gogolian situation in "The Overcoat," their urge to
bring things closer to what is probable and possible in real life,
shows their penetrating understanding of the basic mechanics of
Gogol's masterpiece. But it also betrays their inability to grasp
that, given his basic character, Gogol simply could not have
handled the amorous involvement between an older man and a
younger woman in a way that appeared normal and natural to
them. "Diary of a Madman" was his other approach to this
situation and there the man's yearning for the young woman is
seen as hopeless and ridiculous. Only by making the woman an
inanimate object was Gogol able to write his tender and affecting
romance between a man and a garment.

The love-story dimension of "The Overcoat," though semi-
submerged, is nonetheless a sure-fire ingredient to which every
reader of the story responds without fail. Another, equally
sure-fire ingredient is the comeuppance that the character known
simply as "a very important person" gets at the hands of Akaky
Akakievich's ghost for having mistreated and humiliated the
poor clerk when he was alive. Here, for once, Gogol deliberately

undercuts the supernatural element by revealing at the very end that what the "important person" saw as a ghost was in actuality the same robber who stole Akaky Akakievich's overcoat earlier. The revenge of the ghost strikes a responsive chord in all of us, because it is always satisfactory to see the hurt underdog retaliate against his persecutor. But Gogol would not be Gogol if he did not manage to connect both the lesson taught the "important person" and the downfall of Akaky Akakievich himself with punishment for yielding to a heterosexual amorous impulse. The "important person" has his frightening encounter with the supposed ghost just as he is leaving for an evening of dalliance at the home of the German lady he keeps. Terrified by the ghost, the "important person" gives up his plans for the evening and goes straight home. As for Akaky Akakievich, his chaste amorous involvement with his overcoat gradually leads him to do something he has apparently never done in the entire half century he has spent in this world: he starts noticing real women and responding to their sexual potential. The sequence of events is gradual, but unmistakable. After acquiring his longed-for "pleasant, life-long helpmeet," his next step is to take an unprecedented interest in a painting he sees in a shop window on his way to the party his colleague gives in honor of his new overcoat: "He stopped with curiosity before a lighted shop window to look at a painting in which a beautiful woman was shown removing her shoe and thereby baring her entire leg, which did not look at all bad, while behind her back a man with sideburns and a handsome goatee was peeking at her from the door." From the woman in the painting (this same painting, incidentally, had already appeared in "The Nose," where it had an entirely different function), it is but a step to involvement with real women, and this indeed happens as Akaky Akakievich is returning home from the party: "Akaky Akakievich was walking along in a

Alienation and Love: "The Overcoat"

cheerful state of mind; he even started running, for no discernible reason, after a lady who walked past him like a streak of
lightning and every part of whose body was in extraordinary
agitation."

Akaky Akakievich quickly checks his impulse, but the retribution mechanism has already been set in motion by this violently physical female by her mere presence. It is immediately
after his encounter with her that he is robbed of his most precious
possession, the overcoat. He is handicapped in fighting for the
return of his beloved object by his sense of being tainted, which
others seem to be aware of as well: when he is received by the
police official to whom he wants to report the robbery, he is
asked whether he had visited a bawdy house (*neporyadochnyi
dom*) at the time of the robbery. "Akaky Akakievich was totally
embarrassed and went out, not knowing whether the authorities
were going to look into the matter of his overcoat or not." He
has the humiliating encounter with the "important person," falls
ill, and resorts to profanity to express his state of mind as he lies
dying, mourning to the end the loss of his overcoat and, possibly, of his innocence. "The Overcoat" ends the way so many
other love stories involving a man and a woman end in Gogol—
with the death of the male participant.

"The Overcoat" is the most perfect artistic embodiment of the
two constant, cardinal Gogolian themes: the lethal nature of
love and the destructive potential of change—any kind of
change. The happiest environments in his work are always the
ones in which time stands still and each succeeding generation
follows the same familiar and patriarchal mode of existence that
the earlier ones did. Such is the world of "Ganz Küchelgarten,"
of the light opera stories in the Dikanka cycle ("Fair at Sorochintsy," "May Night," "Christmas Eve"), of "Ivan Fyodorovich
Shponka and His Aunt" and of "Old-World Landowners." This

Alienation and Love: "The Overcoat"

was also the world inhabited by the protagonists of "Terrible Vengeance," "Taras Bulba," and "Viy" until the intervention of evil forces made a shambles of their well-adjusted lives. In his reclusive, bivalvelike existence, Akaky Akakievich was perfectly adjusted and happy. "It would be hard to find a man whose life was so totally devoted to his work," we are told at the beginning of the story. "To say that he worked with zeal is not enough—no, he worked with love. There, in his copying, he discerned a whole world of his own, varied and agreeable." Fate cannot touch Akaky Akakievich until he becomes involved with his overcoat. Overcoat spells love and love brings on change, and it is at this point that Akaky Akakievich becomes just as vulnerable as the other protagonists of the St. Petersburg cycle of stories. Acquisition of the overcoat takes him out of his routine, out of his own part of town, and even threatens to take him out of the safety of his social isolation. The underlying idea is of course that safety lies only in withdrawal from current life and in lack of action, an essentially ultra-conservative idea that is basic to all of Gogol's social and political thinking. It is odd indeed that the so-called progressive Russian critics, from Belinsky and Chernyshevsky to their present-day self-styled disciples in the Soviet Union, should extol "The Overcoat" and deplore *Selected Passages from Correspondence with Friends* as an incomprehensible aberration on Gogol's part, for the basic philosophical idea of these two works is one and the same: the desirability of total social stasis.

Like all major masterpieces, "The Overcoat" is capable of conveying new and different meanings to each succeeding epoch. The sentimentalist tirades that so impressed Gogol's contemporaries can now be seen for the literary convention they are. The theme of human solitude and of urban alienation that the story so powerfully sounds can speak much more eloquently to the

Alienation and Love: "The Overcoat"

twentieth-century imagination than it could have to the people of Gogol's time, since we know much more about such things than the nineteenth century ever did. After Dostoyevsky's *Notes from the Underground*, Chekhov's "Heartache" and "My Life," after Kafka's *The Trial* and Nabokov's *The Defense* and *Invitation to a Beheading*, we can see that "The Overcoat" was the initiator of the great modern tradition of writing about the solitary and vulnerable individual human being rejected or threatened by a dehumanized collective. This theme is important and appealing on many levels of modern consciousness and it has implications for many present-day societies. Bulat Okudzhava's song "The Last Trolley" was a big underground hit in the Soviet Union at about the time when the Beatles' "Eleanor Rigby" was a big commercial success in the West. Both of these songs deal in essence with the theme that Gogol developed in his story about a lonely man's loss of his overcoat, a story which was written in 1841.

As a writer of prose fiction, Gogol had to undergo a long, complex evolution from "Saint John's Eve" to "The Overcoat" and *Dead Souls*, gradually gaining in depth and originality and acquiring ever greater artistic individuality. As a playwright, he showed himself as an innovator even in his very first, uncompleted efforts for the dramatic stage. He can be seen in retrospect as one of the two great reformers of nineteenth-century Russian drama, the other being Anton Chekhov. Gogol and Chekhov were the only two Russian playwrights of that century who neither transposed into a Russian milieu the readymade formu-

Russian Comedy

lae of the Western well-made play nor based their conception of drama on standard melodrama or on simplistically understood Shakespeare. To say this is not to belittle the genuinely original achievements and contributions of such fine Russian playwrights of the nineteenth century as Alexei Potekhin, Ivan Turgenev, Lev Tolstoy, Alexei Pisemsky, or Alexander Sukhovo-Kobylin, to name only the most original and creative. But the significance of Gogol and Chekhov is greater than that of any of these other playwrights, if only because their work drastically altered the very conception of what Russian drama could or should be.

The Chekhovian reform at the turn of the century put an end to the school of jerrybuilt and imitative drama and opened the door for the remarkable achievements of the Symbolist playwrights in the early twentieth-century. The effect of the Gogolian reform was not nearly so clear-cut. The dramatic tradition he helped overthrow—that of the Russian Neo-Classical comedy— was by no means worthless; it was already seriously crippled by the advent of Romanticism; and Gogol developed from it and built upon it every bit as much as he had revolted against it.

The introduction of professional theater and modern forms of drama into Russia in the middle of the eighteenth century gave the country the viable tradition it had lacked, ending the time lag that had hindered the development of dramatic literature during the previous hundred years. Despite the popularity of Neo-Classical tragedy, an enthusiasm that eighteenth-century Russians shared with the rest of the Western world, it was in the field of comedy that the Russian dramatic genius manifested itself most rapidly and most successfully. By the last quarter of the eighteenth century, the repertoire of Russian theaters could boast of fine prose comedies by Vladimir Lukin, Denis Fonvizin (two of whose plays, *The Brigadier* and *The Minor*, retain their place as national classics to this day), and Ivan Krylov. Neo-Classical

Russian Comedy

comedy in verse, after a few false starts, hit its stride in the two verse comedies of Yakov Kniazhnin, who was known to his contemporaries primarily as a writer of Neo-Classical tragedies patterned on Corneille, Voltaire, and Metastasio. It was in Kniazhnin's last two comedies, dating from the early 1790s, that the problem of writing fluent and witty Russian dialogue in verse was finally solved. In 1795, following Kniazhnin's example, the poet Vasily Kapnist (a Ukrainian and a close friend of Gogol's father) wrote his remarkable verse comedy *Chicane*, a savage satirical indictment of Russian legal procedures and the finest Russian work for the dramatic stage between Fonvizin's *The Minor* and Griboyedov's *The Misfortune of Being Clever*. By the first quarter of the nineteenth century, Russia had a whole pleiad of writers of witty and elegant comedies, led by Prince Alexander Shakhovskoy, who also has the distinction of being the first important Russian stage director.

Shakhovskoy was occasionally guilty of sloppy versification, which set Pushkin against him, and he made the irreparable blunder of incorporating a lampoon of Vasily Zhukovsky into one of his very best plays, *The Lipetsk Spa* (1815), which earned him the enmity of the entire Romantic generation. But his comedies show a fine sense of dramatic values, are expertly structured, and are very entertainingly written. The weaker aspects of Shakhovsky's plays were overcome and his strong points, the fluency of his dialogue and the mastery of his plotting, were brought to a new level of perfection in the plays of his younger disciples, such as Nikolai Khmelnitsky, Alexander Pisarev, and Alexander Griboyedov.

The Russian Neo-Classical playwrights of the early nineteenth century built on the achievements of Molière and Marivaux and their eighteenth-century French successors, such as Destouches and Beaumarchais, the way Mikhail Glinka built the Russian

Russian Comedy

national opera on Mozart, Weber, and Rossini. Like Glinka, they brought to their art an individuality and a specifically Russian dimension that resulted in a wholly distinctive native contribution to the art of playwriting. Nor were these playwrights quite as exclusively French oriented as their subsequent reputation made them out to be. They knew and valued the plays of Holberg and Goldoni, of Sheridan and Goldsmith, and they learned much from these Western playwrights. In addition to the success Neo-Classical comedy achieved on the stage (which produced a brilliant galaxy of actors and actresses who specialized in this repertoire), it contributed enormously to that purification and focusing of the Russian literary language which posterity so myopically credited to Pushkin alone. A simple reading of Shakhovskoy's *Lipetsk Spa* or one of Khmelnitsky's comedies of ca. 1817 should convince anyone that they are written in the kind of style and diction we associate with *Eugene Onegin* and "Count Nulin." And yet they were written at a time when the young Pushkin's own language was still restricted to the stylistic mannerisms of the Karamzinian poets of the turn of the century. Before Pushkin turned to the neo-Shakespearean manner of *Boris Godunov* (1825), he sketched out plans for several verse comedies in the Shakhovskoy-Khmelnitsky manner, which, as his notes indicate, he intended for the actors and actresses who specialized in plays by these playwrights. In a letter to his brother, Pushkin referred to the comedies of Nikolai Khmelnitsky as his *première amante (pervaya lyubovnitsa)*, and as late as 1831, he called Khmelnitsky, in a letter addressed to him, his favorite poet.

Russian Neo-Classical drama of the early nineteenth century fell victim to two momentous revolutions in artistic taste, the Romantic and the realist, that followed each other within less than two decades. By the mid-1820s literary fashions had changed to such an extent that Shakhovskoy himself took to writing melodramatic Gothic pageants and doing dramatic adaptations of Byron and Scott. By the 1840's, all that remained of Russian Neo-Classical drama, like the tip of a submerged iceberg, was Griboyedov's *The Misfortune of Being Clever* (1828), the finest comedy produced by that tradition, which subsequent critics managed to pigeonhole as either Romantic or realistic, and Pushkin's nostalgic homage to the Neo-Classical school of drama in *Eugene Onegin* (Canto I, stanza xviii). In one of those self-purgations by which the Russians periodically consign some of the finest achievements of their culture to oblivion, the entire brilliant period of Russian drama from Kapnist to Griboyedov was relegated to the dustbin of history. From Vissarion Belinsky in the 1840s to Vladimir Nabokov in the 1960s, the Russian commentators who do mention these plays and playwrights invariably dismiss them as derivative, stilted, and musty, although they are about as stilted and musty as Sheridan or Goldoni. Throughout the rest of the nineteenth century various directors and actors, including such celebrities as Maria Savina, Turgenev's close friend and the most famous Russian actress of the end of the century, made sporadic attempts to revive some of Shakhovskoy's verse comedies, only to be savagely attacked by utilitarian-minded critics for trying to disinter works they considered antiquated and irrelevant. Apart from these people of the theater, no one ever read any of these plays or knew what they were like. When several collections of these comedies were published in the Soviet Union in the 1960s (for the first time in more than a century), the striking elegance of their language and the mastery of their stagecraft came as a total surprise to those who knew them only by their reputation, formed in the 1840s and never questioned or revised since.

Gogol's comedies are traditionally credited with having deliv-

Russian Comedy

ered the *coup de grace* to the moribund Neo-Classical dragon. What is not usually realized is that his comedies are also the direct descendants and legitimate heirs of the Shakhovskoy-Khmelnitsky-Griboyedov school. Of the three leading dramatic genres of the Romantic age in Russia, only Neo-Classical comedy both appealed to Gogol and suited his talents. He vehemently rejected the Romantic melodrama in which his one-time classmate Kukolnik was to score his great but transient successes. The neo-Shakespearean historical tragedy, pioneered by Pushkin's *Boris Godunov*, greatly attracted Gogol, but his two efforts in this form were, to put it charitably, unpromising. Neo-Classical comedy, however, was a genre with which he had been intimately involved since his childhood. At a very early age he got to know Kapnist's *Chicane*, meeting the author on several occasions when the playwright was a guest of his parents at Vasilievka. During his school years in Nezhin, Gogol had his first taste of popularity when he played major roles in comedies by Fonvizin, Krylov, and Khmelnitsky. The leading actors with whom Gogol made friends in Moscow and St. Petersburg, including such celebrated figures as Mikhail Shchepkin and Ivan Sosnitsky, had all built their reputations primarily on the plays of Shakhovskoy and his disciples. It is from this tradition that Gogol learned his craft as a playwright, the sureness of his structure and plotting, the art of his witty and entertaining dialogue, and the vividness of his characterizations. Of course he added his own specifically Gogolian dimensions to what he had learned from his predecessors—his own brand of realism, his Surrealism, and his Absurdist metaphysics—taking Russian drama light years ahead of Shakhovskoy and Griboyedov in the process. But it is on the achievement of these predecessors that his innovative stagecraft was based.

Gogol's conception of drama diverged from that of Shakhov-

Love in Gogol's Plays

skoy school in several important ways. He did not care for
their tendency to restrict the purview of their comedies to
princes, magnates, countesses, and wealthy heiresses. Where
Shakhovskoy and Khmelnitsky were content to divert and to
entertain, Gogol wanted to use the stage as a forum for moral
and social preaching, being in this respect closer to such eighteenth-century Russian playwrights as Fonvizin and Kapnist,
who also wanted to instruct their audiences while amusing them.
The Neo-Classical convention against which Gogol revolted
most violently was the requirement that one include a love intrigue in every play and end every comedy with an obligatory
marriage of two of the protagonists.

Gogol's aversion to heterosexual love and marriage is self-
evident in all of his prose fiction from *Mirgorod* on. Since he did
not make an open issue of it, this antipathy was not generally
noticed by his contemporaries. The deliberate omission or parodistic burlesquing of the traditional love interest in his plays,
however, could not be overlooked, if only because Gogol himself raised this aspect of his plays to a sort of ideological mani-
festo and saw in it a cornerstone of his dramatic reform. A number of contemporary critics complained of the absence of love
interest in *The Inspector General*, among them the influential
and arch-reactionary Osip Senkovsky, who wrote in his review
that Gogol could have improved the structure of his play and
increased the dramatic interest by including among his characters a young woman—a friend or an enemy of the mayor's
daughter—with whom Khlestakov could fall in love. In the
dramatic dialogue *After the Play*[19] Gogol replied by having a
character styled as "Second Amateur of the Arts" attack the
entire notion of the necessity for love intrigue in drama: "It is
high time we stopped leaning on this eternal love intrigue. All
you have to do is to take a good look around. Everything

Love in Gogol's Plays

changed in this world long ago. Today drama can be more actively propelled by the desire to obtain an advantageous situation, to shine, and to eclipse others at all costs or to obtain revenge for having been disdained or mocked. Does not a high position, money, or a lucrative marriage generate more electricity today than love?" Later on in the dialogue, this "Second Amateur of the Arts" contrasts comedy's potential for meaningful social commentary with the obligatory requirement of the love element, which Gogol and his spokesman see as a crippling limitation: "At its very inception, comedy was a civic and national concept. At least that was how its father, Aristophanes, showed it to us. Only later did it enter into the narrow gorge of private intrigue and bring in the love gambit, that indispensable love interest. But how feeble this intrigue is even in [the work of] the best comedy writers! How insignificant these theatrical lovers are, with their cardboard love!"

For his principled rejection of the love interest, Gogol has been lavishly praised by generations of Russian critics as a bold innovator. Although this was indeed a highly original stylistic departure, it never occurred to these critics to see its obvious causes, its self-evident origin in Gogol's own psychosexual orientation. Since most of the important Russian playwrights of the remainder of the nineteenth century were heterosexually oriented, Gogol's much vaunted innovation found no followers, and Russian playwrights from Ostrovsky to Chekhov went on incorporating a love interest into their most important plays. Gogol himself was not inclined to face the causes of this particular aversion, and this was why he repeatedly argued, not entirely convincingly, one might add, that including in a play a love affair terminating in marriage was somehow incompatible with projecting the play's social or moral dimensions.

In comparison with the human insights of Gogol's plays, with

Uses of Theater

their magnificent flights of imagination and their verbal splendor, the didactic and moralizing aims which Gogol ascribed to them and to theater in general cannot but strike one as primitive and simplistic. "Theater is a great teacher and its task is a profound one," Gogol wrote in his essay "The St. Petersburg Stage in 1836." "It teaches a great, living lesson to an entire crowd, to a thousand people at once; in the glitter of festive lighting, to the thunder of music, it shows the ridiculous side of customs and vices and the highly touching qualities of human virtues and lofty sentiments." The ultimate purpose of teaching these lessons from the stage is spelled out in the same essay: "The Monarch's eye will look down benevolently upon the writer who, moved by the pure desire of good, will undertake to expose the lowly vices, the unworthy frailties and customs in various strata of our society and thus provide aid and wings to His just rule." These sentiments, expressed at the time of the first performance of *The Inspector General*, were reiterated in a somewhat more elaborate form ten years later in Gogol's essay on theater in *Selected Passages from Correspondence with Friends*. In another essay of that volume, "What, Finally, Is the Essence of Russian Poetry and Wherein Resides Its Peculiarity?" Gogol singled out Fonvizin's *The Minor* and Griboyedov's *The Misfortune of Being Clever* as the two most important Russian plays. While Gogol gave the plays of Kniazhnin, Kapnist, Shakhovskoy, and Khmelnitsky their due in that essay, he preferred the plays of Fonvizin and Griboyedov, not because of superior literary art or greater dramatic value, he made clear, but because of the seriousness of their moral purpose and their high level of social significance. Yet, interestingly enough, the didactic and moralistic criterion which Gogol stressed so heavily in his theoretical writings about the theater and drama can be applied—and very approximately at that—to only two of his own plays, *The Inspector General*

The Medal of St. Vladimir

and the unfinished *The Medal of Saint Vladimir, Third Class*. Only the most unbridled kind of wishful thinking could ever discern any kind of moral lesson in *Marriage* or *The Gamblers*.

All in all, Gogol undertook writing for the stage on a total of six occasions. He brought only three of these projects to completion: *The Inspector General, Marriage,* and *The Gamblers*. His two attempts to produce Romantic tragedies on historical subjects remained stillborn. Far more interesting are his sketches for the unfinished comedy, *The Medal of Saint Vladimir, Third Class*, which he began at about the same time as *Mirgorod* and which, had he completed it, might well have ended up as one of his most original works for the stage. Gogol had conceived it as a play laid out along generous lines, with a large cast and at least three subordinate plots in addition to the central one. The principal plot was to be about the efforts of an ambitious St. Petersburg government official, named variously Barsukov (Mr. Badger) or Burdyukov (Mr. Wineskin), to be nominated for the medal that provides the title for the comedy (the medal of St. Vladimir usually was awarded to civil servants of the highest rank for distinguished achievements). Frustrated in his ambition, Barsukov was to go insane at the end of the play and imagine that he himself had become the coveted medal. The first subplot had to do with the lawsuit brought against Barsukov by his brother, a provincial landowner, over an inheritance left to them by their aunt. The second subplot concentrated on the affairs of Barsukov's widowed sister, a powerful matriarch who tyrannizes her obedient and dutiful son. Still another subplot traced

The Medal of St. Vladimir

the plans of Barsukov's large domestic staff to organize a servants' ball, to which only the better class of servants would be
invited and from which their socially undesirable colleagues
would be excluded.

There were two main reasons why Gogol never completed
The Medal of Saint Vladimir. One was that it touched on topics
that the drama censorship of the time would not permit to be
represented on the stage. But an equally valid reason for abandoning the play was Gogol's realization that he would not be
able to coordinate the numerous and unwieldy subplots and
integrate them in a coherent manner. A few years later, Gogol
decided to salvage the completed portions of *The Medal of Saint
Vladimir* by converting what he had already written into four
separate one-act plays. These reworked dramatic fragments are
usually included in the Russian editions of Gogol's collected
writings, and some of them were occasionally performed by
nineteenth-century Russian actors.

The first of these dramatic fragments, *The Morning of a Man
of Affairs*, outlines the hero's ambition to be awarded the medal
and some of the lobbying he does to achieve his aim. *The Lawsuit* shows the visit of Barsukov's (here, Burdyukov's) brother to
the home of an official who is his brother's rival and enemy in
order to discuss the feasibility of legally challenging their aunt's
last will and testament. The grounds for the proposed lawsuit
constitute a piece of Gogolian fancy that has become proverbial
in Russian: the late aunt was named Eudoxia, but instead of sign-
ing this name on her last will and testament, the dying woman
wrote "dip it, please" (*obmokni*). The issue discussed in this fragment is whether "dip it, please" should be considered a valid signature on a legal document. The third fragment, *Servants' Quarters*, was thoroughly reworked by Gogol in 1839 or 1840 and
amounts almost to a new play in comparison with the sketch for

The Medal of St. Vladimir

The Medal of Saint Vladimir on which it was based. It is a rather nasty satire on the servant class as a whole. All the servants, whether free or enserfed, are shown as spoiled, pampered, lazy, and rude people who do everything in their power to avoid doing any work whatsoever for their employers. Social prejudices and snobberies are far worse among the domestics than among the upper-class people for whom they work and whom they despise and constantly cheat. Not quite as blatantly chauvinistic as Gogol's treatment of the Jews in "Taras Bulba" or of the Germans in "Nevsky Prospect," the playlet still amounts to a wholesale indictment of an entire class of human beings, who are clearly seen as less than fully human. A character called "The Pot-Bellied Majordomo" outlines a philosophy of divinely ordained social immobility: a person born into the servant class has a duty to remain a servant all his life, for this is God's will, and anyone seeking to change his social position makes himself laughable. The statement sounds like pointed satire, but unfortunately this is the very philosophy Gogol was later to advance in all seriousness in *Selected Passages*. Despite the total difference of his outlook from Gogol's, it is highly likely that Lev Tolstoy took a good look at *Servants' Quarters* before writing the scenes that involve the domestic servants in his own comedy *The Fruits of Enlightenment* (1889).

The most interesting splinter from *The Medal of Saint Vladimir*, and the best-realized one artistically, was originally called *Scenes from the Life of High Society*, with the title later changed by Gogol to simply *A Fragment*. For all its brevity, the piece contains a fully developed, masterly portrait of the kind of female character that has become a great favorite of twentieth-century American playwrights, as exemplified by Sidney Howard's *Silver Cord* and *Suddenly Last Summer* by Tennessee Williams—the outwardly civilized, but ruthless and power-mad

The Medal of St. Vladimir

matriarchal figure who sacrifices her son to her need for ego-gratification and her social snobbery. The main motivation in the life of Barsukov's sister Maria Alexandrovna is to keep her position within the pecking order of other society hostesses. Her appealingly presented, sensitive, corpulent, and socially awkward thirty-year-old son, Misha, is merely a pawn in her games of social ascendancy. Because the son of a rival hostess is a dashing army officer, the clumsy Misha is steered into a military career for which he is obviously unsuited. His way of dressing and his mode of life are determined by what the children of the other ladies of his mother's circle have been wearing or doing, rather than by his own preferences or inclinations. The slightest objection on Misha's part is instantly checked by accusations of ingratitude and threats of a hysterical tantrum. The long-suffering son goes along with most of this tyranny, but he draws the line at marrying the half-wit daughter of a prince merely because this marriage would enhance his mother's social position. It turns out that he is already in love with the daughter of a poor government clerk. This off-stage romance of Misha's is Gogol's single concession in his works for the stage to the convention of including a love interest; but even so, a love affair between a fat man and a woman who does not appear in the play is not exactly the standard romantic fare of Gogol's or any other time. At the end of A Fragment, Maria Alexandrovna, miffed at her son's resistance to her plans, engages the services of a professional blackmailer, a man she herself despises, to manufacture slanderous gossip about the woman her son loves and thus to ruin her in his eyes.

In Gogol's gallery of forceful elderly women who specialize in pushing unwilling males into marriage and other forms of distasteful involvement with young women, Maria Alexandrovna is probably the most formidable. Her grimmer aspects may have

The Medal of St. Vladimir

served Dostoyevsky as a model for his characterization of Colonel Rostanev's mother in *The Manor of Stepanchikovo* (also translated as *A Friend of the Family*). Her more humorous sides find their reflection in the typically manipulative and gossipy older women that are frequently found in the stories of the twentieth-century humorist Nadezhda Teffi. Although Maria Alexandrovna appears in a minor and fragmentary work, this overwhelmingly vivid figure offers us one more important slant on the multifaceted challenge that the female sex continually created for Gogol by its mere presence in this world. Apart from the dramatic fragments, a few other leftovers from *The Medal of Saint Vladimir* found their way into Gogol's prose fiction. The hero's craving for the medal and his conversation with his lapdog eventually turned up in "Diary of a Madman," in the episode where Sophie's father discusses his prospects for a medal with the dog Madgie. The idea of a civil servant going insane and imagining that he has become an independently acting medal may well contain the germs of both "Diary of a Madman" and "The Nose."

In the summer and fall of 1835, after abandoning *The Medal of Saint Vladimir*, Gogol went into a veritable frenzy of playwriting. He sketched out a play he called *The Suitors*, an early version of *Marriage* containing most of that play's subordinate characters, but none of the principal ones, and very little of the plot as it appeared in the final version. He also wrote two acts of a historical tragedy called *Alfred*, a pallid homage to Pushkin's *Boris Godunov* and the novels of Scott. Dealing with Anglo-Saxon resistance to the Danish invasion, it reads like a dull history lesson in dramatic form. Nikolai Chernyshevsky, with the unparalleled critical blindness typical of the Russian critics of the 1860s, considered *Alfred* "masterful" and wrote that "historical veracity is scrupulously maintained." Actually, Gogol's pagan

Danes speak like characters in a fairy tale, while the Anglo-Saxons sound like poor but recognizable imitations of the Cossacks from "Taras Bulba." There is not a single line in the entire fragment that is worthy of Gogol, and it is hard to believe that anything so contrived and lifeless could be produced by the man who was writing the St. Petersburg cycle of stories at about the same time.

On October 7, 1835, Gogol wrote to Pushkin, asking him to return the draft of *The Suitors* which he had submitted to Pushkin for his comments and which he hoped to show to some actors in order to get them interested in producing the play. In that letter, Gogol also wrote: "Do me a favor, give me some sort of subject, funny or unfunny, as long as it is a typically Russian anecdote. In the meantime, my hand is trembling from the desire to write a comedy." Pushkin obliged by providing Gogol with a story of how an acquaintance of his passed himself off as an important government official while visiting a small town in Bessarabia. After Pushkin's death, there was found among his papers a fragmentary outline for either a play or a story that reads in part: "Crispin goes to a fair in a provincial town and gets mistaken for . . . The governor is an honest idiot, some hanky-panky between him and the governor's wife. Crispin asks for the daughter's hand in marriage." This fragment is generally considered the point of origin of *The Inspector General*.

This may well be so; but, on the other hand, this sort of mistaken-identity situation was standard fare for both Neo-Classical comedy and the picaresque novel throughout the eighteenth and early nineteenth centuries. As a young boy Gogol appeared in Ivan Krylov's *A Lesson to Daughters*, which is about a young peasant masquerading as a French marquis, a situation that Krylov based on a similar one in Molière's *Les Précieuses ridicules*. A Ukrainian comedy by Grigory Kvitka-Osnovyanenko, which

The Inspector General

Gogol is not likely to have known, since it was written in 1827 but not published until 1840, has a plot that is superficially very similar to that of *The Inspector General*. A more likely source with which Gogol may have been familiar is the unfinished comedy *The Geese of Arzamas* by Nikolai Khmelnitsky. Portions of the first act, which is all that exists of this play, were published in a literary journal in 1829. They show a corrupt provincial judge and his wife who discuss their comfortable way of life, paid for by bribes and other forms of graft, and talk about the prospects of getting their daughter married. A gossipy acquaintance of theirs, a character remarkably similar to Gogol's Bobchinsky and Dobchinsky, barges in to announce the rumor that an inspector general (the actual word *revizor* is used in Russian) is expected in their town.

Whatever initial impetus Gogol may have derived from Pushkin, Khmelnitsky, Krylov, and the picaresque novel tradition, the uses to which he put these familiar situations were so original, indeed unprecedented, that it took actors, directors, and critics an entire century to perceive the full magnitude of his departure from the dramatic conventions and philosophical presuppositions of his age in *The Inspector General*. Gogol himself may well have believed that he was writing an amusing comedy about graft and corruption that would entertain audiences, improve morals, and help the tsar achieve a more just form of government. His subsequent attempts to read additional philosophical, metaphysical, and even religious significance into this comedy, unconvincing as some of them may be, testify to his awareness that the play had deeper recesses of meaning than could be expected in a topical satirical comedy. Many of Gogol's contemporaries saw the play as the first genuinely realistic Russian work for the stage, an opinion that prevailed until the early twentieth century. Boris Warnecke, who in his 1914 book *His-*

The Inspector General

tory of the Russian Theater (the least perceptive Russian book ever written on the subject, but also the only one translated into English) complained of the lack of realism and dramatic plausibility in Chekhov's plays, wrote of *The Inspector General*: "One can hardly point out a single feature in this play that was invented rather than transcribed directly from real life." The more imaginative Russian commentators of the early twentieth century, however, such as Merezhkovsky, interpreted the play as a vision of cosmic banality, as the revelation of metaphysical evil inherent in pettiness and stupidity.

From the vantage point of the second half of the twentieth century it can be seen that the most remarkable thing about *The Inspector General* is the constantly maintained tension between its vividly imagined surface realism and the recurrent lapses into absurdism and surrealism which sporadically disrupt and undermine the superficially realistic texture of the play. The action is situated in a generalized small provincial town located somewhere in Russia. The town's mayor says that you can gallop from it in any direction for three years without coming to the border of any foreign country. This is one of those easily overlooked Gogolian absurdities, similar to the statement in "Terrible Vengeance" that the river Dnieper is so wide that "rare is the bird that can fly halfway across it." The town has a schoolmaster who needs to smash a chair in order to teach his students about Alexander the Great; these chairs are accounted for in the municipal budget. Explanation offered and accepted: he does not spare himself in his devotion to learning. A municipal clerk always smells of vodka. Explanation given and accepted: he was dropped on his head when he was a baby. The only doctor in the municipal hospital takes poor care of his patients and uses tobacco as an all-purpose medicine. Explanation given and accepted: the doctor is a German and cannot be expected to communicate with his patients since he speaks no Russian. Gogol casually springs all this on his audience in the very opening scene of the play, to show them the kind of reality they will be facing.

Within the play's Neo-Classically symmetrical structure, Gogol repeatedly lulls the audience into accepting the proceedings as a semblance of real life, only to project some piece of surrealistic absurdity against this carefully contrived quasi-realistic background. The mayor writes his wife a note on a restaurant bill and she reads of her husband's hope for Divine mercy in payment for two dill pickles and a half portion of caviar. The sequence of bribery scenes dissolves into absurdity when the false inspector and his servant accept as bribes first large sums of money, then a silver tray, then a loaf of sugar, and finally a worthless piece of string. Khlestakov reinforces his courtship of the mayor's wife with a wildly inappropriate quotation from Karamzin's morbid Gothic tale "The Isle of Bornholm" about laws that condemn incest. Asked by the mayor's daughter to inscribe a poem in her album, he offers a passage from Lomonosov's grim "Ode from the Book of Job" about the futility of complaining about Divine Providence. (These quotations were instantly identifiable by Gogol's contemporary audiences.) Asked what he has published in the magazines, Khlestakov names *The Marriage of Figaro*, *Norma*, and *Robert le Diable*. No matter how imaginative Khlestakov may be, no one but his creator could have thought of passing off operas for magazine articles.

An unwary reader or spectator may assume that *The Inspector General* deals with a confrontation of two widespread conventions or stereotypes: a clever swindling impostor of the picaresque tradition takes in a townful of corrupt administrators familiar from satirical literature and muckraking journalism. But Gogol's comedy continually cheats the audience out of its tradition-based expectations. The most effective way of indicting cor-

The Inspector General

ruption and venality in a work of literature is to show the villains as ugly and evil and to build up sympathy for their victims, who are usually shown in an attractive light. This was the path chosen by Kapnist in *Chicane*, where the unscrupulous machinations of corrupt legal officials are powerfully contrasted with the predicament of the honest and appealing army officer whom they are trying to victimize and whose side the audience instantly takes. Alexander Sukhovo-Kobylin, one of Gogol's finest successors and disciples, also resorted to a similar procedure in his great trilogy of plays about moral corruption in the government. Compared with the villains in the plays of Kapnist and Sukhovo-Kobylin, Gogol's mayor and his cronies in *The Inspector General* seem about as ugly or threatening as a troupe of Russian dancing bears. They may be uncouth and not particularly admirable, but on the other hand they are consistently amusing and occasionally verbally brilliant. The victims of their oppression whom we do get to see and with whom we might be expected to sympathize—the blackmailed merchants, the foulmouthed Mrs. Poshlyopkina (the locksmith's wife) who is the Great Russian reincarnation of Khivrya from "The Fair at Sorochintsy," and the unjustly flogged Mrs. Ivanova—are, if anything, even more unpleasant, pushy, and opportunistic than the officials.

Nor is Ivan Khlestakov, the false inspector general, by any means a clever swindler or picaro, fleecing the gullible provincials by pretending to be a high and powerful official. Some of the earliest performers of this role tried to play him as a sly rogue, much to Gogol's annoyance and disgust. Actually, this flighty young man, one of Gogol's most memorable and perfectly realized creations, is one of the finest portraits of a creative but disinterested liar in the whole of world literature. Dmitry Merezhkovsky quite correctly compared Khlestakov's lies and bragging to the inspiration of a poet, for they are indeed a kind of art for art's sake with him. To credit adroit maneuvering or mercenary motives to Khlestakov is to misunderstand the play and all of its central relationships. Self-righteous and moralizing critics of the nineteenth century saw Khlestakov as immoral and despicable. The present-day émigré poet George Ivask drew a portrait of Gogol's hero in a poem devoted to him that is a reply to that critical view and is probably closer to the author's own conception:

> A phantom, a fop, Khlestakov,
> I levitate, holding on to my coattails,
> I wave my greetings to cows,
> I'm a playful boy, not scum.
>
> I have no wish for wintery satire,
> I'm rococo, I'm March and April,
> I'm a rake, not a trouble-maker,
> A darling cupid from St. Petersburg![20]

The Khlestakov of Gogol's comedy is not the inspector general, but he is indeed an emissary from St. Petersburg—not from the real St. Petersburg to a real provincial town, but from the ephemeral St. Petersburg of "The Nose" and "Diary of a Madman" to the equally unreal but more weighty and dense provincial town of "The Carriage," "The Two Ivans," and *Dead Souls*. A close cousin of Kovalyov from "The Nose" and of Lieutenant Pirogov from "Nevsky Prospect," but more pleasant and appealing than either of them, Khlestakov sees in attaining Kovalyov's rank of collegiate assessor and in being awarded the medal of Saint Vladimir the summit of success. Looking after him in his modest St. Petersburg apartment is the cook-housekeeper Mavra, whom we last saw when she was employed by Poprish-

The Inspector General

chin in "Diary of a Madman." A government clerk, Khlestakov holds roughly the same rank as did Poprishchin and Akaky Akakievich. But these two older men were broken in spirit and had no hopes, while Khlestakov is young and jaunty, has a well-to-do father, whose estate he will one day inherit, and has hopes to spare. Kovalyov and Pirogov were allowed to escape only after undergoing their respective catastrophes, but Khlestakov escapes in the most stylish way of all: with impunity, in a troika, with all his loot, and after having dazzled and held spellbound an entire town.

Khlestakov's success and escape, every bit as absurd as the escape of Major Kovalyov with his nose intact, are the very opposite of the successes and escapes of swindlers and conmen. He walks into his good luck like some sort of bouncy sleepwalker, having no idea why he suddenly can get away with anything and everything. His getaway is made possible by the advice of his clever manservant, without whom Khlestakov would have been caught and ignominiously exposed. The lack of discernible motivation for most of Khlestakov's actions, his inexplicable success, and his escape effected in the absence of all intelligent planning take The Inspector General out of the province of Neo-Classical comedy which it so much resembles structurally and bring it into the realm of twentieth-century Theater of the Absurd. The inner logic of the play works not because of the not very plausible psychological explanations of the characters' motives which Gogol provided for the second edition of the play, but because of the carefully contrived and highly entertaining difference in specific gravity between the modes of thinking and personalities of the butterflylike Khlestakov and the clumsy, ursine city fathers. This consistently realized contrast between their respective lightness and heaviness is one reason why the play is as alive today as it was the day Gogol wrote it, a far more convincing reason than

The Inspector General

the sociological dimensions to which his countrymen have obsessively tried to restrict the play's ultimate significance (how many people today really deeply care that there was graft and corruption in the administration of pre-reform Russia?).

One of the most authentically absurdist and most purely Gogolian aspects of *The Inspector General* is Khlestakov's compulsive simultaneous courtship of the mayor's wife and daughter. As we can gather from his daydreams in Act II and from the letter to his St. Petersburg friend Tryapichkin which is read at the end of the play,[21] Khlestakov's obsessive flirtations are prompted not by a real desire to seduce a woman or to win her love, but by the need to make conquests he can boast about to his male friends. The point of experiencing love for a woman is not loving a woman but being able to tell a man about it—here again Khlestakov is an artist for art's sake. There is actually something in his attitude akin to that of Plato in "Woman," *toutes proportions gardées*. Left alone with either the mayor's daughter or his wife, Khlestakov goes into fits of wooing as a sort of reflex action conditioned by literary usage and social custom (no English translation so far has done justice to the inspired lunacy of his pursuit of the wife and to her responses). But all Khlestakov wants or needs is the verbal consent of the mayor's wife to his proposition and of the daughter to his marriage proposal. He certainly does not intend, nor would Gogol have allowed him, to actually carry out any of these amorous plans. The moment his ego is gratified by the women's verbal acquiescence, he flies off in his troika and disappears from their lives forever.

This aspect of *The Inspector General* was understood and realized on the stage for the first time by Vsevolod Meyerhold in his epoch-making production of the play in 1926. Hailed by Vladimir Mayakovsky and Andrei Bely as the first genuinely Gogolian interpretation of the play, the production was savagely attacked by many leading theatrical and literary critics accustomed to the traditional view of the play as realistic social satire. To emphasize the play's surrealistic dimensions, Meyerhold departed not only from previous stage tradition, but occasionally from Gogol's own text, interpolating passages from discarded variants and drafts of the play itself and also from *Dead Souls* and *The Gamblers*. In the scene between the mayor's wife and daughter and Khlestakov, in particular, Meyerhold heavily stressed the erotic element. The daughter made herself explicitly available sexually, while her mother pressed Khlestakov to her ample bosom so violently that he had to fight free to avoid being strangled. The relatively liberal People's Commissar of Education, Anatoly Lunacharsky, who liked the production very much, could not help wondering as he watched these love scenes "whether Meyerhold might be attacking love itself, eroticism in all its forms in general."[22] If this was indeed Meyerhold's intention, it shows an insight into the essence of Gogol unparalleled in the Russian tradition.

After the text of *The Inspector General* was completed, Gogol's protectors at the tsar's court, Zhukovsky and especially Count Mikhail Vielhorsky, a courtier and dilettante musician who at various times had been a friend and associate of Beethoven, Liszt, and Berlioz, brought the play to the monarch's attention. Nicholas I read the play, liked it very much, and saw nothing objectionable in it: he was, after all, opposed to bribery and graft, and the play ended with the culprits about to be punished by the emissary of the tsar. He authorized the play's production and the first performance took place in St. Petersburg on April 19, 1836. Despite a highly unsatisfactory staging and inept performances which irritated Gogol and which he strongly disliked, the success of the play was overwhelming. It would not be an exaggeration to say that *The Inspector General* was seen by contemporaries as the most important theatrical and literary event of the decade.

Much of the popular opinion of the day, however, interpreted the play in a way that neither the tsar nor the playwright had foreseen: people saw in it a wholesale indictment of Russian social institutions and of the existing form of government. Antigovernment dissenters such as Herzen and Bakunin (and, a few years later, the influential critic Belinsky), who welcomed such an indictment, stressed the play's realism and verisimilitude, while defenders of the status quo, such as the monarchist journalists Bulgarin and Senkovsky, insisted that the play was improbable and that the Russia it portrayed was unreal and fantastic. From the very beginning, the reputation of *The Inspector General* as an unvarnished transcript of Russian reality in the raw came to be linked with a critical attitude toward the tsarist regime and its institutions, and this traditional connection has prevented many subsequent Russian commentators from realizing that, unattractive though their political motives may have been, Bulgarin and Senkovsky were making a valid aesthetic point when they insisted that the Russia depicted in the play existed to a large extent only in the author's imagination. No one in the nineteenth century realized that what Bulgarin and Senkovsky saw as shortcomings were actually the play's strongest points, a breakthrough in creative imagination that enabled Gogol to anticipate in advance both Surrealism and the Theater of the Absurd.

Gogol was deeply outraged that anyone could consider him a rebel and an incendiary. "Everyone is against me," he wrote ten days after the play's opening to Mikhail Shchepkin, who was preparing the Moscow production of *The Inspector General*. "Elderly and respectable officials shout that I must hold nothing sacred, since I had dared to speak of civil servants in

The Inspector General

such a tone. The policemen are against me, merchants are against me, literary men are against me. They berate me and go to see the play; there is not a ticket to be had for the fourth performance. If it were not for the august protection of our sovereign, the play would never have been staged, and there were people who tried to get it banned. Now I see what it means to be a writer of comedy. The slightest trace of truth, and you set against yourself not just one individual, but entire social classes." To Mikhail Pogodin, Gogol wrote on May 10, 1836: "No prophet is honored in his own country. What dismays me is not that all social classes have so decisively arisen against me, but it is depressing and saddening to see your own countrymen whom you love turn against you so unjustly, to see how false and distorted their perception of everything is, making them take the particular for the general, the exception for the rule." Since the play was such an unqualified success, Gogol's sense of being persecuted can only be explained by the dismay he felt at being seen as an enemy by the very people he had assumed to be his ideological allies.

Gogol's bitterness about the play's reception is expressed again and again in the letters he wrote to Pogodin and Shchepkin in the next few months. His reaction to the success of *The Inspector General* took exactly the same external form as his reaction to the failure of "Ganz Küchelgarten": in a state of near-panic, he suddenly left Russia and went to Western Europe. This time round, however, his escape gradually turned into a permanent residence abroad. As the reputation of *The Inspector General* grew and expanded in subsequent years and as its interpretation as a militantly subversive play gained ever wider currency, Gogol repeatedly tried to counter this view in critical articles, in the elaborate debates of *After the Play*, and in two versions of a short polemical play called *The Inspector General's Dénouement*

Marriage

(1846 and 1847), where he argued that the characters in his play were meant to be allegorical representations of human passions and that the real inspector general announced at the end stood for Divine Justice. His desire to correct what he felt was a distorted reading of the play also motivated certain polemical passages in *Dead Souls* and the pro-monarchy arguments in the revised version of "The Portrait." By and large, Gogol's vehement protestations of loyalty to the regime did little to change the popular attitude toward the play, which may well be the reason why he so resolutely stayed away from governmental and administrative spheres of human activity in his other two plays.

It took Gogol about two months to write *The Inspector General. Marriage*, his supreme statement in dramatic form of his fear of women and loathing of matrimony, was in the works for almost nine years. It began as a simple satirical comedy about a woman who wants to get married; it ended up as an ambiguous and many-layered play about a man who doesn't. But through all the stages of the play's gestation Gogol never once lost track of the basic impulse that brought this particular work to life: to show up once and for all the arbitrary absurdity of the institution which had taken away from him the friends of his youth, turned his younger sisters into incomprehensible strangers, and deprived him of his rightful place in the human community.

The earliest version of the play, dating from 1833-1835, was called *The Suitors*. It was planned as a slapstick comedy, centered on a crude and rambunctious provincial noblewoman who is so desperate for a husband that she dispatches a matchmaker

Marriage

to the county fair with orders to bring her anyone at all, provided he is "a gentleman and of decent family." When the suitors arrive, the heroine excuses herself for keeping them waiting by explaining that she was engaged in fisticuffs with her cook in the kitchen and could not get away. Pratfalls for women (discussed, rather than shown on the stage) are a constant source of humor in *The Suitors*: the matchmaker claims that she had been kicked by horses and tossed out of her carriage while running her errand, and the heroine's maid supposedly had taken a tumble while climbing over a wattle fence, an event which prevented her from tidying up the room where the guests are received. Male characters engage in mutual insults that almost lead to a comical duel between two of them. The existing draft of *The Suitors* ends with the heroine's announcement that she loves all four of her suitors and accepts all four of their proposals. Gogol apparently had no idea where to take the play from there, so he abandoned it temporarily.

The Suitors contains four of the important secondary characters which were to appear in *Marriage*. The corpulent, practical-minded civil servant Yaichnitsa ("Mr. Omelet," or, more precisely, "Mr. Fried Eggs, Sunny Side Up") is a landowning nobleman in this earlier incarnation, but he already has his name, his corpulence, and his personality as they are found in the final version of the play. The sentimental former naval officer Baltazar Zhevakin ("Lt. Chewer"), the retired infantryman Anuchkin (spelled more correctly as "Onuchkin" in *The Suitors*; the name is derived from a contemptuous variant of *onucha*, a footcloth peasants wear inside their bast shoes), and the matchmaker who is called Mavra in this version are likewise already present. But five other equally important characters, including the hero and the heroine of *Marriage*, have not yet been created. Compared to the final play, *The Suitors* cannot but strike one as

Marriage

a crude and obvious piece of theater, devised for the purpose of demonstrating that people who like getting married are also crude and obvious, choosing their partners for the length of their noses, for their corpulence (viewed as a sign of beauty in both males and females), and for their property holdings.

Gogol set *The Suitors* aside in order to concentrate on writing *The Inspector General.* When he returned to it some years later, he had the benefit of an extremely important suggestion made by the actor Shchepkin. Shchepkin proposed that the bride be a woman of the merchant class and that Gogol show her against the background of her own merchant-class subculture, thus making for an effective contrast between her views and values and those of her noblemen-suitors. Merchants in nineteenth-century Russia were, like the clergy, a separate caste. Of peasant antecedents, they were less well educated than the gentry, far less Westernized and more tradition-bound and patriarchal. But many merchant families were wealthier than some of the nobles, whose inferiors they supposedly were. Since apart from social snobberies there was no barrier to intermarriage between members of different classes, merchant heirs and heiresses occasionally attracted those impoverished members of the gentry who regarded marrying them as a means of improving their fortunes.

The merchant-class milieu and its customs had been portrayed in the Russian theater with considerable realism for several decades prior to *Marriage*, particularly in one of the best-known comic operas of the end of the eighteenth century (Mikhail Matinsky's *St. Petersburg Bazaar*) and in a popular early nineteenth-century melodrama by Pyotr Plavilshchikov. Gogol, like Ostrovsky after him, is frequently given credit for introducing the merchant milieu to the stage by those who are not familiar with the development of Russian drama. What was new about

Marriage

Marriage, however, was its theme of the social and erotic inter-
action between the two classes.

The young woman who replaced the boisterous noblewoman
of *The Suitors* in the final version of *Marriage*, Agafya Tikhonovna Kuperdyagina, is probably as close to being a believable, convincingly presented female protagonist as Gogol could
ever get. She is a comical, at times even a laughable character,
but she has a social and psychological identity and understandable motivations, and her reactions to her predicament are as
sensible and logical as are to be found anywhere in Gogol. The
only child of a well-off merchant, Agafya has inherited her
father's property and is as free and independent as a woman of
her time and social status could hope to be. Because her father
was a domestic tyrant who drove her mother to a premature
grave with his beatings and brutality (apparently a frequent
enough type in the merchant milieu of the time, to judge from
the literature of the period), Agafya resists her aunt's suggestions
that she accept the proposal of the dashing young merchant
Alexei Starikov ("Mr. Oldfolks"), who has no mercenary
motives in seeking her hand and who is the only suitor in the
play to care for Agafya for her own sake. Starikov's role was far
more extensive in the earlier drafts of the play in comparison
with the almost walk-on part to which it was later reduced. But
even so, this pleasant and handsome young man is clearly the
best possible choice Agafya could have made. For Agafya, however, Starikov is merely a potential wife-beater; the beard he
wears (customary among merchants) reminds her both of her
own violent father and of the peasant origin of all merchant
families.

At twenty-seven, Agafya is dangerously close to becoming an
old maid. Custom and social pressure require that she marry (in
The Suitors, this social imperative was expressed by Yaichnitsa

Marriage

in terms of a legal requirement: "You absolutely must have a husband, madam; the law requires it."). So she hires a professional matchmaker to bring some noblemen into her life, using her dowry and property as bait. Although Gogol sympathizes with her position, he nonetheless punishes her with the final humiliation of being left in the lurch by the nobleman she chooses. Social climbing is something Gogol would not condone, even when he himself left his character no alternative. But then, for all the ostensible realism with which her predicament is outlined, Agafya remains a Gogolian creation, with her uncritical acceptance of her aristocratic suitors, no matter how unattractive they may be physically (Yaichnitsa and Zhevakin) or irrational psychologically (Podkolyosin and Anuchkin), and her desire to make up one ideal man by combining various physical features of these four. A simple comparison of Agafya's reasoning and reactions with those of Anna Akimovna in Chekhov's "A Woman's Kingdom"—a young woman of the same class and in more or less the same situation—will show how far from any meaningful social or psychological realism Gogol's writing manner ultimately is.

If in creating Agafya Tikhonovna Gogol ventured into what was for him totally new territory, the two principal male characters of *Marriage*, the reluctant bridegroom Podkolyosin and his busybody friend Kochkaryov, could easily have appeared in any of the *Mirgorod* or St. Petersburg cycle stories. Ivan Kuzmich Podkolyosin ("Mr. Under-the-Wheel") is a placid, phlegmatic civil servant, holding the same rank as Kovalyov in "The Nose." Unlike the protagonists of the St. Petersburg stories, Podkolyosin is not stalked by any nameless terrors. His nose is where it should be, he has a comfortable overcoat or maybe even two, and he has no interest in either prostitutes or stray German housewives. He is entirely adjusted to his situation and doing well at his job. His one and only worry is his public image. For a man in his position, marriage is the unavoidable next step. But Podkolyosin has not the slightest desire to marry. Like several other of Gogol's protagonists (Shponka, Chartkov, Akaky Akakievich, Chichikov), Podkolyosin seems to be totally devoid of any sexual urge, so that when Kochkaryov tries to talk him into marrying by appealing to his sensuality, the only response Podkolyosin can manage is: "Yes, it is nice if a pretty lady sits next to you" and "They do have nice hands." Kochkaryov's assurance that married life usually consists of more than sitting next to each other and holding hands only baffles and embarrasses Podkolyosin.

Reluctant as he is to go through with a marriage, Podkolysin is at the same time extremely anxious to be known as a man who is contemplating matrimony. This is the gist of his several conversations with his servant at the very beginning of the play in which he inquires whether his tailor and the salesman at the grocery store are aware that he might be planning to marry. This is why he has engaged the services of the matchmaker Fyokla Ivanovna, who comes to see him periodically but whose every effort to bring him together with any prospective brides he stubbornly resists. In the next-to-the-last draft of *Marriage*, Gogol provided an unexpectedly plausible motivation for Podkolyosin's ambivalent attitude to matrimony by having Kochkaryov tell Agafya: "The director of his section, his superior, loves him so much that he sleeps in the very same bed with him." Such an open reference to physical homosexuality (offered by Kochkaryov as evidence of Podkolyosin's solvency and job security, with an understandably comic effect) could not possibly have passed the censorship of the time, as Gogol well knew. He deleted this line in the final version, but it is surely interesting that he could not resist putting it down on paper in the first

Marriage

place. The deletion leaves us with the usual vague and undefined fear of women and marriage, so typical of the rest of Gogol's work, as Podkolyosin's chief psychological motive.

The witty and colorful matchmaker lacks the power to get Podkolyosin off his sofa so that he can meet Agafya. Then Podkolysin's closest friend steps in and takes over her function, acting as an unpaid male matchmaker himself. In earlier drafts Kochkaryov was called Kokhtin, a phonetic spelling of Kogtin, "Mr. Claws" (the name comes from Kapnist's *Chicane*, where it was given to a rapacious and corrupt law clerk). He and Podkolyosin have been friends since their childhood. Kochkaryov is married, but his attitude to marriage is established the moment he makes his first entrance:

(*Kochkaryov runs in*)

Kochkaryov.	Podkolyosin, what are you . . . (*Seeing Fyokla*) How do you happen to be here? Why, you! Listen, what the devil did you get me married for?
Fyokla.	What's wrong with that? You did the legal thing.[23]
Kochkaryov.	The legal thing! What's so special about a wife? As if I couldn't manage without her!
Fyokla.	But you yourself kept pestering me: get me married to someone, granny, you just have to do it.
Kochkaryov.	Why, you old rat!

Kochkaryov is clearly unhappy in his marriage and considers it a mistake. Yet he plunges into the project of marrying off his closest friend with overwhelming energy and gusto. By alternately cajoling and bullying him, he drags the protesting Podkolyosin off to meet Agafya. Kochkaryov makes up his mind to marry his friend to her without ever having seen her or knowing

anything about her. He persuades Agafya to choose Podkolyosin over the other prospects. By intriguing and lying, Kochkaryov alienates or scares off the rest of the suitors. No one seems to
be able to withstand his whirlwind energy. Yet, at first glance,
there seems to be no discernible motive for all of his pushing and
manipulating.[24] Even Kochkaryov himself professes to be puzzled by his own behavior in the angry Act II soliloquy he recites
after Podkolyosin obstinately insists on departing after his
tongue-tied interview with Agafya. But at the end of that same
soliloquy, Kochkaryov's true motivation becomes clear to the
audience, if not to himself: "Here is what's annoying: he left and
he hasn't a care in the world. It's all like water off a duck's back
for him—this is really insufferable! He'll go back to his apartment, stretch out, and smoke his pipe. What a disgusting creature! [. . .] But I won't have it, I'll bring back that good-for-
nothing! I won't let him sneak out of it, I'll bring the scoundrel
back!" Even though Kochkaryov himself dislikes marriage and
feels trapped in it, the fact of being married has turned him into
an obedient servant of the matriarchate. Himself miserable, he is
determined to reduce his oldest friend to the same state of mis-
ery. His resourceful maneuverings are a transposition into a
comical key of the activities of the colonel-father, the Cossack
guards, and the other male accomplices of the dead witch in
"Viy" who drag the protesting Homa Brut into the village and
the church so that he may be sacrificed on the altar of female
power.

Vsevolod Setchkarev has wittily compared the action of *Marriage* to repeatedly stretching a rubber band and then letting it
snap back. Podkolyosin is the unwilling band which Kochkaryov keeps pulling toward Agafya and marriage. "Six times,
with ever increasing force, Kochkaryov causes him to lose his
balance and six times Podkolyosin springs back with equal force
into his original position," Setchkarev writes. "Kochkaryov's

Marriage

last and most powerful attack, which apparently brings complete victory, is followed by the catastrophe: a springing-back that literally hurls Podkolyosin out the window." Podkolyosin's leap from the second-story window and his departure in a hired cab mark his escape from matrimony and the preservation of his freedom and at the same time punish Agafya for her presumptuous desire to escape her social status. This dramatic leap is also the culmination of a series of sudden precipitous escapes by horse-drawn conveyances that Gogolian characters effect in order not to have to face intolerable or dangerous situations. The narrator of "The Two Ivans" leaves Mirgorod in a hired cart when reconciliation between the two heroes is no longer thinkable; Poprishchin in "Diary of a Madman" imagines that he is fleeing from the madhouse in an airborne troika; while Khlestakov in *The Inspector General* and Chichikov in *Dead Souls* avoid both matrimony and criminal charges by galloping off in real troikas. But Podkolyosin's escape is the most genuine and triumphant of all: nothing has changed, no punishment is haunting him, and the status quo, that highest Gogolian nirvana, has been re-established.

Podkolyosin was drawn to marriage solely by his concern for his public reputation—it had no other attractions for him. Among Agafya's other suitors, Yaichnitsa-Omelet sees marriage as a business transaction: he is selling Agafya his status as a nobleman and a government official, and in return he is getting some real estate and some household articles. When he is informed by the lying Kochkaryov that the dowry has a lower market value than that quoted by Fyokla, Yaichnitsa indignantly cancels the deal. Anuchkin is a one-issue maniac, interested in neither marriage nor Agafya, but in his own obsession with the French language, knowledge of which is a status symbol. Unable to learn French, Anuchkin intends to acquire a spouse who will speak French for him by a kind of proxy.

Marriage

Baltazar Zhevakin is also obsessed—in his case by Sicilian beauties whom he had observed several decades earlier during his service in the navy and who had aroused his sensuality so powerfully that he had not been able to think of anything else since that time. This overaged Cherubino, who cannot speak to or about women without lapsing into cloying endearments and diminutives ("cutie-pie" and "honeybunch" as used by an elderly Miami Beach gallant would be the present-day American equivalents of Zhevakin's *raskrasotochki* and *rozanchiki*) is one of Gogol's most pathetic creations. His libido in a constant state of genteel and indiscriminate arousal, Zhevakin is willing to settle for Agafya or for almost any other woman as a means of assuaging his persistent sexual itch.

None of the motivations or purposes associated with perpetuating the institution of marriage in human society is even remotely present in the thinking of the male characters of this play. Love is nonexistent, companionship between a man and a woman is an impossibility, sensuality (as personified by Zhevakin) is a pitiful joke, and the joys of procreation and parenthood are ridiculed in the Act I dialogue between Podkolyosin and Kochkaryov as a comical and selfish urge. Gogol's mockery of this basic human institution is so sweeping and illogical in the play, his revulsion so fundamental, that the earliest readers of *Marriage*, the first actors who played in it, and the audiences who saw it on the stage simply did not know what to make of it. By 1842, when the play was finally published and produced in both Russian capitals, Gogol's reputation as a social critic, based on a misreading of *The Inspector General* and *Dead Souls*, was firmly established. His contemporaries, accordingly, chose to see *Marriage* as a simple satire of marital customs, concentrating their attention on such secondary themes as social climbing and status seeking, but overlooking the play's central core and its principal thrust. This was the way Russian criticism

Marriage

understood this play throughout the nineteenth century. Nor were the creative writers who drew on *Marriage* as an example and stimulus for their own work any more discerning than the critics. Alexander Ostrovsky incorporated some of the more obvious features of *Marriage* into his merchant-milieu melodramas and Ivan Goncharov derived the basic conception of his celebrated novel *Oblomov* from its initial scenes, but neither of them showed the kind of perception of the play's theme and content that is found in Turgenev's and Dostoyevsky's ripostes to "The Overcoat," in *The Bachelor* and *Poor Folk*, respectively. With the advent of Russian Marxist criticism, *Marriage* was placed in a convenient sociological pigeonhole which is, if anything, even more simplistic than the nineteenth-century views of the play: Agafya was now seen as a symbol of nascent capitalism, trying to take over feudalism (Podkolyosin), but meeting with some resistance.

The insights of such later thinkers as Nietzsche, Strindberg, and Freud into the relationship between the sexes could obviously contribute much to our understanding of Gogol's meaning in *Marriage*. But Russian criticism has so far preferred to abide by the utilitarian or Marxist platitudes. While the wit and the brilliance of its verbal texture are self-evident to anyone who can read it in the original (no English translation even begins to do justice to the idiosyncratic magnificence of the subtly fractured Russian of the play's dialogue), *Marriage* remains to this day perhaps Gogol's single most misunderstood work.

Gogol's last play, *The Gamblers*, was conceived and sketched out prior to his departure from Russia in 1836, but it was given its final form in Bad Gastein in 1842 during the final burst of creativity that also produced "The Overcoat," *Marriage,* and the revised versions of "Taras Bulba," "The Portrait," and *The Inspector General.* Shorter and simpler than the two earlier comedies, *The Gamblers* is in some important ways their continuation and culmination.

On the surface, this play is a familiar and always satisfying tale of a swindler caught in his own nets. The basic plot is similar to that of Ben Jonson's *Volpone* and to that of the story of Gianni Schicchi's turning the tables on Simone, as evoked by Dante in the thirtieth canto of the *Inferno* and in Puccini's opera based on that episode. The milieu in which Gogol situated the play—Russian noblemen addicted to card playing for high stakes—had been previously explored in depth by both Pushkin (his stories "The Shot" and "The Queen of Spades") and Lermontov (his play *Masquerade* and his verse tale "The Treasurer's Wife of Tambov"). But as he had so often done in the past, Gogol took these familiar and fashionable literary ingredients and put them to his own unique and highly unexpected uses. His gamblers are not simply the card-table addicts of Pushkin or Lermontov, but professional cardsharps who live in a special subculture of their own and regard their trade as a form of artistic expression. Gogol takes particular pains to establish at the outset that the play's principal character, Ikharyov, is an affluent landowner, the owner of a large number of serfs, who engages in cheating at cards not out of material need but for the emotional and aesthetic satisfaction it gives him. Ikharyov is an artistic, creative cheat, just as Khlestakov was an artistic liar. When he and the other professional gamblers decide to join forces, they discuss their calling and its finer points in terms that befit artists exchanging subtle suggestions on how to improve their art forms.

In *The Gamblers,* Gogol returns once more to the all-male

The Gamblers

microcosm that he had previously described in "Taras Bulba" and the opening passages of "Viy." This time round, however, the camaraderie of the all-male society is deceptive, and it has acquired a mean and vicious inner core, unthinkable in the *Mirgorod* stories. The world of *The Gamblers* is not unlike the world of Jean Genet's *Haute Surveillance* or *Notre-Dame des Fleurs*. Gogol's gamblers pretend to be friends, allies, or relatives, but their affability can easily turn into mutual betrayal. One can only speculate about Gogol's disappointment in his close friendship with the poet Yazykov, which took a turn for the worse just before *The Gamblers* was completed, or about his complex but insufficiently studied relationships with several Russian painters in Rome and the ways these personal experiences could have conspired to produce this bleak view of friendship between men.

The two central metaphors on which *The Gamblers* is constructed can be grasped in the second half of the twentieth century with far greater ease than they could have been in Gogol's time. The work of Genet can unlock for us the metaphor of friendship as betrayal, an idea which both Gogol and Genet develop against the background of an underground, all-male criminal subculture. The play's other basic metaphor, that of criminal endeavor as a work of art, makes much better sense to those familiar with Vladimir Nabokov's *Despair*, a novel which treats the hero's plans to commit a murder and an insurance fraud in terms of planning and gestating an artistic creation. Like Nabokov's Hermann, Gogol's Ikharyov also falls into the trap he has set for others; like him, he is also a failed artist who is undone by insufficient command of his artistic medium and inattention to essential details.

Traditional Russian criticism has been unaware of these important dimensions of *The Gamblers*. Even as perceptive a his-

---

The Gamblers

torian of Russian literature as D. S. Mirsky proclaimed it vastly inferior to Gogol's other two comedies: "It is an unpleasant play, inhabited by scoundrels who are not funny, and, though the construction is neat, it is dry and lacks the richness of true Gogol." Others have denied Gogol's ability to handle plot and character in *The Gamblers*, referring to the the three stooges who impersonate the intended victims, but who are actually participants in the conspiracy to fleece Ikharyov. The supposed flaw of the play, it was claimed, is that the audience never gets to meet two of these three characters in their true identities and is thus misled and fooled as badly as Ikharyov. But if one realizes that the illusory nature of everyone's identity is one of the central themes of this play (and of the whole of Gogol's work), this alleged deficiency can be seen as the astute literary stratagem it actually is. Ikharyov and the other three gamblers are delineated very carefully and emerge as individualized characters. The stooges who appear under false identities, however, are not individual characters, but broad literary stereotypes. The virtuous father, Glov-senior, a sort of parody of the elder Germont from Verdi's *La Traviata* written a full decade before that opera was composed, and his weak, easily swayed putative son, Glov-junior, babbling about his future amorous conquests and military exploits as he gambles away the money entrusted to him, are both the very stuff of the most obvious late eighteenth-century melodrama. The cynical, bribable city hall official Zamukhryshkin is an obvious take-off on the corrupt law clerks from Kapnist's *Chicane*. Gogol deliberately emphasized the familiar, hackneyed qualities of these three characters. By falling for their clumsy act, Ikharyov exposes his failure as a confidence man, which on the metaphorical level of the play also represents his failure as a creative artist.

Love and marriage are totally absent from the gamblers'

The Gamblers

world, but Gogol manages to insert a bit of subtle ridicule of them just the same. Glov-senior's sentimental eulogies of the joys of family life and his concern for the marital happiness of his sweet, innocent daughter, and Glov-junior's hot-blooded heterosexual desires are in the end exposed as so much play-acting by hired stooges incapable of experiencing such emotions. Their passion for gambling and the satisfaction of planning and executing clever swindles provide these men with all the amorous excitement they need. Cards have explicitly taken over the place of women in their lives. The one female character in the otherwise all-male cast of *The Gamblers* is Ikharyov's specially marked deck of cards, bearing the elegant German-Russian name of Adelaida Ivanovna (the Russian word for deck, *koloda*, is feminine in gender). Adelaida Ivanovna and her major role in the play are the culmination of the sequence of nonhuman wives and mistresses in Gogol's work: Ivan Shponka's bolt-of-cloth wife, Chertokutsky's carriage-mistress and the general's Agrafena Ivanovna in "The Carriage," Chichikov's strongbox in *Dead Souls*, and Akaky Akakievich's overcoat. Ikharyov addresses endearments to Adelaida Ivanovna when he first unpacks her, he introduces her to his new friends, and he pleads for her help and support in moments of crisis. Adelaida Ivanovna is endowed with the highest virtue that a female character can possess in a work by Gogol: like Pulcheria Ivanovna in "Old-World Landowners" and Agrafena Ivanovna in "The Carriage" (could the identical patronymic of these three be entirely accidental?), she is totally incapable of making any sexual demands on the man in her life.

When the other gamblers get to meet Adelaida Ivanovna, one of them suggests that because of her German first name she would make a suitable wife for another gambler who is named Krugel. Krugel rejects the idea with a typical Gogolian non sequitur: "What sort of German am I? My grandfather was a German, but even he could not speak German." He may be willing to betray and swindle Ikharyov, but he knows better than to try to get between him and his helpmate. Yet for all of her resourcefulness and loyalty, Adelaida Ivanovna is but a woman: she is no match for the combined assault of the three master criminals Ikharyov believes to be his friends and their three stooges he thinks are his victims. He loses and in his fury he turns against her, screaming: "To hell with Adelaida Ivanovna!" There follows a stage direction, impossible to carry out in actual performance, which is nonetheless one of the most important and revealing lines in all Gogol: *He grabs Adelaida Ivanovna and flings her at the door. Queens and deuces fly to the floor.* The second sentence of this direction is a set of *double entendres* in Russian. The word for "queens" in a card deck is actually "ladies." The word for "deuces" can also mean "couples" or "pairs." The expression "fly to the floor" (*letyat na pol*) can be interpreted to mean "collapse." The phrase is thus the climax of the headlong flight from women, love, and marriage which gathered ever greater momentum in each of Gogol's succeeding plays. Khlestakov fled from marriage in a troika, Podkolyosin in *Marriage* escaped it by jumping out the window, while at the end of *The Gamblers* the very possibility of associating with "ladies" (either real ones or those made of cardboard) and forming "couples" with them falls on the floor and collapses.[25] With all of Gogol's amazing thematic variety and stylistic versatility, this one obsessive idea managed to insinuate itself in one form or another into almost every one of his mature stories and plays.

Russian tradition credits Gogol's plays with being the point of departure for Russian realist drama. And, indeed, productions of his plays undoubtedly contributed to the emergence of a more realistic mode of staging and acting. However, the playwrights who tried to follow his example noticed only the most obvious and superficial aspects of Gogol's innovative dramatic method: the satire on corruption in the civil service in *The Inspector General*, the matchmaking customs of Russian merchants in *Marriage*, and the image of society as a menagerie of mutually destructive predators in *The Gamblers*. Gogol's reversals of logic, his sense of metaphysical absurdity, and the sexual component of his plays went unnoticed in the nineteenth century, with two significant exceptions. Alexei Pisemsky's first comedy, *The Hypochondriac* (1851), and the last play of Alexander Sukhovo-Kobylin's trilogy, *Tarelkin's Death* (1868), are the only nineteenth-century plays whose authors truly understood the essence of Gogolian comical style and built their own dramatic conceptions upon it. Both of these plays were angrily attacked for their supposed "absurdities" and "improbabilities" by nineteenth-century critics, who failed to see their Gogolian aspects, since Gogol was regarded as the epitome of photographic realism at the time. The far more important and innovative *nonrealistic* aspects of Gogol's plays came to be recognized only in the early twentieth century; the impact of this recognition can be seen in such remarkable achievements of twentieth-century Russian drama as Sologub's *Nocturnal Dances*, Zamyatin's *The Flea*, Mayakovsky's *Bathhouse*, and Erdman's *Mandate*.

By the time of Gogol's departure from Russia in 1836, his name had become a household word throughout the country. Yet very few people could claim to have known him well as a person. His sociability, his highly visible participation in the lit-

Gogol's Underground Life

erary life of his time, went hand in hand with a reluctance to reveal his inner self even to his closest associates. "Those whom he did admit to a kind of intimacy," writes Donald Fanger, "found themselves, so to speak, in small rooms that did not communicate; thus the most useful memoirs—Aksakov's, Annenkov's, Smirnova's—give convincing but often contrasting pictures, and the key that would reconcile them is missing."[26] Elsewhere in the same perceptive essay Fanger points out that "Gogol's few attempts to speak frankly in his letters were all attempts to speak *about* frankness, and one feels in them the anguished desire of a man bewildered by his own chronic evasions and mimicry to find his 'real' voice and discover what it might have to say."

Another present-day commentator, Helen Muchnic, expressed the same idea in somewhat stronger terms. "Gogol lied to himself as well as to others," she writes. "Lying was his way of life, the essence of his genius."[27] The critic Pletnyov, one of Gogol's most steadfast champions and supporters, replied to Gogol's request for a frank appraisal of his character as follows: "So you finally want to hear some truths. Very well then, be my guest. What are you like? As a person you are a secretive, egotistical, arrogant, and mistrustful being, who sacrifices everything for the sake of fame. As a friend, what are you like? But then, can you have any friends?" (Pletnyov's letter to Gogol of October 27, 1844). Gogol replied to Pletnyov's accusations with a long, convoluted, not very coherent letter in which he pleaded mitigating circumstances, but on the whole recognized that Pletnyov's charges were not without foundation.

The evasions and concealments, the deceptions and mistrustfulness are a constant theme of Gogol's biographers, who usually see this entire complex as an odd, inexplicable feature of his personality. But actually there is nothing unique or specifically Gogolian about it. Recent psychological studies of the adapta-

Gogol's Underground Life

tion patterns to which homosexuals are forced to resort in Western societies[28] show that dissimulation is a frequent survival strategy, which male homosexuals in particular instinctively use in order to avoid recognition and detection. The need to dissimulate had to be especially strong in a case like Gogol's, where personal moral and religious scruples combined to reinforce existing social strictures. The toll in nervous stress and tension was predictably high,[29] and it is to this stress that we can attribute the digestive difficulties and ailments, real and imaginary, that plagued the last fifteen years of Gogol's life.

And yet, a close reading of Gogol's correspondence and of memoirs about him will reveal a few chinks here and there in the carefully contrived façade; through these chinks can be glimpsed what Dostoyevsky, in a moment of insight whose full implications he probably did not realize, called Gogol's "underground life." For example, the beginning of Gogol's letter to Alexander Danilevsky of December 20, 1832, in which he thanks fate for never having experienced love, "for this flame would have turned me to dust in one instant," has been quoted in innumerable critical essays and biographies. No one ever quotes the following puzzling passage from the end of the same letter: "Having received your letter, I was reminded of you so vividly that, meeting a junior ensign walking near the Blue Bridge, I thought to myself: I ought to drop by and see him. He probably has not been allowed out because of failure to pay the fee for [illegible]. So I turned toward the school and had already asked the soldier on guard whether the Grand Duke had stopped by and whether he is expected today, but then I came to my senses and went home." Annotating this passage in Volume X of the USSR Academy of Sciences edition of Gogol (1940), Vasily Gippius limits himself to informing the reader that the grand duke in question was Mikhail Pavlovich, the younger brother of Nicholas I and the director of the school for the Corps of Pages, as well as of all the infantry cadet academies. One possible way of understanding this passage, then, is to assume that the "him" does not refer to the junior ensign near the Blue Bridge, but to a cadet or a page whom Gogol had been seeing clandestinely. An inspection visit by the Grand Duke would interfere with Gogol's intended visit to this person.

Equally curious are the circumstances of the death in Rome of the young architect Mikhail Tamarinsky (or Tomarinsky), as described in the memoirs of Pavel Annenkov and of Fyodor Iordan. As far as anyone knew, Gogol and Tamarinsky were no more than casual acquaintances. During the two weeks of Tamarinsky's fatal illness, Gogol inquired repeatedly about his condition, but refrained from either visiting the dying man or attending his funeral. The day before the funeral, however, Annenkov met Gogol on the Spanish Steps in a state of utter despair over Tamarinsky's death and on the verge of a nervous breakdown. At Gogol's request, Annenkov hired a cab and drove him to Albano. "During the trip and in Albano," Annenkov reports, "Gogol appeared entirely calm, and he offered no explanation for his desperate words, as though they had never been said." The violent reaction, which Annenkov found so puzzling, becomes understandable if we assume that Gogol either had a secret crush on Tamarinsky or had a closer relationship with him than he cared to admit. Gogol's refusal to visit the dying architect or to come to his funeral can then be explained by his fear of betraying his true emotions in public.

Embittered by the adverse criticism of *The Inspector General* and by the widespread misunderstanding of his intentions in

Life Abroad

writing the play, Gogol left Russia in June of 1836. Accompanied by his old school friend Alexander Danilevsky, he traveled leisurely through Germany and Switzerland. He spent the winter of 1836-37 in Paris, a city he never learned to like. Gogol found the free discussions of any political topic, the unconstrained advocacy of political and social reforms in French cafés and salons, both distasteful and incomprehensible. The spring of 1837 found him in Rome, where he was to settle for many years.

In some areas of his life, foreign travel had the kind of broadening effect on Gogol that it is traditionally reputed to have. For the first time, he began acquiring female friends and correspondents. In Baden-Baden he encountered Maria Balabina, who had once been his pupil at the Patriotic Institute, and her French-born mother, Varvara Osipovna. The Balabin ladies were accompanied by Princess Varvara Repnina, whose brother was related to the Balabins by marriage. All three of these women became Gogol's ardent admirers and assiduous correspondents. In Paris Gogol met for the first time Alexandra Smirnova, née Rosset (a russification of the originally Italian name Rossetti). A lady-in-waiting to two Russian empresses and a friend of Pushkin and Zhukovsky, Smirnova eventually became one of Gogol's closest friends. Her memoirs are one of the most informative sources we have about Gogol's person; it was to her that he addressed the highest accolade and the greatest mark of confidence that he ever granted any woman: calling her "my beautiful brother" in one of his letters. The topic of mutual interest that brought Gogol together with all these women friends was their shared interest in religion. At one time or another, Gogol played the role of religious preceptor (one is tempted to say "guru") in the life of each. This was also the case with some of his relationships with women in later years, such as his epistolary friendship with the elderly and pious Nadezhda Sheremeteva.

Another group of new friends were the Russian painters he

Life Abroad

met in Rome. With some of the most celebrated artists of the time, such as Ingres and Thorvaldsen, in permanent residence, Rome was considered a major artistic center, and the government of Nicholas I supported there a considerable number of Russian painters, engravers, and architects, at times over long periods, for the purpose of perfecting their abilities through close, first-hand study of the Italian masters. One of the most respected and admired of these resident artists was Alexander Ivanov, a painter of mythological and biblical subjects. Of morose and unsociable disposition, Ivanov devoted most of his life to painting a single huge canvas, "Christ's Appearance before the People" (also referred to in more recent times as "The Appearance of the Messiah"), a work in whose conception and gestation Gogol was profoundly involved. Women were all but absent from Ivanov's life. When they appeared in his work, it was often in a far from flattering light: Potiphar's wife contemptuously rejected by Joseph, Delilah divesting Samson of his locks and his strength, and Magdalene kneeling at the feet of Jesus were treated by Ivanov in several variations each. Pre-adolescent boys were his very favorite subject, usually appearing naked, singly or in groups in one canvas or sketch after another, year after year, throughout Ivanov's career. His first major painting, based on the mythological theme of Apollo, Hyacinthus, and Cyparissus which shows Apollo affectionately fondling two nude and sun-tanned ten-year-olds, gives more than a hint of Ivanov's probable pedophilia.

The close relationship that Gogol and Ivanov formed in Rome was reflected in the work of both. Ivanov's huge canvas and his ideas about the function of art appear in the revised version of "The Portrait." Gogol's essay on Ivanov, first published separately and later included in *Selected Passages,* is a handsome tribute and a testament to his friendship and admiration. It was

Iosif Vielhorsky

probably Gogol's later mysticism that helped Ivanov break out of the academicism that is otherwise typical of his work and create in the 1850s his beautiful and visionary watercolors and drawings on biblical subjects, in which Ivanov becomes the precursor of the magnificent visionary art of the turn-of-the-century Russian painter Mikhail Vrubel.

In Paris and during his first year in Rome Gogol worked steadily on *Dead Souls*, which he had begun before leaving Russia. The realization that he was producing his most ambitious and possibly most important work to date, his growing infatuation with Rome and its art treasures, his friendship with Ivanov and other Russian painters, and his newly discovered capacity for friendly contact with women must all have conspired to loosen Gogol's emotional restraints and prepare him for the most profound personal involvement of his life.

In the spring of 1838, the heir to the Russian throne, the future Alexander II, embarked on a grand tour of Western Europe. He was accompanied by his tutor, the poet Zhukovsky, and by Iosif Vielhorsky. The latter was the twenty-three-year-old son of Count Mikhail Vielhorsky,[30] the dilettante musician and courtier who had been so helpful in bringing *The Inspector General* to the attention of the tsar and thus in getting it past the censorship. The young Vielhorsky was of a studious disposition, and the tsar therefore decreed that he be educated together with Alexander so as to provide an example of seriousness and diligence. Actually, the two young men seemed to care little for each other's company. Iosif Vielhorsky was a serious student of history, engaged in a historical research project, and he felt his position at court was a hindrance to his scholarly progress.

In the course of the tour, it was discovered that Iosif Vielhorsky had tuberculosis. He left the royal party and throughout the summer consulted German doctors at various spas. In Novem-

Iosif Vielhorsky

ber, he came to Rome and settled at the villa of Zinaida Volkonskaya, a friend of his parents and one of the most remarkable
Russian women of the age. A celebrated beauty and one-time
mistress of Alexander I, Zinaida Volkonskaya was also a gifted
poet, composer, and singer. Rossini admired her performance of
contralto roles in his operas, which she sang in private performances not open to the public; Pushkin, Mickiewicz, and Baratynsky described her in their poetry and dedicated poems to her. In
1829, she was converted to Roman Catholicism and thereby incurred the wrath of Nicholas I. The tsar allowed her to keep her
property, but forbade Volkonskaya to reside in Russia. She decided to settle in Rome, where her magnificent villa soon became
an important literary salon and a magnet for all resident and visiting artists and intellectuals.

It was at Volkonskaya's villa that Gogol first met Iosif Vielhorsky on December 20, 1838. The meeting marked the beginning of what seems to have been the happiest and most fulfilling
period in Gogol's life. Throughout January and February of
1839, Zhukovsky was in Rome, and Gogol acted as his guide. In
March, Zhukovsky was replaced by Pogodin. Gogol's pleasure
at the company of these two old and admired friends and his
gradually growing closeness with Iosif Vielhorsky are reflected
in some of his letters of the period and in Pogodin's memoir "A
Year Abroad." Pogodin was introduced to Vielhorsky and was
highly impressed by his potential as a historian. "The young
Count Vielhorsky showed me his materials for a bibliography of
Russian history," Pogodin wrote in his memoir. "He's doing fine
work, but will the Lord allow him to bring it to completion? The
red color in his cheeks bodes no good. Nevertheless, he's working continually."

With the turn of Vielhorsky's illness for the worse in April,
Gogol moved in with him at Volkonskaya's villa in order to devote his entire time to nursing him. "I learned at that time that

"Nights at the Villa"

[Gogol] was on terms of intimacy with the young Vielhorsky,"
wrote Alexandra Smirnova in her memoirs, "but I saw him
rarely then and did not try to find out how and when this relationship came about. I found their intimacy *comme il faut*, most
natural and simple." There is a tinge of defensiveness or perhaps
justification in Smirnova's tone that implies, as Henri Troyat has
pointed out, that the arrangement may have raised a few eye-
brows. But for once, Gogol was beyond caring for appearances.
He had at last found a friend whose need for shared closeness
and affection was equal to his own. His love was reciprocated;
but he fully realized that the days of his loved one were num-
bered. "I live now only for the sake of his dwindling days," Gogol wrote to Maria Balabina on May 30. 1839. "I catch his every
minute. His smile or his momentary joyous expression make an
epoch for me, an event in my monotonously passing day." And
in the postscript of a letter to Stepan Shevyryov, also at the end
of May: "I spend my days and nights at the bedside of the ailing
Iosif, of my Vielhorsky. The poor boy cannot bear to spend a
minute without me near him."

Gogol kept a journal of his vigils at Volkonskaya's villa. Two
manuscript fragments from this journal were eventually discovered in Mikhail Pogodin's archive. They are usually printed in
complete editions of Gogol's works in Russian under the title
"Nights at the Villa." Russian critics, both pre-revolutionary and
Soviet, often refer to "Nights at the Villa" as a fragmentary work
of fiction.[31] It is, however, clearly a part of a larger personal
diary, the remainder of which, given the explicit nature of the
surviving portions and the attitudes of the Victorian age, may
well have been destroyed. Here is the text of these fragments:

They were sweet and tormenting, those sleepless nights. He
sat, ill, in the armchair. I was with him. Sleep dared not touch
my eyes. Silently and involuntarily, it seems, it respected the

"*Nights at the Villa*"

sanctity of my vigil. It was so sweet to sit near him, to look at him. For two nights already we have been saying "thou" to each other. How much closer he has become to me since then! He sat there just as before, meek, quiet, and resigned. Good God! With what joy, with what happiness I would have taken his illness upon myself! And if my death could restore him to health, with what readiness I would have rushed toward it!

. . .

I did not stay with him last night. I had finally decided to stay home and sleep. Oh, how base, how vile that night and my despicable sleep were! I slept poorly, even though I had been without sleep for almost a week. I was tormented by the thought of him. I kept imagining him, imploring and reproachful. I saw him with the eyes of my soul. I hastened to come early to him and felt like a criminal as I went. From his bed he saw me. He smiled with his usual angel's smile. He offered his hand. He pressed mine lovingly. "Traitor," he said, "you betrayed me." "My angel," I said, "forgive me. I myself suffered with your suffering. I was in torment all night. My rest brought me no repose. Forgive me!" My meek one! He pressed my hand. How fully rewarded I was for the suffering that the stupidly spent night had brought me! "My head is weary," he said. I began to fan him with a laurel branch. "Ah, how fresh and good," he said. His words were then . . . what were they? What would I then not have given, what earthly goods, those despicable, those vile, those disgusting goods . . . no, they are not worth mentioning. You into whose hands will fall—if they will fall—these incoherent, feeble lines, pallid expressions of my emotions, you will understand me. Otherwise they will not fall into your hands. You will understand how repulsive the entire heap of treasures and honors is that attracts those wooden dolls which are called people. Oh, with what joy, with what anger I could have trampled underfoot and squashed everything that is bestowed by the mighty scep-

"Nights at the Villa"

ter of the Tsar of the North, if I only knew that this would buy a smile that indicated the slightest relief on his face.

"Why did you prepare such a bad month of May for me?" he said to me, awakening in his armchair and hearing the wind beyond the windowpanes that wafted the aroma of the blossoming wild jasmine and white acacia, which it mingled with the whirling rose petals.

. . .

At ten o'clock I went down to see him. I had left him three hours before to get some rest, to prepare [something] for him, to afford him some variety, so that my arrival would give him more pleasure. I went down to him at ten o'clock. He had been alone for more than an hour. His visitors had long since left. The dejection of boredom showed on his face. He saw me. Waved his hand slightly. "My savior," he said to me. They still sound in my ears, those words. "My angel! Did you miss me?" "Oh, how I missed you," he replied. I kissed him on the shoulder. He offered his cheek. We kissed; he was still pressing my hand.

THE EIGHTH NIGHT

He did not like going to bed and hardly ever did. He preferred his armchair and the sitting position. That night the doctor ordered him to rest. He stood up reluctantly and, leaning on my shoulder, moved to his bed. My darling! His weary glance, his brightly colored jacket, his slow steps—I can see it all, it is all before my eyes. He whispered in my ear, leaning on my shoulder and glancing at the bed: "Now I'm a ruined man." "We will remain in bed for only half an hour," I said to him, "and then we'll go back to your armchair." I watched you, my precious, tender flower! All the time when you were sleeping or merely dozing in your bed or armchair, I followed your movements and your moments, bound to you by some incomprehensible force.

How strangely new my life was then and, at the same time, I

"Nights at the Villa"

discerned in it a repetition of something distant, something that once actually was. But it seems hard to give an idea of it: there returned to me a fresh, fleeting fragment of my youth, that time when a youthful soul seeks fraternal friendship with those of one's own age, a decidedly juvenile friendship, full of sweet, almost infantile trifles and mutual show of tokens of tender attachment; the time when it is sweet to gaze into each other's eyes, when your entire being is ready to offer sacrifices, which are usually not even necessary. And all these feelings, sweet, youthful, fresh—alas! inhabitants of a vanished world—all these feelings returned to me. Good Lord! What for? I watched you, my precious, tender flower. Did this fresh breath of youth waft upon me only so that I might suddenly and irrevocably sink into even greater and more deadening coldness of feelings, so that I might become all at once older by a decade, so that I might see my vanishing life with even greater despair and hopelessness? Thus does a dying fire send its last flame up into the air, so that it might illuminate with its flickering the somber walls and then disappear forever.[32]

Iosif Vielhorsky died in Rome on May 21, 1839. His last moments were darkened by Zinaida Volkonskaya's ill-advised efforts to effect a deathbed conversion to Catholicism. Gogol's opposition to this move earned him Volkonskaya's subsequent enmity. On June 5, Gogol wrote to Alexander Danilevsky: "A few days ago I buried my friend, one whom fate gave me at a time of life when friends are no longer given. I speak of my Iosif Vielhorsky. We have been long attached to each other, have long respected one another, but we became united intimately, indissolubly, and utterly fraternally only during his illness, alas." The relationship left Gogol with some of the most cherished memories of his life. It apparently also saddled him with a lasting sense of guilt.

The extent of his guilty feelings and the form they took can be

Gogol and Ivanov

partially surmised from the reflections of the affair in the work of Gogol's friend Alexander Ivanov. At the time of Vielhorsky's death, Ivanov had already produced more than a hundred preparatory studies for his magnum opus, "Christ's Appearance before the People." The essential conception of the canvas did not change from one preliminary version to another. All of them depict Saint John the Baptist in the foreground, preaching to a crowd that includes some of the future apostles, contrasted with the small and solitary figure of Christ, who is quietly approach-

Alexander Ivanov: Study for the figure of the crouching slave in "Christ's Appearance before the People," which is a portrait of Gogol.

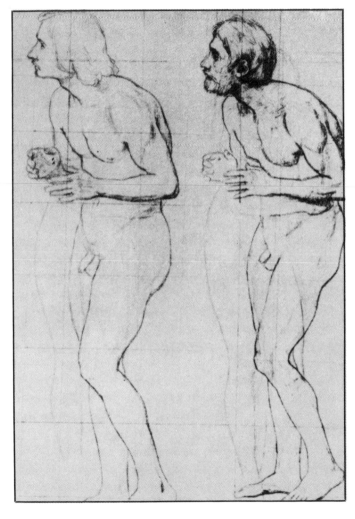

Alexander Ivanov: Two studies for "Christ's Appearance before the People." The figure on the left has Gogol's head.

Gogol and Ivanov

Alexander Ivanov: Head of a young man, assumed to be a portrait of Iosif Vielhorsky.

ing the crowd from a distance. It had long been noticed that in a study for the painting that dates from ca. 1839-1841 (it is now at the Russian Museum, Leningrad), the figure of the gloomy peni-tent, located closest to the figure of Christ, is actually a portrait of Gogol. Through the inspired detective work of Nikolai Mash-kovtsev, a long-time student of Ivanov's art, it was later also established that Gogol and Vielhorsky were also depicted in that version of the painting as the nude man and boy who have just been baptized in the Jordan and are seen emerging from the water in the foreground on the right.[33]

Mashkovtsev demonstrated the connection of the elder of the two baptized men with Gogol by pointing out the facial resem-blance between him and a number of earlier sketches Ivanov had made for that figure, including what appears to be a very hand-some sketch of Gogol in the nude (apparently, Gogol's head was superimposed on the body of a professional Italian model). In the fall of 1934, Mashkovtsev discovered on sale in a Leningrad Torgsin store (a special hard-currency store, where only foreign tourists may shop) a study of a young man's head by Alexander Ivanov that turned out to be a portrait of Iosif Vielhorsky. The same head appears in a drawing at the Tretiakov Gallery that also contains a portrait of Gogol and a sketch of St. Christopher carrying the infant Christ. Vielhorsky's head is also identical with that of the just-baptized boy huddling next to the Gogol-inspired nude figure in the Russian Museum study for "Christ's Appearance before the People." However, in accordance with his own aesthetics (and his psychosexual orientation), Ivanov placed the head of the twenty-three-year-old Vielhorsky on the body of a boy who could not be more than twelve.

According to Mashkovtsev, the Russian Museum study for the painting embodies a conception worked out jointly by Gogol and Ivanov and testifies to their close empathy and mutual con-fidence. If he is right, the agonized figure of the penitent near

Gogol and Ivanov

Christ might well represent Gogol's contrition at having given himself over to a love that was not sanctioned by society and that was prohibited by his religion. At the same time the nude baptized pair in the foreground would symbolize Christ's forgiveness and acceptance of this love. None of this found its way into the final version of the painting, however, and Mashkovtsev offers a plausible explanation why. In 1841, Ivanov painted his well-known portrait of Gogol. He was generally reluctant to do portraits, but he acceded to his writer-friend's request and produced two copies of the same portrait, which Gogol wanted to present to Zhukovsky and to Pogodin. The portrait is a relaxed, domestic, and affable variation on the gloomy penitent of the study. Gogol is even wearing the penitent's plum-colored garment in the portrait, but here it is clearly a dressing gown, which Ivanov had disguised as a biblical robe in the painting.

The two copies of the portrait were painted in great secrecy and their recipients were explicitly asked not to put them on public display. In 1844, however, Pogodin allowed his copy to be reproduced simultaneously in two publications. This was the first appearance of a Gogol portrait anywhere, for until that time Gogol had forbidden the publication of any of his likenesses. His rage at Pogodin's breach of confidence becomes fully understandable when one realizes that the portrait's publication made the inclusion of Gogol's and Vielhorsky's quasi-portraits in "Christ's Appearance before the People" an impossibility. In the huge painting that Ivanov finally completed in 1857, the penitent nearest Christ is a handsome young man who bears no resemblance to Gogol and the baptized pair has been replaced by a Semitic-looking father and child, decorously draped in the garments they are putting on. Gogol could not forgive Pogodin the publication of the Ivanov portrait for several years and his anger over the incident accounts for his nasty attack on this old friend in *Selected Passages* in 1846.

A Visit to Russia

Iosif Vielhorsky's father traveled to Rome when he received the news of his son's critical condition. He arrived just in time to be present at Iosif's death. Gogol volunteered to accompany Vielhorsky senior to Marseilles, where his German-born wife, Luise, and their other children were waiting, and to help him break the news to them. Gogol carried with him his most cherished possession: a bible on which his dying friend had inscribed with trembling hand "To my friend Nikolai. Villa Volkonskaya." His emotional state during the boat trip to France can be imagined. Yet an account of his behavior during that trip which we have from a rather unexpected witness shows to what extent Gogol had learned to control and conceal his inner feelings. A man who struck up a chance conversation with Gogol on the deck of the steamship turned out to be the foremost French literary critic of the time, Charles Sainte-Beuve. Sainte-Beuve later recalled that Gogol's conversation during the trip was spirited, knowledgeable, and entertaining.

Several years later, in 1845, Sainte-Beuve described the meeting in his enthusiastic review of Louis Viardot's translations of Gogol's tales into French. The review marked the beginning of Gogol's reputation in the Western world. A curious dividend of that literary encounter on the steamship was the effect it had on the reputation of the Roman poet Giuseppe Gioacchino Belli, who wrote in the proletarian Trasteverino dialect and for whose principal work, Sonnetti romaneschi, Gogol had a very high regard. It was Gogol who informed Sainte-Beuve of Belli's existence, and it was the critic's ensuing enthusiasm that made the Italians themselves sit up and take notice of this poet, demonstrating

A Visit to Russia

once again what unpredictable factors can affect writers' reputations.[34]

Countess Vielhorsky had not been informed of her son's death, and it fell to Gogol to carry out this difficult task. She collapsed on the floor upon hearing the news and went into a state of shock which lasted for two days and out of which Gogol brought her by his gentle ministrations. He was to remain a devoted friend and correspondent of Iosif's mother and his two younger sisters for the rest of his life. Going back to Rome and to his memories was more than he could face. He decided to return to Russia temporarily, stopping at Marienbad on the way for a water cure for his nerves. This was to be the first of his two temporary returns and it was motivated by Gogol's desire to settle the future of his younger sisters. The second return, in the winter of 1841-42, was occasioned by the necessity of making arrangements for the publication of *Dead Souls*.

Throughout his stay abroad, Gogol had corresponded diligently with his mother and sisters, taking a great interest in their affairs while telling them as little as possible of his own. Maria, the oldest of his sisters, was widowed in 1836. Two years later, she was making plans for her second marriage. Gogol, who had strongly advised her against her first marriage, was immediately alarmed. He wrote to Maria, urging her to exercise the utmost prudence and to weigh the material advantages that the new marriage might bring against the loss of freedom it would entail. In a letter he wrote to his mother a few weeks later, Gogol expressed his objections more pointedly. Unless her prospective husband possessed a huge fortune, Maria simply had to be stopped. "She must remember that she will start having children, which bring a thousand worries and cares, so that she will end up thinking with envy of her earlier existence. A girl of eighteen may be forgiven for preferring external appearance, a kind

---

A Visit to Russia

heart, and a sensitive character to everything else, and for disdaining riches and security for their sake. But it is unforgivable for a widow of twenty-four to limit her considerations to them alone" (Gogol's letter to his mother of February 5, 1838). It never occurred to Gogol that his line of reasoning, so reminiscent of Podkolyosin's in *Marriage*, may have had nothing to do with his sister's situation. His reaction to the prospect of marriage—anyone's marriage—was instinctive, gut-level, and invariably negative.

His other two sisters, Anna (Annette) and Elizaveta (Liza), had been accepted as boarding students at the Patriotic Institute when Gogol taught history and geography there. The aristocratic school's exorbitant tuition, which Gogol's family would not have been able to afford, was waived out of regard for Gogol's literary accomplishments. At the time of Vielhorsky's death, Gogol was informed that Annette and Liza were to graduate from the Patriotic Institute early in 1840. Their mother was planning to travel to St. Petersburg to be present at their graduation and then take them back home to the Ukraine. Gogol found that plan all wrong. He saw no point in his sisters' taking the final examinations and then participating in graduation ceremonies. "What is suitable for boys is unbecoming for girls," he wrote his mother in this connection on October 24, 1839. He resolved to take his sisters out of the school prior to the examinations and to place them as *demoiselles de compagnie* with some pious and moral-minded elderly noblewomen. This had to be done because, left to their own and their mother's devices, Annette and Liza might "fling themselves on the neck of the first man who comes along and end up marrying just anyone" (the letter just quoted). It was to save his sisters from this last eventuality that Gogol traveled to Russia in the fall of 1839.

It turned out to be something of a triumphant homecoming.

A Visit to Russia

After Pushkin's death in 1837, Gogol was seen in literary circles as the greatest living Russian writer; some members of the younger generation, for whom Gogol was the fearless social critic of *The Inspector General*, considered him the greatest Russian writer who had ever lived. He was given the star treatment and he soon learned to act the part. Lionized in both Moscow and St. Petersburg, Gogol responded by being difficult and capricious, demanding that special wines be served and dishes prepared if he accepted a dinner invitation, deliberately making people wait for him, and walking out in the midst of a gala performance of *The Inspector General* that was staged in honor of his stay in Moscow. A fledgling poet named Afanasy Fet, later to become one of Russia's finest nineteenth-century poets, tried to see Gogol during his stay in Moscow. He was told by Pogodin to leave his manuscripts and was later sent the message that he had talent and should continue writing, but that Gogol was too busy to see him.

Old friends found Gogol changed outwardly. At thirty he looked older than his forty-eight-year-old mother, who came to Moscow for a reunion with him and who basked in his success and its reflections upon herself with great relish. Gogol's continuing interest in clothes and fabrics now found its expression in the elaborate wardrobe he brought with him from Italy. He particularly liked brocaded and embroidered vests (the art of embroidery had interested him since his early youth, and a considerable portion of his correspondence with his mother during his stay in St. Petersburg is devoted to embroidery patterns and designs). In complete privacy, he apparently took to wearing what in a later age might have qualified as high drag.

When Gogol came to St. Petersburg in November of 1839, he stayed at Zhukovsky's apartment in the Winter Palace. He was surprised in his room there one morning by Zhukovsky and

Sergei Aksakov, who entered quietly and without knocking. "There was Gogol in front of me, wearing the following fantastical costume," Aksakov reported in his memoirs. "Instead of boots, he wore long woolen Russian stockings, reaching higher than the knee; instead of a jacket, a velvet spencer worn over a flannel camisole; around his neck was a large multicolored scarf and on his head was a crimson velvet woman's headdress (*kokoshnik*), embroidered in gold and very similar to the headdresses of Finnish tribeswomen." Gogol did not seem to be particularly embarrassed at being caught in this outfit. He simply asked Aksakov what his business was and then dismissed him by pleading the need to go on writing.

During his years in Rome, Gogol made a study not only of Roman art and architecture, but also of the finer points of Italian cooking. Back in Russia, he became fond of demonstrating his way with various traditional Italian dishes. Aksakov's memoirs contain a detailed description of Gogol preparing macaroni that had been cooked—or rather, undercooked—to his specifications, sprinkling it with butter and grated parmesan that he had brought in his pocket and then seasoning it with salt and pepper, while delivering an interminable lecture to the assembled guests on the method of preparation he was using. "The macaroni was indeed very tasty," Aksakov reports, "but many found it underdone and too heavily peppered. But Gogol pronounced it very successful, ate a lot, and felt none of that heaviness of which some were later to complain."

Gogol's involvement with fabrics, embroideries, and cuisine sets him apart from other major Russian writers of the nineteenth century just as surely as Chekhov's concern for animals, biology, and nature conservation points to the specific differences in *his* psychological make-up. Both Pushkin and Chekhov could write of food with enthusiasm, but it is impossible to

Departure and "Rome"

imagine either of them giving a cooking demonstration. Nor can one picture Tolstoy or Dostoyevsky seriously concerning himself with fabrics or fashions. On the other hand, none of these writers could have managed the rich and numerous culinary passages and enumerations in *Dead Souls*, a work that Andrei Bely qualified as "not an Iliad, but a Gobble-iad" (*ne Iliada, a Zhratviada*). Nor could any of them have attained the sheer brilliance of Gogol's wonderful mimicry of the two ladies' discussion of the latest styles in women's fashions in Chapter IX of *Dead Souls*.

Gogol's renewed contact with Russian realities proved creatively stimulating. During his 1839-40 visit he began writing "The Overcoat" and made considerable progress on *Dead Souls*. He read the early chapters of his novel at several literary gatherings and was assured that he was producing a work of genius, with some of the younger enthusiasts mentioning Shakespeare and Homer as suitable comparisons. By spring, however, he was ready to return to Rome and took the rather extraordinary step of advertising in a newspaper for a male traveling companion who owned a carriage and was willing to share travel expenses as far as Vienna. The advertisement found no takers, but a young relative of the Aksakov family named Vasily Panov was so overwhelmed by Gogol's reading of the sixth chapter of *Dead Souls* that he canceled all of his personal plans and offered himself to Gogol as factotum and traveling companion.

May 9 was St. Nicholas' Day—Gogol's nameday—and it was celebrated at a garden fête given by Pogodin in Moscow. Besides Gogol, the other guest of honor was a twenty-six-year-old army lieutenant named Mikhail Lermontov, who had come by special permission from the Caucasus, where he had been banished by the government. Lermontov had just published *A Hero of Our Time*, a novel Gogol admired enormously. He thought its prose among the finest in the Russian language and felt that Lermontov, already known as a poet, had a great future as a novelist. Actually, Lermontov had only one year left to live at the time and was to fall in a senseless duel (which may have been a suicide in disguise) before he could produce another novel. In Gogol's honor, Lermontov read his just-written narrative poem "Mtsyri," about a Georgian novice monk who flees the monastery in search of love and friendship but finds indifference, violence, and betrayal instead.

Prior to leaving Russia, Gogol promised his Moscow friends that he would finish *Dead Souls* and bring it back for publication within a year's time. Panov proved to be a helpful traveling companion. Gogol was flattered by this young man's admiration and devotion, but as a person Panov was stolid, pedantic, and unimaginative. If we add that memoirists also describe him as not very bright, we can understand why Gogol failed to form any kind of deep attachment for him, something that would undoubtedly have happened had Panov possessed a more engaging personality. When Gogol came down in Vienna with what was either a case of acute depression or a fit of hypochondria, leading to a crisis that some biographers (for instance, Setchkarev) consider a major turning point in his artistic development, Panov seems to have been of no help at all.

Before succumbing to his crisis in Vienna, Gogol interrupted his work on *Dead Souls* to devote himself to writing a tragedy based on a subject taken from Ukrainian history and bearing a most untragic-sounding title, *The Shaved-Off Moustache* (since the title is in the singular in Russian, it actually refers to only one

half of a moustache). Since this work is mentioned frequently in
Gogol's correspondence and in Panov's letters to Aksakov, it is
odd how little we know about it. Only two sentences from it survive, because Pavel Annenkov happened to see them in Gogol's
manuscript and memorized them: "What did God have to create
women for in this world? The only possible reason is in order to
have the women give birth to Cossacks"—a statement that
would not make a bad epigraph to "Taras Bulba." Later on, Gogol was to read the text of this play to Zhukovsky, who responded by falling asleep. Gogol thanked him for this honest critique and threw his manuscript into the fireplace; Zhukovsky
later commented that it was no great loss.

Another writing project for the sake of which Gogol kept
postponing the completion of *Dead Souls* was his planned novel
about Italy and Italians, which was to be called *Annunziata*. All
that remains of the project is the first chapter, printed in collections of Gogol's stories as a separate work called "Rome." A
paean to the city of Rome, its architectural marvels and its eternal, unchanging essence, the work contrasts the genuine beauty
of Rome with the gaudy tinsel of Paris, with its contending philosophical and political parties and its mindless pursuit of novelty for novelty's sake. While Paris is compared at one point to
an insolent streetwalker who forces herself on the passer-by in a
dark street, Rome is personified by an ideally beautiful working-
class girl from Albano, Annunziata, who catches the eye of the
protagonist, a young Italian nobleman educated in Paris who
dreams of restoring the vanished glories of Renaissance Italy.
Descriptions of Annunziata are the climax of Gogol's tendency
to turn beautiful young women into dehumanized alabaster statues, a tendency which we have already seen in his treatment of
Alcinoe in "Woman" and of the Polish beauty in "Taras Bulba."
As Louis Pedrotti has wittily demonstrated in his essay "The

Departure and "Rome"

Architecture of Love in Gogol's 'Rome',"[35] Annunziata is not merely a living statue, as her predecessors were. She is actually metamorphosed by Gogol into a set of architectural details, blending imperceptibly into the landscape of the city and becoming a work of architecture herself. Gogol's own love for the city and its buildings is thus disguised in "Rome" as the protagonist's love for a woman; but a close reading of the text, such as Louis Pedrotti's, can uncover the plaster under the supposed flesh.

Gogol overcame his Vienna crisis by dint of a firm resolution "not to die among the Germans." As soon as he started for Italy, his condition improved. Once in Rome, he proceeded with the long-delayed task of completing *Dead Souls*. Freed by Vasily Panov's loyal ministrations from all daily chores, Gogol felt genuinely inspired, even elated, as he wrote these chapters. "A wondrous work is being created and conceived in my soul," he wrote to Sergei Aksakov on March 5, 1841, "and my eyes were full of tears of gratitude more than one time. I can clearly see in it the sacred will of God. Such inspiration cannot come from man—no man could have thought up such a theme!" Later in the same letter, Gogol compared himself to a cracked and fragile clay vessel containing a treasure and, therefore, deserving to be cherished and preserved.

During his earlier years in Rome, Gogol's support came primarily from the two-year artist-in-residence fellowship that Nicholas I granted him in 1837 through Zhukovsky's intercession and also from a series of subsequent royal handouts of two to four thousand rubles that came either from the tsar or from the heir apparent, the Grand Duke Alexander. On one occasion, when Gogol's pleas for money followed one another too closely, the generous Zhukovsky sent him several thousand rubles out of his own pocket, pretending that it was a gift from the Grand Duke. Filled with the assurance of creating a great and useful book, Gogol now had no compunctions about asking his literary friends to finance the completion of his masterpiece. Requests for money went out to Pogodin and Aksakov, who provided sizable loans. Vasily Panov, too, contributed one thousand rubles, even though he had incurred Gogol's displeasure by becoming involved with a Roman charmer named Giulia and neglecting his secretarial duties for her. In May and June of 1841, Pavel Annenkov, who replaced Panov as Gogol's secretary and factotum, made a clean copy of the first half of the novel and in August Gogol set off for Russia to supervise the book's publication.

He arranged his trip to pass through the German resort town of Hanau so that he could spend some time there with the poet Nikolai Yazykov. Gogol had been involved with Yazykov's poetry since his school years, and Yazykov had always been, after Pushkin, his favorite contemporary Russian poet. Six years older than Gogol, Yazykov had made a literary name for himself during the 1820s, while still a student at the University of Dorpat, by writing some of the most vivid erotic poetry ever written in Russian. Gogol was won over by Yazykov's colorful, almost baroque, imagery, and he greatly valued the occasional religious strain in his poetry, even though the central theme of Yazykov's most memorable poems, which can be summed up very

Nikolai Yazykov in Hanau in 1841. Lithograph by Franz von Hanfstaengl, after a painting by Peter von Cornelius.

Gogol and Yazykov

simply as "Wine, Women, and Song," could not have been congenial to Gogol. The woman in Yazykov's poetry is the very opposite of the disembodied Romantic ideal of other poets of the period. She is very much a creature of flesh and blood—a promiscuous young girl gracing with her presence a gathering of Dorpat students, an easy-going circus rider, a seductive provincial housewife. Her main qualities are her beauty and her availability. In fact, a woman's physical availability is a constant source of the poet's joy, conveyed in Yazykov's poetry again and again, with irresistible candor and obvious gratitude. Leafing through a volume of his lyrics, one realizes to what extent the theme of carnal love disappeared from Russian poetry after Yazykov's and Pushkin's time.

Gogol and Yazykov had met briefly in person a year earlier when Gogol passed through Hanau during his previous journey to Russia in June of 1839. Yazykov was taking a cure in Germany for a disabling affliction that made walking difficult. Because of his sexually active early life and the erotic content of much of his poetry, it was widely rumored at the time that he was suffering from the effects of syphilis. Actually the disease was tuberculosis of the spinal column. Gogol's and Yazykov's dislike of the Germans, their shared political conservatism, and their admiration for each other's writings provided the ground for the initial meeting of the minds. In Moscow, Gogol sought out Yazykov's sister, Ekaterina, the wife of the Slavophile poet and philosopher Alexei Khomyakov. She was to become one of Gogol's closest and dearest friends in the last years of his life. "Gogol is in raptures over your poem 'Epistle to Pavlova'[36] and has learned it by heart," Ekaterina Khomyakova wrote to her brother. "He begs you to write to him in Vienna. When you return to Hanau, he will make a point of coming there. He loves you terribly and speaks of you with as much admiration as he does of Italy."

Gogol and Yazykov

In September of 1841, Gogol indeed visited Yazykov in Hanau. Learning that Yazykov's brother Pyotr was planning to return to Russia at the end of the month, Gogol decided to travel with him and postponed his return in order to spend a few weeks in Hanau with the Yazykov brothers. "We have become good friends with Gogol," Nikolai Yazykov wrote Ekaterina on September 19, 1841. "He has promised to live together with me, that is, to share an apartment after my return to Moscow. He has apparently written many new things and he is going home to get it all published. He is most charming and I am glad that my brother Pyotr Mikhailovich will not undertake the long journey all alone, but will have a companion with whom one cannot be bored and who has traveled abroad and who knows all German customs and folk beliefs."

Later during the same month, Yazykov wrote to one of his other brothers: "Gogol has told me about the oddities of his (probably imaginary) illness. He supposedly harbors the rudiments of every possible illness. He also spoke of the peculiar structure of his head and of the abnormal position of his stomach. He was supposedly examined and palpated in Paris by celebrated physicians, who discovered that his stomach is located upside down. In general, there is much in Gogol that is strange—at times I could hardly understand him—and odd. But he is very charming just the same. He promised to live together with me."

For Yazykov, this promise was apparently no more than a plan for a future joint housing arrangement. Gogol, however, chose to see in it a pledge of love and devotion, such as Yazykov was not only incapable of giving, but which he probably could not even have imagined. Reaching Dresden after leaving Yazykov in Hanau, Gogol addressed to him an enraptured letter in which he poured out his newly found love and his conviction that the days he had just spent in Hanau were a turning point in his life:

Gogol and Yazykov

. . . I am now all alone, enjoying the coolness after coffee, and many things come to my mind: things I cannot speak of to anyone, things I speak of with you; one time there even flashed [through my mind] an elongated house in Moscow, with a row of rooms heated to fifteen degrees [Centigrade] and with two secluded private studies. No, Moscow must not now frighten you with its noise and annoyances. You must remember that I shall be waiting for you there and that you will not be coming for a visit but are coming straight home. Your path is firm and it is not in vain that a staff was given you as a pledge for these words.[37] Oh, have faith in my words! I have not the strength to say to you anything but this: oh, have faith in my words! I myself dare not disbelieve my words. Wondrous and incomprehensible things exist . . . but the sobs and the tears of a deeply agitated noble soul would have kept me forever from saying everything I have to say . . . and my lips would grow mute. No human thought is capable of imagining even a hundredth part of that boundless love that God bears for man. That is all. Henceforth your gaze should be radiantly and alertly lifted upward—that is what our encounter was for. And if at our parting, when we shook hands, a spark of my spiritual strength did not separate from my hand and enter your soul, that means that you do not love me. And if you should ever be vanquished by boredom and cannot overcome it by remembering me, that means that you do not love me; and if a temporary ailment overcomes you and causes your spirit to droop downward, that means that you do not love me. But I am praying, praying fervently in the depths of my soul this very minute that this may not befall you and that any dark doubt about me may leave you and that as often as possible your soul may experience that same radiance that suffuses my entire being this very minute.

Goodbye. I send you many kisses *in absentia*. Let me know in Moscow that you have received this letter; I would not want it to be lost, for it was written in a heartfelt moment.

Your Gogol

Gogol and Yazykov

After he reached Moscow (following a detour to St. Petersburg, where he visited the Vielhorsky family), Gogol sent Yazykov another letter about their future life together:

> . . . the days are sunny, the air is fresh and autumnal, before me is an open field, there is not a carriage, not a droshky, not a soul—paradise, in a word. I embrace and kiss you several times. Our life here can be fully beautiful and serene. I have brought the coffee I make to perfection, there are no annoying flies and no disturbances from anyone. I do not know how this happens, but it is true that when a person is ripe for secluded life, something appears in his face, his speech, and his actions that separates him from everything that is quotidian, and people who are engrossed in quotidian talk and passions involuntarily withdraw from him. Write and describe everything. We both have few external events, but they are so closely connected to our internal events that everything is mutually interesting for us. My mood is good and radiant. May God grant that you have as good and radiant a mood during your Hanau seclusion. I pray for that with all my heart and I am sure that an invisible hand will keep you in good health and deliver you to me in good health. God alone knows, perhaps it shall be our lot to reach old age hand in hand—anything is possible.
>
> Goodbye. I kiss you with my heart and soul and await your letter. (Letter to Yazykov of October 23, 1841)

Many actions and attitudes in the life of this supposedly soberly realistic writer can all too easily be qualified as unrealistic. Gogol's selection of Yazykov, of all people, as the object of his passion, however, seems misguided to the point of absurdity. It demonstrates that even after his experiences with Vielhorsky, Gogol was still not prepared to face fully the implications of the nature of his affections.[38] The resolutely heterosexual Yazykov,

Gogol and Yazykov

who in an early poem turned none other than Plato into a dashing skirt-chaser, was even less able to respond to Gogol's love
than Gerasim Vysotsky and Mikhail Pogodin had been when
they were in the same situation some years earlier. At the same
time, Yazykov's literary star had declined considerably since the
1820s, and the effusions of the foremost writer of the day and
his offer to share a residence could not but flatter him. He responded to Gogol's letters in the only way and the only tone he
was capable of, that is, by writing his verse epistle "To N. V.
Gogol." The epistle, which Gogol allowed Pogodin to publish in
his journal *The Muscovite* early in 1842, begins with the lines:

> Blessed be your return
> From this heathen Germany
> To Russia, to the holy shrines on the Moskva River!

The poem continues with some humorous anti-German dia-
tribes, describing Yazykov's favorite diversion, which is watching the local Germans slip and fall on an icy path outside his
window:

> An eloquent picture
> For Russian eyes! Love it!

and concludes with a two-line envoi that can perhaps be ren-
dered into modern Anglo-American idiom as:

> Well then, buddy-boy, let us arrange
> Those lodgings and start living it up!

But the two writers' plans for a joint residence in Moscow
were not fated to materialize. Yazykov's doctors insisted that he
remain in Germany for further treatments. In the meantime,

Gogol and Yazykov

Dead Souls ran into unexpected censorship difficulties, an obstacle that Gogol had not even remotely foreseen. During his absence from Russia, the censorship regulations had grown far more stringent than before. The decade of the eighteen-forties, just beginning, was to be the time when Russian literature was more severely censored than it would ever be again until Soviet times. An elderly censor took a look at the book's title and decided that it must be directed against the Christian religion's teaching that the soul is immortal. Other censors had even more petty objections. Gogol wrote a desperate letter to the Minister of Education, Uvarov, and showed a fine diplomatic hand by addressing a similar request to Uvarov's lover, Prince Dondukov-Korsakov, under whom he had worked at St. Petersburg University. Dondukov-Korsakov indeed responded by taking up Gogol's cause. It was the help of Gogol's friends with connections at the tsar's court, however—Vladimir Odoyevsky and Count Mikhail Vielhorsky (Iosif's father)—that proved decisive.

It is indeed curious the way Nicholas I repeatedly supported and championed Gogol. The most repressive and the least imaginative of all the Romanovs, Nicholas regarded the arts with suspicion and believed that they should be controlled by the state. Hector Berlioz dedicated the *Symphonie fantastique* to him, unaware that the only musical instrument for which Nicholas had any use was the bass drum, as being helpful in keeping soldiers in step during military drill. In the 1830s, Heinrich Heine somehow managed to view the tsar's suppression of the Decembrist Rebellion as evidence of his liberality and concern for the common people. Heine did not realize that at that very same time Nicholas was subjecting Pushkin, Lermontov, and Bestuzhev-Marlinsky to ugly persecution and that the wonderful German-Russian poet and playwright Wilhelm Küchelbecker had been removed by the tsar from life and literature and buried alive for the rest of his days, first in a prison cell, then in remote Siberian exile. Gogol, however, was the one Russian writer in whom Nicholas had full confidence. He supported him financially, held a high opinion of *The Inspector General*, and disregarded the horrified objections of his own censors and of the pro-government critics and journalists to the publication of *Dead Souls*, which at the time he had, curiously enough, not even bothered to read.

Later on, in 1845, when Alexandra Smirnova tried to convince the tsar to grant Gogol a pension (and succeeded in doing so), she actually got him to read some passages from *Dead Souls*. He was reportedly particularly taken with the scene at the end where the troika that carries Chichikov away is compared to Russia, speeding toward its future, with all the other nations stepping respectfully aside. It seems not to have occurred to the monarch that his country was being compared to a conveyance in which an unapprehended swindler was fleeing from justice. Be that as it may, the tsar made no objections and his censors authorized the publication of the novel. Not only the tsar, but his dreaded chief of secret police, Count Alexander Benckendorf, who had played such a sinister role in Pushkin's life, also showed a most touching solicitude for Gogol's predicament during the three months that it took to get *Dead Souls* through the censorship hurdles. Even though he could not spell Gogol's name correctly, Benckendorf petitioned the tsar to authorize a grant of five hundred rubles to help tide Gogol over the period of uncertainty.

The delays with the publication of the novel took up most of the winter of 1841-42. Despite the imperial authorization, the censors insisted that the title be changed to *Chichikov's Adventures, or Dead Souls* and they managed to find fault with the interpolated novella about Captain Kopeikin, demanding altera-

Gogol and Yazykov

tions and rewrites. Gogol fretted and grew irritable. Each new obstacle postponed his reunion with the friend for whose company he longed more than anything else. The Aksakovs found him difficult. His relationship with Pogodin turned sour, preparing the way for Gogol's angry break with Pogodin over the publication of his portrait two years later. Throughout that time he kept sending Yazykov affectionate letters, telling him of the wonderful life together they would have as soon as the publication of *Dead Souls* was settled. By the spring of 1842, Gogol's impatience was almost more than he could bear: "I swear that the last gloomy cloud is about to depart from you, for I want to see you badly, so badly that I have never yet yearned for anything as much [in my life]. Something that is this powerful can never turn drab or dull. I embrace you *in absentia*, until the time that I can embrace all of you in person and as closely as should be," Gogol wrote to Yazykov between the eighteenth and twenty-third of May, 1842. His other letters to Yazykov dating from this period all end with some such formula as: "I embrace and kiss you and am burning with the impatience to do both in person" (from the letter of February 10, 1842).

Gogol's other important project during that winter was the preparation of the revised, definitive edition of the stories and plays he had published up to that time. Supervising the printing of this edition required Gogol's presence in Russia during the summer, which would have delayed his reunion with Yazykov still longer. In his eagerness to depart for Germany, Gogol hit on the idea of appointing a school friend from his Nezhin days, Nikolai Prokopovich, to act as his agent, putting him in charge of editing and publishing his collected works. Prokopovich had had no previous experience in the publishing field and he botched things badly. The printer's shop produced twice the number of copies he had ordered. Delivering one half to Prokopovich, the printer offered the other half to the booksellers at a reduced

Gogol and Yazykov

price. The result was that, although the collected works enjoyed excellent sales, Gogol made almost no money from the edition and had to support himself and pay off his numerous debts from the proceeds of *Dead Souls* alone.

Within a week after *Dead Souls* went on sale in St. Petersburg, Gogol was on his way to Germany. A letter he sent to Zhukovsky from Berlin on June 26, 1842, is permeated with Gogol's sense of joy, euphoria, and assurance of his own literary powers. Yet, with his usual habit of covering up his traces, Gogol informed Zhukovsky that he was traveling to Bad Gastein only to take a water cure on his doctor's orders. Actually, he did not need any such treatment at the time. "Gogol arrived at Gastein on July 14," Yazykov wrote to his brother Alexander on July 21. "He settled in the same house with me and we live together like two brothers. He is, thank Heaven, well, does not need a cure, and he came to this hole solely for my sake. This heroic deed of his is a blessing for me and it constitutes an epoch in my foreign wanderings and in my life in general. He urges me to come and spend the winter with him in Rome; otherwise Gogol will accompany me to Russia." Reunited with Yazykov, Gogol clearly did not care where he was to live as long as he could be with his friend. "Gogol consoles, refreshes, and cheers me up with his example and his conversation," Yazykov wrote in the letter just quoted. "He has brought me *Dead Souls,* which I am enjoying all the more because I consider this work to be extremely useful to our beloved fatherland." Yazykov's other letters to his relatives dating from July and August of 1842 are full of expressions of his admiration for Gogol and of gratitude for his presence. Still, Yazykov could not resolve to settle with Gogol in Rome, as Gogol was urging. In his indecision, he consulted his serf valet Sylvester. "And why shouldn't we take a trip to Rome?" was Sylvester's reply.

As for Gogol, he seems to have realized soon enough that the

Gogol and Yazykov

relationship of which he had dreamed all his life was once again eluding him. The embraces, kisses, and endearments that he had been showering on Yazykov in his letters of the previous fall and winter failed to become reality once the two writers were actually reunited. Yazykov was plainly not able to respond in that way, and Gogol, however great his disappointment may have been, had to adjust to the situation. In the humorous letter Gogol sent to Yazykov on August 3, when he left him for a brief trip to Munich, we find no trace of the amorous and sentimental effusions that characterized his earlier letters. Cheated of his hopes for a mutually loving relationship, Gogol had to settle simply for Yazykov's company.

His deeper inner reaction to this disappointment can be surmised from the fact that within a few weeks after his reunion with Yazykov Gogol sat down to work on the final version of *The Gamblers,* which up to that time had existed only as a few inconclusive sketches. The play, on which Gogol worked throughout August and which he completed in time for it to be published in the multivolume edition of his collected works Prokopovich was preparing in St. Petersburg, offers a view of friendship and companionship between men that is totally new for Gogol. The warm and rewarding camaraderie described in his earlier writings, especially in "Taras Bulba," becomes in *The Gamblers* a sham and a pretense, a bait that the other male characters hold out to the protagonist in order to trap and to cheat him. It can hardly have been a coincidence that Gogol conceived this play's image of friendship between men at this particular juncture of his emotional biography.

Nevertheless, the two writers traveled together to Venice in September. In his letter to his family of September 26, 1842, Yazykov wrote from Venice: "I don't know how to thank Gogol for everything that he does for me: he takes care of me and looks

Gogol and Yazykov

after me as if I were a relative. Without him here with me, I would have been totally exhausted. It is probable, it is even more than probable, that I will resolve to spend the winter with him in Rome."

Gogol and Yazykov came to Rome early in October and settled at Gogol's old apartment in the Via Felice. A year earlier, Gogol had written to Yazykov that moving in together was all that either of them needed to be completely happy: "An indestructible confidence in you has entered my heart and I was all too happy, for the voice of my heart had not yet ever deceived me" (letter of September 27, 1841). One year later they both knew that voice to have been illusory. The difference in temperament and in respective emotional expectations was too great. "I'm cold and bored and annoyed with myself that I heeded Gogol's flattering words and came to Rome where he intended to and had promised to settle me in the best possible manner," Yazykov wrote to his family in the fall of 1842. "It turned out quite differently."

In a letter written to one of his brothers at about the same time, the picture looks even more grim:

I did not find in Rome the sort of peaceful and carefree existence that Gogol had promised to arrange for me. He loves giving orders and keeping house, but he gives orders and keeps house in an extremely slovenly and disorganized way. I am crowded and cold; there is not even a separate cubbyhole for Sylvester, the fireplace lacks a flue and it is the only one for two rooms. It is between +9° and -1° [Centigrade] here; getting up in the morning can hardly be pleasant even for a healthy person, and can hardly be wholesome for a sick one. I shiver, shake, and yawn. Gogol, his nose blue from the cold, walks about the room and keeps assuring me that we are very warm. It goes without saying that all my affairs have to be transacted through him owing to Sylvester's and my unfamiliarity with the local language and that the result, therefore, is three bags full of nonsense. He is constantly being cheated and swindled and fleeced by the Italians, whom he trusts as if they were honest and whom he respects exceedingly. He spends money as if it were dirt and fusses and bustles, being quite sure that he outsmarts everyone and buys everything cheaper than the others, and takes pathological offense if he is contradicted in anything. I feel like a prisoner here and wait with impatience for the autumn months and then for December and January to pass. Then I would feel warmer and more accustomed to these bad domestic arrangements (all this is strictly between us).[39]

In the meantime, a vague rumor began circulating in Moscow about Yazykov's excessive dependence on Gogol. "What has been going on between you and Gogol?" Alexander Yazykov asked his brother in his letter of March 8. "Please write in greater detail, we are all interested. And why is it that you write so little, and so briefly and vaguely? There is a widespread opinion here that you cannot return to Moscow alone. Is this true?" "The rumor that is being spread in Moscow to the effect that I supposedly cannot return home alone has been fabricated and put into circulation by one of my well-wishers, whose name and patronymic I do not have the honor of knowing," Yazykov replied to his brother on April 20, 1843.

The last straw in the floundering relationship was provided by Sylvester, who had ideas about looking after his master that clashed with Gogol's. The valet's constant meddling in Gogol's household dispositions led to the parting of the ways. Yazykov left for Bad Gastein in the spring; he returned to Russia permanently late in 1843. Gogol continued to admire his poetry, but the letters the two writers occasionally exchanged until Yazy-

The Sexes *in* Dead Souls

kov's death in 1846 were restricted almost entirely to literary and medical topics.

Dead Souls is regarded by general consent as one of the great Russian novels of the nineteenth century. Apparently because Gogol considered its topic to be of national importance and because the book contains numerous lyrical digressions written in rhythmical prose, he subtitled it *poèma*. Translating this word into English as "a poem," as is occasionally done, is both mistaken and misleading, for in Russian the primary meaning of *poèma* is "an epic." Gogol intended the book to be an epic of Russian provincial life of his time, a survey and a panorama of the rural landowning class in all of its complexity and variety. His contemporaries were so dazzled by the book's linguistic virtuosity, its irrepressible humor, its larger-than-life characterizations (most of the book's characters became proverbial from the day of its publication) that they believed its form and structure to be totally new and unprecedented. Actually, the structure of *Dead Souls* utilizes and puts to its own purposes the familiar and widespread genre of the traditional picaresque novel. Like the novels by Lesage, Fielding, and Defoe that made the genre popular and like its Russian predecessors written in this form—Mikhail Chulkov's *The Comely Cook; or, The Adventures of a Depraved Woman* (1770), Vasily Narezhny's *The Russian Gil Blas* (1814), and Faddei Bulgarin's *Ivan Vyzhigin* (1829)—*Dead Souls* has an amoral central character who travels around trying to regain his lost fortune by swindling those who have established themselves in society, but who are shown to be

The Sexes in Dead Souls

morally no better than he. The structure allows the writer to place his protagonist in a variety of environments and to contrast him with a gallery of diverse human types. The one traditional ingredient of the picaresque novel formula that is glaringly missing in _Dead Souls_ is the hero's promiscuity and his usual numerous sexual adventures.

A vast literature exists about every conceivable aspect of _Dead Souls_—there is even an entire book devoted to its use of similes and metaphors[40]—and there is no need to recapitulate it here. For the purpose of the present study, it should suffice to examine the book's view of sexuality, such as it is, and its treatment of the relationship between the sexes. To begin with, Pavel Ivanovich Chichikov, the unflappable purchaser of dead serfs who is the book's central character, is entirely devoid of any sexual instinct. According to both Andrei Bely and Vladimir Nabokov, Chichikov is wedded to his (feminine gender) strongbox, in which he carries his money and the titles to his purchases. He certainly has little interest in real women. His reaction to receiving a sentimental anonymous love letter from an older noblewoman is simple curiosity. At the governor's ball he examines the women present, trying to discover the letter writer's identity; otherwise he takes no notice of the ladies at the ball, most of whom have put on their best finery to impress him, and he earns their enmity by his uncivil lack of attention.

Chichikov's momentary interest in the governor's sixteen-year-old daughter at the time of their carriage accident in Chapter V is expressed in one of Gogol's most overtly misogynous passages:

"A nice girlie," he said, opening his snuffbox and taking a pinch of tobacco. "But what is the main thing that is so attractive about her? The attractive thing is that she is just out of a

The Sexes in Dead Souls

boarding school or an institute, that there is nothing female (*nichego bab'ego*) in her yet, that is, none of the very thing that is most unpleasant in them. Now she is like a child, everything about her is simple, she'll say whatever comes to her mind, she'll laugh where she feels like laughing. One can make her into anything, she may become a marvel and she may end up a piece of trash—and she *will* end up a piece of trash! Just let those mammas and aunties have a go at her. Within a year they will so fill her up with every kind of femaleness (*vsyakim bab'em*) that her own father won't be able to recognize her."

Chichikov's meditations on the future of the governor's daughter end with the admission that if her parents were to offer a two-hundred-thousand-ruble dowry to her prospective husband, she could conceivably make some decent man happy. The next time Chichikov sees the girl is at a ball in her parents' home. The narrator stutters, digresses, and becomes almost incoherent in his effort to describe this encounter. The reader is not told the subject of their conversation, but gets instead a long list of young women with improbable names to whom Chichikov, we are informed, had spoken of similar things at various times in the past. The girl is so bored that she keeps yawning. Nevertheless, it is implied that in some not entirely clear way Chichikov is attracted to her. This nebulous attraction is enough cause for Gogol to unleash his usual punishment: the governor's daughter becomes the unwitting agent of Chichikov's undoing and disgrace.

The role of the governor's daughter in the scheme of the novel is a good illustration of Gogol's resourcefulness in avoiding the traditional love interest in his mature work, of his way of playing with the readers' expectations and then offering them a cleverly devised substitute for a romantic relationship. In a novel by anyone else, the governor's daughter would have been the heroine with whom the male protagonist becomes romantically involved. What we get instead is a character who is as close to being a total blank as a pivotal character in a novel can be. At her first appearance, her face is compared by the narrator to a translucent, newly laid egg. Her character and personality are as devoid of features as this egg. She has nothing to say during any of her appearances in the novel, and the reader does not even learn her name (although he is told the names of a whole crowd of young women of whom she reminds Chichikov and who have no other function in the book). Instead of a heroine, we get a sort of anti-heroine, notable primarily for her lack of all traits. Compared with the overwhelmingly vivid people who surround her, she all but fades into the wallpaper; yet she is the character on whom the plot and the dénouement of the book hinge.

In the first half of *Dead Souls* we are introduced to five supposedly typical landowning households that Chichikov visits in his search for dead serfs to buy. In contrast to the populous landowning families we meet in the novels by Turgenev and Tolstoy, we find that three of the five estates in *Dead Souls* are inhabited by widowed persons—Nozdryov, Plyushkin, and Korobochka —living alone except for their serfs and other retainers. Only two out of the five—Sobakevich and Manilov—are married. The crude and dishonest Sobakevich is actually shown in his marital bed with his wife, Feodulia Ivanovna—one of the two forays Gogol made into this uncongenial territory (the other being the scene in "The Carriage" where Chertokutsky was too drunk to respond to his narcissistic wife's endearments): "Even Sobakevich, who seldom had anything good to say about anyone, as he returned from the town quite late, got entirely undressed, and climbed into bed next to his skinny wife, said to her: 'I've been to a party at the governor's, darling, and had din-

The Sexes in Dead Souls

ner at the police chief's and met the collegiate assessor Pavel Ivanovich Chichikov—a most pleasant person!' To which his wife replied 'Hmm!' and gave him a kick with her foot." The reader laughs and reads on, but within the whole of Gogol's work that kick is only to be expected: how else does a Gogolian woman react to the news that a man likes another man? Feodulia Ivanovna's second appearance in the novel occurs when Chichikov visits the Sobakevich estate and is introduced to her: "Chichikov stepped up to kiss her hand, and she almost shoved it inside his mouth, giving him the opportunity to notice that she washed her hands in pickle brine."

A full-scale close-up of married life and love, as viewed by Gogol, is to be found in Chapter II of *Dead Souls*, in which Chichikov visits Manilov and his wife, Liza, at their estate. There is more than a touch of malice in the description of the treacly bliss in which this impractical and vacuous couple live out their days:

They were entirely satisfied with each other. Although more than eight years had passed since they were married, they would still bring each other a piece of apple or candy or a hazelnut and say in a touchingly tender voice that expressed perfect love: "Open your little mouth, sweetheart, so that I may put this little piece there." It goes without saying that the little mouth would be opened in such cases in a particularly graceful manner. For birthdays, a surprise would be prepared: some kind of beaded case for a toothpick. And very often, as they sat on the sofa, suddenly, for no discernible cause, one of them would put aside his pipe and the other her needlework if it happened to be in her hands, and they would imprint on each other such a languid and prolonged kiss that one could smoke to the end a small straw cigar during its duration. In a word, they were what is called happy. Of course it could be

The Sexes in Dead Souls

pointed out that there are many other things to be attended to in the house, besides lengthy kisses and surprises, and many questions could have been asked on that score. Why, for example, are the meals so stupidly and wastefully prepared in the kitchen? Why is the pantry empty? Why is the housekeeper a thief? Why are the servants slovens and drunkards? Why is the household staff allowed to sleep unmercifully late and to give itself over to debauchery the rest of the time? But all these are lowly subjects and Manilova is a woman of good upbringing.

Up to a certain point, this situation is a recognizable parallel to the one in "Old-World Landowners." In that story Gogol had also described a landowning couple whose love and attachment for each other prevent them from realizing that their household is poorly run and that their retainers are stealing from them. Nor were Afanasy and Pulcheria any more practical-minded or useful to surrounding society than the Manilovs. Yet they were depicted with tolerance and affection, while the Manilovs are subjected to biting satire. One possible reason for the difference is that Afanasy and Pulcheria were old and chaste, while the Manilovs are sexually active and are producing children. Their cloying love for each other is not the main object of Gogol's satire, to be sure, but it is clearly shown as one of the principal causes of their impracticality and their empty-headed, Pollyanna-like constant good humor. Apart from Afanasy and Pulcheria, the Manilovs are Gogol's sole developed portrait of a man and a woman happily in love. It is not a flattering portrait, needless to say.

Not only are the Manilovs happy lovers, they are also happy parents. Their two little sons represent Gogol's first attempt at portrayal of children since "Saint John's Eve," where the principal function of the little boy Ivas was to get himself murdered.

The Sexes in Dead Souls

The Manilov boys bear the pompous, patently impossible names of Alcides (that is, Hercules) and Themistoclus (a "partially Greek name," which the parents ostensibly concocted by attaching the inappropriate Latin suffix -*us* to the name of the Athenian statesman and then pronouncing it with a French *u* and a French-style stress on the last syllable). In earlier drafts, Gogol had planned to call them Alcibiades and Menelaus. Of course, none of these names was in the calendar of the Orthodox saints, and in real life both custom and ecclesiastical law would have prevented the Manilovs from naming their children in this manner. The grandiose names stand in deliberate contrast to the children's described behavior. Themistoclus gives inane answers to the simplistic questions his father asks him in order to show him off before Chichikov; a butler has to wipe his nose lest a "considerable drop of foreign matter" fall into his soup; and he viciously bites his little brother on the ear (a sinister activity, previously associated with the harridan Agafya Fedoseyevna in "The Two Ivans"). Alcides gnaws a mutton bone that makes both of his cheeks glisten with mutton fat. All in all, Gogol's portrayal of these two children gives us a fair idea of what he thought he was rescuing his sisters from when he so resolutely warned them against getting married.

Extramarital heterosexual sex is associated in *Dead Souls* primarily with the widowed landowner Nozdryov, a bully, braggart, and carouser who hangs around provincial fairs ogling actresses and assorted flouncy ladies and who keeps a pretty nursemaid in the house for reasons that are, it is implied, not entirely connected with the care of his children (not shown in the novel). Nozdryov's womanizing is seen as an integral component of his volatile and dangerously violent character. His violence and his involvement with women, perceived as alien and threatening by the peaceable and asexual Chichikov, are

The Sexes in Dead Souls

what make Nozdryov an unwitting member of the otherwise all-female coalition that causes Chichikov's fall from grace and precipitates his hasty escape. Nozdryov in a sense carries out the same function in *Dead Souls* that the elemental demon Viy does in the story named after him and that the busybody meddler Kochkaryov does in *Marriage*. All three are blind instruments of women's wiles and all three betray other males into women's hands. In Nozdryov's case the betrayal occurs through irresponsibility more than anything else, but it is hardly accidental that this boozy libertine starts the unmasking of Chichikov with his drunken revelations at the governor's ball.

Both the causes and the mechanism of the hero's punishment in *Dead Souls* follow with remarkable consistency the pattern of Gogolian retribution for sexual involvements in the *Mirgorod* and St. Petersburg stories. The hero's interest in the governor's daughter constitutes his transgression. Immediately after Chichikov's tongue-tied tête-à-tête with her at the ball, Nozdryov blurts out the story of the purchases of dead souls. At the same time Squiress Korobochka arrives in town in her watermelonlike carriage to expose Chichikov's machinations still further. By the next morning the two gossipy ladies of Chapter IX, who had been miffed by Chichikov's preference for the governor's daughter and his lack of interest in their own persons and finery, have enough material to launch the all-out attack by conjecture and slander which leads to Chichikov's downfall. In earlier, discarded, drafts, they were to accuse Chichikov of raping Korobochka; in the final version they settle for spreading rumors that he intends to elope with the governor's daughter. Chichikov is refused entry to the governor's mansion immediately after his reverie about the governor's daughter, just as Akaky Akakievich was divested of his overcoat right after taking an equally playful interest in the agitated lady who passed him in the street. At this

The Sexes in Dead Souls

point in the plot, the usual Gogolian formula, as exemplified in "Viy," "Nevsky Prospect," and "The Overcoat," among other works, would require that the male protagonist die. But *Dead Souls* is a comical picaresque novel, so the hero has to be allowed to escape. Yet the element of death is so indissolubly connected to this sort of situation in Gogol's mind that he causes another male character to die by proxy, as it were, for Chichikov. The city's public prosecutor inexplicably falls dead upon hearing of Chichikov's predicament and Chichikov learns that the townspeople hold him responsible for this death.

Except for Nozdryov, the characters who cause Chichikov's downfall are, as already noted, all female. Anastasia Korobochka is the familiar Gogolian figure of a meddlesome and dim-witted old woman. The energetic younger matrons in Chapter IX, initially introduced to the reader as "a simply pleasant lady" and "a lady pleasant in all respects," are something of a new departure for Gogol. His greater personal knowledge of women enabled him to depict female characters in such later works as *Marriage* and *Dead Souls* with greater insight and verisimilitude than he had attained in earlier works. The encounter of the two ladies in Chapter IX is probably the most overwhelmingly real portrayal of women in Gogol's entire work. It is also a brilliant verbal *tour de force*; performed by two capable actresses in Mikhail Bulgakov's dramatization of *Dead Souls* for the Moscow Art Theater, this scene invariably brings down the house, even though this is the only scene in which they appear.

Not only magnificently resourceful and inventive verbally, these two women are also strong-willed and independent-minded. Their independence is amusingly illustrated by their refusal to go along with the narrator's resolve not to reveal their names to the reader. In their dialogue they go ahead and tell us they are Anna Grigorievna and Sophia Petrovna, in violation of their creator's decision. That much independence in a female character bodes no good in a work by Gogol, as readers of the four *Mirgorod* stories should realize. When we put Chapter IX of *Dead Souls* side by side with *Mirgorod*, we see that the function of Anna Grigorievna and Sophia Petrovna in the novel is not only comical and satirical, but also punitive. In these two strong women whom he had barely noticed at the ball, Chichikov has met his nemesis.

The sexual implications and aspects just pointed out may not have been central to Gogol's basic conception of *Dead Souls*. Still, these are elements that propel the action of the novel and form its plot. At the time of the book's first publication, both Gogol and his contemporaries were far more interested in its social criticism. As he traced Chichikov's adventures, travels, and encounters with the Manilovs, Sobakevich, Plyushkin, Korobochka, and Nozdryov, it was Gogol's intention to satirize the laxness and inefficiency of these serf owners and their failure to take their obligations to their serfs and their own best economic interests seriously enough. Most of his contemporaries chose to read the book as a merciless indictment of the entire institution of serfdom. They did this, as Donald Fanger has so aptly suggested, because it would not have occurred to any Russian at that point in history to write a satirical book about serf owners and not indict the institution itself. For Gogol, however, serfdom had always been a divinely ordained fact of Russian life which he could not imagine being either abolished or changed. When he realized how his views on this subject had been misunderstood by his readers, he hastened to disabuse them in his next book, *Selected Passages*. A reading of Gogol's letters to his mother and to his youngest sister, Olga, about how to run their estate at Vasilievka and how to treat their serfs will instantly dissipate any illusions that Gogol was a champion of the serfs or a

The Sexes in Dead Souls

partisan of their emancipation, as will an examination of the way the serf characters are treated in *Dead Souls*.

Another misunderstanding about Gogol that the publication of *Dead Souls* helped consolidate was that Gogol was the foremost realistic chronicler of the Russian life of his time. With his overwhelmingly powerful imagination, Gogol managed to conjure up an image of life in the Russian provinces (which he did not know and had not visited) and make it as vivid and believable as he did German life in "Ganz Küchelgarten." The book's brilliant imagery and its inexhaustible verbal inventiveness[41] made readers as intelligent as Turgenev and Herzen mistake Gogol's highly idiosyncratic vision for a photographic transcript of existing conditions. Russian criticism of the early twentieth century and particularly the three major fiction writers of the present century who wrote critical studies of Gogol—Bely, Remizov, and Nabokov—did not find it hard to show the illusory nature of Gogol's supposed realism and to demonstrate the unique and consummate literary art with which the illusion that misled Gogol's contemporaries was achieved.

Gogol's year-long infatuation with Yazykov coincided with the highest point of his career as a playwright and writer of imaginative fiction. In addition to publishing *Dead Souls*, Gogol wrote "The Overcoat" and "Rome" during this period, edited and prepared for publication *Marriage*, and produced revised and greatly expanded new versions of "Taras Bulba" and "The Portrait." In the already mentioned letter to Zhukovsky of June 26, 1842, Gogol wrote that he considered *Dead Souls* and his other writings up to that point a makeshift porch, devised by a provincial architect for the colossal edifice of his future literary productions. The letter makes ironic reading, because with the writing of *The Gamblers* that summer and the completion of *After the Play* in October, Gogol's literary career, inaugurated

Gogol and Smirnova

twelve years earlier with "Saint John's Eve," came to a virtual end. The rest of his life was to be devoted to nonfictional writings and to unsuccessful efforts to produce a sequel to *Dead Souls*. Gogol's prodigious productivity during the time when he had high hopes for a life-long loving relationship with Yazykov and the failure of his literary powers when those hopes were dashed indicate that this particular relationship may have had a significance in Gogol's emotional and artistic biography that was greater than his biographers have until now realized.

He went on living in Rome after Yazykov's departure, traveling frequently to Germany to consult doctors and taking a variety of cures for his largely psychosomatic digestive and circulatory ailments. We know of no further attempts on Gogol's part to establish a close emotional relationship with another man after the fiasco with Yazykov. In the fall of 1842, he wrote to Alexandra Smirnova that he wanted to visit her in Florence, where she then lived, but was unable to come because the ill Yazykov needed his presence. Gogol pleaded for her to come to Rome. At the end of January of 1843, Smirnova, accompanied by her brother and her children, moved to Rome. Gogol was overjoyed and arranged to take her on a series of guided tours of Rome's historical sites and art treasures. Their paths crossed again that summer, when they traveled independently to visit Zhukovsky in Baden-Baden. Both Gogol and Smirnova stayed in Nice with the Vielhorsky family from November 1843 to March 1844.

It was during this period that their friendship became genuinely close and durable. Smirnova was unhappy in her marriage and subject to frequent periods of depression. Gogol's fervid religiosity, his sermons about giving up all hope for personal gratification and about entrusting oneself to the will of Providence, suited her situation and her mood. Gogol became her per-

Gogol and Smirnova

manent spiritual guide and preceptor. "She is a pearl among Russian women," Gogol wrote to Yazykov about Smirnova on June 5, 1845. "But hardly anyone seems to have the strength to appreciate her as she deserves. Even I myself, having always respected her and been friends with her, came to know her well only recently, during the moments of her and my suffering. She was truly my consoler at such times when anyone else's words would hardly have consoled me; at times our souls were as similar as two twin brothers."

Gogol's friends in Moscow and St. Petersburg, long puzzled by the absence of any women in his life, decided that the inevitable had at last happened—Gogol must have found the right woman and fallen in love. Not everybody was happy about his supposed choice. The Aksakov family regarded the aristocratic Smirnova as a potentially undesirable influence and deplored what they took to be Gogol's infatuation, fearing that it would distract him from what they admiringly called his "monastic way of life." The carnal-minded Yazykov was not to be taken in by Gogol's words about spiritual affinity: "According to all the rumors that reach me, she is simply a siren who floats on transparent waves of seduction," he wrote to his brother Alexander about Gogol's involvement with Smirnova. Gogol's most faithful correspondent, the seventy-year old Nadezhda Sheremeteva (she was the maternal aunt of the poet Tyutchev and she and Gogol exchanged lengthy letters on religious and theological topics), was clearly alarmed:

It is your wish that I state my misgivings concerning you [she wrote to Gogol from Moscow]. Very well, having said my prayers, so I shall. You must know, my friend—the rumors might be unfounded, but everyone coming from where you are says and writes the same thing—that you have given yourself over to a certain person, who has spent her life in the great world and has now withdrawn from it. Spending so much time with that person, will the conversation be for the good of your soul? I fear that in such company you might be deflected from the path that you have by the grace of God elected. This, my friend, is my confession to you of something that has distressed me greatly and long. It could be that you are concerned with her conversion; may the Lord help you and may God grant it that she and we and everyone be saved.

The rumors reached Gogol's old school friend Alexander Danilevsky in the Ukraine, where he had settled at his family estate. Danilevsky wrote to Gogol, asking him whether the rumors about him and Smirnova were true. "Surely you must have been joking when you wrote that," Gogol answered, "because you know that side of me well enough. And even if you didn't, you could still add up all the data and arrive at the correct answer. Besides, it is hard for a person who has already discovered what is best for him to start chasing after what is worse" (letter of April 13, 1844).

Gogol's initial experience of love for another human being was fraternal—his love for his little brother Ivan. This remained the only kind of love he was capable of for the rest of his life. In the person of Alexandra Smirnova he found the one woman he could love—at least on a spiritual plane—as he could love a man. But to do so, he had to start thinking of her as if she were, in fact, a man. As Victor Erlich has pointed out, Gogol's addressing of Smirnova in his letter of May 30, 1844, as "my beautiful brother" was by no means a slip of the pen. Equally significant is the statement in the letter to Yazykov, quoted above, that Gogol's and Smirnova's souls were "as similar as two twin brothers." Their mutual need and affection are beyond doubt; but since Smirnova was, after all, a woman, Gogol could not conceive for her the kind of passionate infatuation that throbs in the pages of "Nights at the Villa" and in some of his letters to Vysotsky, Pogodin, and Yazykov. Nor do we find in Gogol's letters to Smirnova anything like the easygoing, fond camaraderie of his correspondence with Danilevsky. There was an impenetrable barrier in his dealings with women beyond which he could not go. Because of his habit of keeping his true feelings secret even from his closest friends, it is understandable that some of them (including Danilevsky and Yazykov, both of whom should have known better) chose to see his relationship with Smirnova in terms of a conventional love affair.

Much of the decade of the 1840s was devoted by Gogol to futile efforts to write a sequel to *Dead Souls*. As he was completing the final chapters of the novel, he came to see it as the first part of a trilogy. The widespread interpretation of the novel as a critique of serfdom and of the social evils of tsarist Russia confirmed Gogol's resolution to continue and expand this work. According to the testimony of the critic Vyazemsky, Gogol came to regard the published novel as the equivalent of the *Inferno* portion of Dante's *Divine Comedy*. This was the book that depicted the evil and unattractive aspects of Russian reality. As Gogol saw it, the shortcomings he had shown could all be corrected under existing conditions by the simple force of moral example. The projected second novel of the trilogy was then to be the equivalent of Dante's *Purgatorio*. Chichikov would now encounter worthy models, efficient and practical-minded landowners who took their social and religious obligations seriously,

Continuing Dead Souls

in contrast to the slack and impractical Manilovs and Nozdryovs of the first part. In the third part, Chichikov and even the senile miser Plyushkin were to be reformed by associating with virtuous aristocrats and saintly millionaires.

To judge from the surviving drafts for _Dead Souls_, Part II, and from the descriptions of the destroyed chapters of the novel in the memoirs of Alexandra Smirnova and her half-brother, Lev Arnoldi, Gogol had intended to incorporate into his book two love affairs. One of these affairs involved an inactive, Oblomov-like young landowner, Tentetnikov, who gets himself mixed up in a political conspiracy (all he does is listen to some subversive talk), and Ulenka, a young woman of high moral principles who follows Tentetnikov to Siberia, proves his innocence to the authorities, marries him, and cures him of his inactivity. The other affair was a star-crossed encounter between a Byronic young man named Platonov, who is bored with life because he is so exceptionally handsome that things are made too easy for him, and a worldly society lady too jaded to take Platonov's sudden passion seriously.

While Gogol had no trouble imagining the grotesque and comical aspects of Russian provincial reality in the original _Dead Souls_, picturing the attractive and constructive sides of this reality was something else. He found himself compelled to fall back on the method he had used for his early Ukrainian stories: he resorted to researchers and informants. Nikolai Yazykov's brother Pyotr, a landowner in the Simbirsk area, supplied Gogol with long lists of local facts, figures and names. Alexandra Smirnova, whose husband had in 1845 been appointed governor of Kaluga Province, where she joined him, got a stream of requests for local customs and incidents.

Gogol's notebooks from that period teem with factual information: the administrative hierarchy, religious customs, forms

Continuing Dead Souls

of economic dealings between landowners and serfs, commerce, methods of jurisprudence, clothing, names of local fish and birds. It is as if Gogol had suddenly become a total stranger to the country he had described with so much assurance in the published portion of *Dead Souls*. In the introduction to the 1847 edition of the book, Gogol pleaded with his readers to send him corrections of any factual errors his book might contain and suggestions about what he had omitted, as well as descriptions of life in the upper social stratum. "I need to know this class, which is the flower of our people," Gogol wrote. "I cannot publish the latest volumes of my book until I acquire some knowledge of all the aspects of Russian life, at least to the extent I need to know it for my work in progress."

Clearly, Gogol had accepted the role of factual chronicler of Russian life in which he had been cast by the critical reception of his book. Rather than undertake a first-hand study of Russian life and society, however, Gogol preferred to get to know it by correspondence while remaining in Italy. Unable to discover in the welter of regional terms and disjointed facts his informants sent him that upright, edifying type of landowner he needed to justify the existing serf-owning system, Gogol decided to create such a paragon all by himself, with the aid of partly literary, partly real-life models. The figure of Konstantin Kostanzhoglo, the enterprising, go-getting landowner of Greek descent, was to be the second volume's answer to all the inefficient and dishonest characters of the original *Dead Souls*. (Gogol derived this character partly from a millionaire tax farmer of Greek origin, Dmitry Benardaki, whom he met at a German resort, and partly from a literary prototype most of his contemporaries would have considered downright disreputable—the benevolent and patriarchal landowner Rossianinov in Bulgarin's *Ivan Vyzhigin*.) The very embodiment of what in the twentieth century has come

Continuing Dead Souls

to be known as the Puritan or Protestant work ethic, Kostan-zhoglo works his peasants harder than anyone in the district, restricts their activities to agriculture (no new-fangled Western-style trades or manufactories), prevents them from learning to read or write, and sees to it that they have decent housing and clothing. No charity handouts of any kind are allowed: the peasants have to work for everything they get. Any questions that might arise are instantly squelched by an appropriate quotation from the Bible, chosen to demonstrate that the existing social system is divinely ordained. Kostanzhoglo's serfs are depicted as prosperous, happy, and not wishing to change their situation in any way.

The difficulty of making a character like Kostanzhoglo either believable or appealing was undoubtedly one of the obstacles to the successful completion of a sequel to *Dead Souls*. The other was the self-imposed task of portraying love affairs between men and women—and eventually even a marriage—in an attractive light. This task went against the grain of Gogol's nature. He had managed to avoid dealing with such situations since the operatic romances of the Dikanka stories. By the mid-1840s, a whole school of younger Russian realist writers—Turgenev, Goncharov, Herzen, and Dostoyevsky—had begun to achieve prominence. Their novels and stories invariably featured love affairs between men and women as a basic, essential feature of contemporary reality. In a misguided effort to become the kind of realist writer his contemporaries took him to be, Gogol spent eleven years trying to make himself over into a second-rate Turgenev or Goncharov.

Throughout the last decade of Gogol's life his mysticism colored more and more everything he thought and wrote. He had always been deeply religious, but it was after the failure of his plans for a life-long union with Yazykov that Gogol systematically assumed the pose of a religious prophet who is in direct

Homosexuality and Prophecy

contact with the will of Heaven. The prophetic tone can already be found in some of Gogol's letters of the late 1830s to his sisters Annette and Liza and in his letter to Danilevsky of August 7, 1841, where advice on how to run Danilevsky's family estate is interspersed with such exclamations as: "But hearken to my words, you must hearken to my words now, for my words are doubly powerful over you and woe unto whosoever does not hearken to my words!"; and later in the same letter, "My words are henceforth invested with the highest power. Everything can disappoint, deceive, and betray you, but my words shall never betray you."

This self-righteous, Old Testament tone becomes particularly frequent in Gogol's correspondence from 1844 on. When he sent Alexandra Smirnova a set of instructions on how to dress, what to read, and what manner to use when speaking to people, and she failed to provide a detailed report on how she had carried out these instructions, he wrote to her: "How dare you not answer my letters! Don't you realize who is speaking to you through my letters?" Late in 1843, Gogol discovered the two Thomases of the Catholic tradition, Aquinas (which he preferred to spell "Aquintus") and à Kempis. In January of 1844, identically worded letters went out to Pogodin, Aksakov, and the literary historian Shevyryov, ordering them to read a chapter from *De Imitatione Christi* every day, preferably after tea or coffee. "I am 53 years old," Sergei Aksakov wrote to Gogol, having waited three months to simmer down after receiving the letter. "I read Thomas à Kempis before you were born. . . . And here you sit me down to read him, knowing nothing of my views on the subject. And how? At a prescribed time, having divided it into chapters like lessons. This is both ridiculous and irritating." Gogol's Moscow friends began to fear seriously for his sanity.

Numerous theories have been advanced to account for

Homosexuality and Prophecy

Gogol's turn to mysticism and his ever-growing conviction that he had been elected to deliver a message of salvation to his friends and to the whole of Russia. One of the most provocative views on this subject is to be found not in a biography or a critical essay, but in a work of imaginative fiction, Olga Forsh's historical novel *The Contemporaries*. The novel's fictitious hero, a painter who has been a fellow student of Alexander Ivanov and who associates with Gogol in Rome in the late 1840s, muses on the hidden motives in his own life and in the lives of the people around him. He formulates Gogol's hidden motive as follows: "Gogol has raised a personal peculiarity, his inability to fall in love with a woman, as any imbecile can, to a state of consciousness, similar to those of the stylites. From this he has concluded that he is a 'chosen vessel' and to avoid ending up in Sodom, he aims to land in the calendar of saints."[42]

The insight that Olga Forsh ascribes to her fictitious character is indeed revealing. Gogol may well have tried to rationalize his sexual peculiarity by seeing it as an aspect of the messianic role he was fated to play in his country's history. Such a view can be supported by numerous precedents in many countries and in various historical periods. From the blind seer Teiresias of Greek mythology, whose prophetic gift was connected with his ability to enjoy sex either as a man or as a woman, to the *berdaches* and transvestite shamans of various Native American and Siberian tribes and the flamboyant "Prophet" Jones, who in the 1950s vied for popularity with Father Divine in America's black ghettoes, a number of cultures have connected male homosexuality with prophetic and mystical abilities. Russian eschatological religious dissenter sects of the eighteenth and nineteenth centuries, especially the Khlysty (Flagellants) and Skoptsy (Castrates) had recognizable bisexual and homosexual components in their tradition. The major twentieth-century poet Nikolai Klyu-

Homosexuality and Prophecy

ev, whose work continues and develops much of these two sects' lore, combined in his poetry a frankly homosexual strain with the assertion of his own prophetic and visionary powers.[43]

There has always been, then, a type of homosexual male who has aspired to a position of power and authority and who has chosen the role of religious leader, mystical healer, or shaman and magician, depending on the culture in which he lives. Once this entire complex is understood, it can be seen why Gogol's religious preoccupations and insights so often shade off into the prophetic, the magical, and the shamanistic. The possibility of predicting the future by constructing tall buildings (as postulated in the 1835 essay on architecture), Gogol's belief that he could transform his friends' lives by assigning material to be read at certain prescribed hours, and the magical function ascribed to the word "forward" in the Tentetnikov chapter of the second part of *Dead Souls* all fall within this area.

Once, during their stay in Nice in the winter of 1843-44, Gogol read to Smirnova some of the subsequently destroyed portions of the second and third volumes of *Dead Souls*. As he was reading the chapter that described the marital happiness of Ulenka and Tentetnikov and the edifying moral influence they had on each other, a clap of thunder was heard and a storm began outside. As described by Smirnova, Gogol was utterly terrified and shook violently. "When I subsequently pleaded with him to read to me the rest of the chapter, he refused with the remark: 'God Himself did not want me to read out loud what was not yet finished and had not received my inner approval. Admit it, were you frightened then?' 'No, my Ukrainian baby (*hohlik*), it was you who were frightened,' I said. 'I was not frightened of the storm, but of reading to you that which I had no business reading to anyone, so that God in His wrath gave me a warning.' "

Late in 1844, Gogol's old friend Alexander Danilevsky was

married in the Ukraine. Aware of Gogol's attitude toward such matters, Danilevsky kept him in the dark until after the wedding, and Gogol learned of the marriage from his mother. Sending Danilevsky his congratulations, Gogol demanded a complete account of the newlyweds' financial situation and an hour-by-hour report of how they spent their time together, apparently believing that he could use this information to direct and guide Danilevsky's marital life from Italy. When Pogodin lost his wife at about the same time, Gogol wrote him a letter of condolence outlining a program of moral betterment for Pogodin that he believed the late wife would have approved and speaking almost as though he were in touch with the dead woman and personally informed of her posthumous wishes. Early in 1845, Zhukovsky's young wife was expecting the delivery of her second child (in 1841, Zhukovsky, who was then fifty-eight, had married the eighteen-year-old daughter of a German painter; according to Alexandra Smirnova's testimony, the young bride was afraid to be in Gogol's company, sensing his hidden hostility despite his outwardly civil behavior toward her). The delivery of their first-born had impaired his wife's health, and Zhukovsky was understandably worried. The letter that Gogol wrote to him on January 11, 1845, was meant as a talisman: Zhukovsky was advised to keep it about his person, as it would help him during the ordeal and presumably assure the safe birth of the baby. It is in letters such as these that the witch-doctor-like aspects of Gogol's mentality can be most clearly seen, aspects that became more pronounced during the last decade of his life.

Selected Passages

As early as 1842 Gogol had spoken to his friends about his wish to make a pilgrimage to Jerusalem in order to pray for divine guidance at Christ's Sepulcher. By 1846, plagued by ill health, loneliness, and his inability to complete the second part of *Dead Souls*, he was ready to undertake the trip. To defray the expenses, he conceived the idea of publishing a volume of his essays interspersed with moral sermons culled from his personal correspondence. The book, which bore the unwieldy title *Selected Passages from Correspondence with Friends*, began as a fund-raising project, but gradually came to be seen by Gogol as the most important statement of his life, destined to eclipse everything else that he had written. He prepared himself for it by studying the writings of a number of religious authors, ranging from St. John Chrysostom to St. Dmitry of Rostov (a Russian church dignitary and playwright of the early eighteenth century). He also read the lives of various Orthodox saints. During the actual writing, he forgot his ailments and experienced the same sense of inspired euphoria that he had felt while writing the first part of *Dead Souls*.

Selected Passages, published late in 1846, consists of thirty-two essays couched in epistolary form. Some of them are reworkings of actual letters Gogol had written earlier to, among others, Smirnova, Zhukovsky, Yazykov, and Gogol's sister Olga. Others were newly written for the book and are disguised as letters to fit into the overall format. Thematically, the book's contents can be broken down into three categories: literary criticism, religious meditations, and essays on social and ethical topics that contain prescriptions for individuals and entire social classes on how to act and what to believe. The critical essays,

Selected Passages

like the corresponding pieces in *Arabesques*, are often perceptive and stimulating. Particularly fine are the essays on the poetry of Derzhavin and Yazykov and the essay on Russian theater, which anticipates some of Stanislavsky's reforms. The religious essays, overlooked at the time of the book's publication, were rediscovered and re-evaluated at the beginning of the twentieth century, after the political passions aroused by the book's social aspects had had time to die down. Lev Tolstoy thought highly of several of them, and such later commentators as Merezhkovsky and Mochulsky have pointed out that there was in Gogol an original and innovative Orthodox theologian. The two essays that compare and contrast the Orthodox and Roman Catholic traditions (Letters VIII and XXXII) can be read with interest even by people not normally concerned with theology.

Two highly instructive essays that show Gogol's thinking at its most bizarre are Letter VII ("On *The Odyssey* Translated by Zhukovsky") and Letter XXIV ("What a Wife Can Be for Her Husband under the Existing Order in Russia"). Zhukovsky's version of *The Odyssey*, on which he worked during the mid-1840s with the aid of German interlinear translations, was apparently Gogol's first introduction to this poem (his good knowledge of the *Iliad* is attested in the memoirs of Smirnova and by the borrowings from it found in "Taras Bulba"). His enthusiasm knew no bounds. *The Odyssey*, he declared, is the finest and most highly moral work in all of world literature; the *Iliad* is but a footnote to it. In the virtuous and patriarchal life depicted by Homer, Gogol found exactly the kind of worthy moral example that he thought all the strata of Russian society had been yearning for and the kind he himself had hoped to offer in the sequel to *Dead Souls*. So in his essay he quite seriously predicted that thorough social and moral changes would occur throughout Russian society as soon as Zhukovsky's translation was made

Selected Passages

available to the entire population. Language, literature, the arts, and the fabric of social life would revert from their nineteenth-century forms to the forms of classical antiquity, and Gogol, for one, was overjoyed at the prospect.

In Letter XXIV, Gogol casts himself in two of the least appropriate roles imaginable, those of a marriage counselor and a financial expert. The letter is addressed to a recently married young woman (she may possibly have been one of Iosif Vielhorsky's sisters, Sophia, who married the minor novelist and memoirist Count Vladimir Sollogub) who wrote to tell him how happy her marriage was. Gogol replies by telling her that her happiness cannot last, because it lacks a firm foundation: "Neither one of you possesses character, if one considers strength of will as character. Your husband, sensing this defect in himself, married in order to find in his wife the stimulus for his every deed and exploit. You married him so that he could stimulate you in your daily activities. Each expects from the other what neither one has. I say unto you: your situation is not only not blissful, it is actually dangerous. You will both melt and dissolve in life like a cake of soap in water."

The only way to avert catastrophe and to save the marriage, says Gogol, is for the wife to take charge of the family finances. She is to figure out their needs at the beginning of each year in even, rounded figures and to divide next year's income into seven equal piles. Pile 1 will contain the money for lodging, heating, water, firewood, and cleaning of the house and the yard. Pile 2 is the money for food, the groceries, the cook's salary, and the nourishment of "all living beings in your house." Pile 3 is for transportation: "the carriage, the coachman, horses, oats, hay, and everything else needed along these lines." Pile 4 is for the wardrobe: "everything the two of you need in order to appear in society or to stay home." Pile 5 is the wife's pin money (which is, one should note, the same amount as the yearly food or lodging expenses). Pile 6 contains the "money for special expenditures that might occur: a new set of furniture, the purchase of a new carriage, or even helping out financially some of your relatives, should the need arise." Pile 7 "belongs to God: that is the money for the Church and for the poor."

The purpose of this division is to enable the young wife to build up her character and will power by keeping these seven piles separate at all times and not on any account borrowing from one of them to pay for items listed under another: "Even if you should witness pictures of heart-rending misfortune and see for yourself that monetary assistance would help, don't you dare touch the other piles, but rather drive all over town, visit all of your friends, and try to arouse their pity. Beg, implore, be ready to humiliate yourself, so that this may serve you as a lesson, so that you may always remember how you were driven to the cruel necessity of turning unfortunates down and how, because of that, you were subjected to humiliation and public ridicule." This system, Gogol assures his correspondent, is sure to cut down her household expenses, strengthen her character, and save her marriage.

As so often with Gogol's advice on practical matters, there is here a sort of magical relationship between the means and the aim that is not amenable to ordinary pragmatic logic. This logical disjunction is especially apparent when Gogol wants to write seriously about economic or financial matters, as in the essay just described or in the Kostanzhoglo chapter of *Dead Souls*, Part II. But it also appears in more hidden forms in some of Gogol's ostensibly more realistic writings. In his brilliant examination of the economic aspects of "The Overcoat," Richard Peace,[44] by applying simple arithmetic to the figures provided in the story and consulting the salary scale of the Russian civil service during the period of the story's action, showed that Akaky

Selected Passages

Akakievich could not possibly have been destitute or have gone to a pauper's grave with the income the story itself tells us he received.

The essays that most startled and shocked Gogol's contemporaries and the ones on which the reputation of *Selected Passages* rested for the remainder of the nineteenth century were the four sociopolitical ones. Perhaps the most famous single essay in *Selected Passages* is Letter XXI, "What Is a Governor's Wife?" a distillation of several of Gogol's letters of advice to Alexandra Smirnova, written in connection with her husband's gubernatorial appointment to Kaluga. In a number of his previous writings, including "The Two Ivans" and *The Inspector General*, Gogol had made it clear that he considered bribery to be Russia's most pressing social problem. In "What Is a Governor's Wife?" Gogol claimed that he had discovered the roots and causes of this unsavory practice. Bribery, he maintained, was the result of the spread of foreign fashions in clothes, which required the wives of high officials to maintain expensive, ever-changing, foreign-style wardrobes, thus driving their husbands to accept bribes. (Several historians immediately pointed out that bribery was far more prevalent in pre-Petrine Russia, when upper-class women were cloistered, inherited their clothes from their mothers and grandmothers, and wore the same dresses all their lives, since fashions did not change.) Gogol's solution was to have Smirnova wear only the cheapest fabrics and appear at all public functions wearing the same dress. In a passage that was removed by the censors, Gogol urged Smirnova to inform the fashion-minded ladies of Kaluga that Her Majesty in St. Petersburg had taken to wearing cheap cotton frocks, which had become the height of style in all the European capitals. This simple expedient, Gogol assured his readers, would quite easily take care of the bribery problem.

The rest of "What Is a Governor's Wife?" offers Smirnova

Selected Passages

advice on how to help her husband serve the government and maintain the status quo. She was directed to form alliances with virtuous matrons and with local priests, two groups Gogol believed to be privy to much useful gossip. In this manner, the governor's wife would be able to expose any subversive or dissident talk and nip all possible opposition to government policies in the bud. Small wonder that the essay became proverbial as the epitome of sanctimonious hypocrisy. Turgenev's radical-Nihilist hero Bazarov in *Fathers and Sons* (1862), after having spent some time in the company of conservative-minded landowners, remarks: "Since I've been here, I've been feeling as wretched as if I had to read Gogol's letters to the wife of the governor of Kaluga." This reference in Turgenev's popular novel led a number of other writers to refer to the whole of *Selected Passages* as "Letters to a Governor's Wife." This is the title under which Anton Chekhov mentions the book in his letter to Suvorin of September 8, 1891, in which he expresses his indignation at Tolstoy's puritanical, ascetic-minded "Afterword" to *The Kreutzer Sonata* by saying: "I'm damned if it isn't sillier and more stultifying than the 'Letters to a Governor's Wife,' which I despise."

Most shocking of all for many Russians of the 1840s were Letter XXII, "The Russian Landowner," and Letter XXV, "Rustic Justice and Punishment." From Alexander Radishchev's anti-serfdom tract *A Journey from Petersburg to Moscow* (1790) to Pushkin's impassioned plea for the abolition of that institution in his poem "The Village" (1819) and Nikolai Pavlov's novella "The Nameday Party," the tragic story of a serf musician, Russian writers repeatedly took the opportunity to point out the inhumanity of such slavery. Ivan Turgenev's stories about cruel serf owners and oppressed serfs, which later formed his *Sportsman's Sketches*, began appearing in literary journals the year *Selected Passages* was published. For most thinking Russians of the late

1840s the only imaginable justification for continuing serfdom was economic: its abolition would ruin the country's gentry. Gogol's defense of serfdom, however, advances ethical and religious grounds for its maintenance. The addressee of "The Russian Landowner" is urged to explain to his peasants that they are serfs because such is the will of God, as expressly stated in the Bible. The landowner requires his serfs to work for him and to support him because this is his religious duty: "Tell them then that you force them to labor and work not because you need the money for your own pleasure, and as proof burn some banknotes right before them, so that they may actually see that money is of no concern to you, but that you force them to labor because God has commanded that man earn his bread by toil and sweat, and read this to them in the Holy Writ to make them see."

The peasants are to be taught respect for their more obedient and hard-working neighbors. Those who fail to show respect for the wealthier serfs are to be addressed by the landowner as "Why, you dirty-faced swine!" (*Akh, ty, nevymytoe rylo!*). The village priest is to accompany the landowner on his rounds, explaining to the serfs that their master represents a divinely ordained institution and carrying a Bible from which he may cite appropriate chapter and verse. The landowner and the priest should prevent the peasantry from learning to read, lest they get their hands on those "empty booklets published for the people by [West] European humanitarians." In case some of the peasants have already learned to read, the existence of books other than religious ones should be kept secret from them.

In "Rustic Justice and Punishment" Gogol addresses himself to the landowner's right to pass judgment in cases where his serfs commit offenses against each other. Legal authorities at the time concerned themselves only with criminal offenses committed by

Selected Passages

serfs, leaving lesser cases involving only other serfs—assault and battery, for example, or minor thefts—to the discretion of the owner. The addressee is urged to attend to all such cases on his estate in person and not to entrust them to his bailiff or manager. Regardless of the nature of the case, the offender *and* the victim must in all cases be punished by the landowner. The victim, reasons Gogol, must surely have done something to provoke the offense; by lodging a complaint, he shows that he has failed to forgive his fellow man, as Christ commanded. Gogol finds this principle superior to any of the Western quixotic conceptions of legality and personal rights. He ends the essay by citing the passage from Pushkin's novel *The Captain's Daughter* wherein the heroine's mother advises a soldier sent to investigate a fight at the public baths: "Be sure to find out who was right and who was wrong and then punish both." Pushkin had intended this as an amusing comment on the remoteness from civilization of the fortress in which the action of his book takes place. Gogol, however, who had already quoted this remark in some of his earlier letters, saw in it the very essence of the native Russian sense of justice.

In the brief but vitriolic Letter XXVII, "To a Myopic Friend," the solemn tone and the Church Slavic diction that characterize much of the book give way to shrill abuse: "You arm yourself with the views of contemporary myopia and think that you are judging the situation correctly. Your conclusions are rotten; they were reached without God. What do you refer to history for? History for you is dead, it is a closed book. Without God it will yield no great conclusions, but only petty and minor ones." The poor wretch to whom this is addressed was apparently a statesman who had drafted a project for financial reform in Russia and, what is worse, consulted French and English economic journals, which, Gogol says, contain only "dead thoughts." Reform

Selected Passages

in any area of Russian life is seen by Gogol as harmful, and in any case he feels that such matters should be left up to God. So the man who devised the project is accused of pride and presumption and told to pray for God to send him some misfortune or personal humiliation as the only way of overcoming these sins.

As the essay on the translation of *The Odyssey* shows, Gogol firmly believed that literary art had the power to transform the world. His previous books, from *Evenings on a Farm near Dikanka*, Part I, to *Dead Souls*, Part I, were tremendous literary successes. But these successes did not satisfy Gogol's urge to deliver to his countrymen a morally uplifting, prophetic message, one that would visibly move all of Russia to change its ways and become righteous. Hence his disappointment at the general misunderstanding of the moral regeneration message that he so persistently tried to read into *The Inspector General* and *Dead Souls* after those works were published and acclaimed. Konstantin Mochulsky postulates that Gogol's sudden departure from Russia after the success of *The Inspector General* was caused by his dismay that the immediate social transformation he had expected did not occur: "Couldn't one assume that Gogol had counted, perhaps half-consciously, on *The Inspector General* to produce some sort of an *immediate and decisive reaction*? Russia will recognize its sins in the comedy's mirror, and all of it as one person will fall on its knees, shed tears of repentance, and be instantly transformed" (Mochulsky's italics).[45]

In *Selected Passages* Gogol decided to deliver his moral message to his country without any fictional or theatrical disguises. Now that Gogol's personal correspondence is available and his writings have been studied by generations of critics, the new revelation that he thought this book embodied can be seen as a detailed restatement of the same philosophy of total stasis and

Selected Passages

social immutability that he had already advanced, in one form or another, in "Ganz Küchelgarten," "Old-World Landowners," *The Servants' Quarters* (the Major-domo's speech), "The Overcoat," and *Marriage*. It amounts very simply to the message: "Leave things as they are." The social and political system is superior to anything that exists anywhere else; there is no way for Russian society to move, except perhaps in the direction of the ideals of Homer's Greece; any attempt to change the existing order is an offense against God and the Orthodox Church.

The émigré scholar Konstantin Mochulsky, whose book is a resolute effort to rehabilitate the religious and moral aspects of *Selected Passages* and to assert its value as a theological document, points out that the social reality with which Gogol thought he was dealing actually had little in common with the grim empire ruled by Nicholas I. Gogol's Russia was instead a Utopian medieval state. "The Gogolian social system," Mochulsky writes, "can be represented schematically as a ladder on which all ranks and social classes are deployed. The people on each rung are the fathers of those below them and the children of those above. The flame of love is passed from hand to hand by those below to those above until it finally reaches the throne. On the throne sits the Monarch, who transmits the love of his children upward to God." The monarch, described by Gogol as one who "sorrows, weeps, and prays day and night for his suffering people," is, needless to say, a wholly mythical figure who resembles the real Nicholas I or any other Russian monarch as little as the Asia and Africa of Gogol's geography lecture resembled the actual continents. The existing reality of contemporary Russia is replaced throughout *Selected Passages* by this medieval Utopia —Gogol's third Utopia, as Vasily Gippius has put it—because this is the kind of simple, patriarchal world (not really dissimilar to the Germany of "Ganz Küchelgarten" and the Ukraine of

"Old-World Landowners") in which Gogol had always felt most at home.

In 1849, *Domostroi*, the famous sixteenth-century household management manual which set up the head of the household as judge and absolute monarch over everyone else in the house and which mingled recipes for jam and sauerkraut with advice on how to beat one's wife and children, was rediscovered and published. For the majority of the Russian intelligentsia, the book's title quickly became synonymous with everything oppressive and obscurantist in Russia's past. But Gogol found in this book the very embodiment of traditional Russian virtues. He advised Anna Vielhorskaya (Iosif's youngest sister) to study Old Russian, so that she could read *Domostroi* and see the superiority of Russian domestic life under Ivan the Terrible to that of the present age.

Gogol seriously expected to be acclaimed as a philosopher and perhaps a prophet with the publication of *Selected Passages*. What happened instead has been compared by Merezhkovsky to an earthquake that pulled the ground from under Gogol's feet and left him standing alone in a void. Only a very few loyal friends, such as Zhukovsky, Pletnyov, and Alexandra Smirnova, wrote to Gogol congratulating him on having written a beautiful and necessary book. Though not agreeing with all of Gogol's views, the critic Pyotr Vyazemsky, one of Pushkin's closest friends and the leading theoretician of Russian Romanticism, nonetheless published an essay defending Gogol's right to express his opinions. An enthusiastic letter came from the elderly critic and memoirist Philip Vigel (1786-1856), widely known for his caustic wit, his open homosexuality, and his political conservatism. Vigel, who had thought *The Inspector General* "insolent and cynical," praised *Selected Passages* as a book of profound wisdom and transcendent poetry. "There was a time when

I knew you long and well," Vigel wrote, "but (woe is me!) did not recognize you." Gogol replied with a gracious letter in which he encouraged Vigel to include his "sincere confession" in his still unpublished, self-revealing memoirs. The servile pro-government critics Bulgarin and Senkovsky, who in the past had attacked every new work by Gogol as grotesque and improbable, thought that in *Selected Passages* he had suddenly manifested a genuine literary talent.

But most thinking Russians, who saw Gogol as the foremost critic of autocracy and serfdom, were flabbergasted. During Gogol's residence abroad, the intellectual elite of the country had split into the Slavophiles and the Westernizers. Gogol had friends and correspondents in both camps. Though they differed in their conception of the path future development would take in Russia, both the Slavophiles and the Westernizers saw the necessity for social reforms and both advocated the abolition of serfdom. Gogol's unexpected defense not only of serfdom, but of the entire status quo, and his statement that "nowhere can the truth be proclaimed as openly as in Russia" were seen by many of his former admirers as an outright betrayal of his former ideals.

Perhaps no one was more outraged by *Selected Passages* than Vissarion Belinsky, the "father of the Russian radical intelligentsia" and one of the most influential Russian critics of the century. Although Belinsky did not value Gogol quite as highly as he did George Sand and James Fenimore Cooper, who were for him the nineteenth-century equivalents of Dante and Shakespeare, he had nonetheless for ten years argued that Gogol was the most truthful of Russian writers, the first one to have shown Russian life as it really was. Belinsky believed in literature's power to transform reality as strongly as Gogol did; by proclaiming Gogol the supreme photographic realist of the age (and willfully ignoring the fantastic and surrealistic aspects of his artistic vision), Belinsky had hoped to use his work to heighten social awareness and bring about improvements. Gogol's image of society and his concept of what was socially desirable were, of course, the very opposite of Belinsky's socialism and atheism. Belinsky's famous Saltzbrunn letter to Gogol, in which he denounced *Selected Passages*, is a brilliant piece of invective and a basic document of the nascent Russian revolutionary movement (it was for reading this letter out loud at an underground political club and for planning to circulate copies of it that Fyodor Dostoyevsky was first sentenced to death and then sent to hard labor in Siberia). But Belinsky's vehement rhetoric in this letter, perhaps the finest piece of writing by this celebrated, but frequently muddle-headed and naive, critic, is all too clearly addressed to the wrong person. Gogol had never claimed to hold any views other than the ones he expressed in *Selected Passages* and had in fact stated them previously in *Arabesques* twelve years earlier. But the accusation of reversal and self-betrayal that Belinsky flung at Gogol was repeated in one form or another by many of Gogol's closest friends, including Aksakov and Pogodin (who despite the rancor he must have felt after having been reviled in one of the essays sent Gogol a serious, reasoned critique of the book).

Gogol's bewilderment at this charge was expressed in the long self-justification he wrote after all the critical opinions were in. In this essay, published after his death under the totally inappropriate title "The Author's Confession" (the title was Stepan Shevyryov's, not Gogol's), Gogol admits his possible mistakes in matters of education, serfdom, and economic relationships, but asserts that *Selected Passages* contains a central core of truth and good will which his friends and contemporaries, to his great sorrow and bitterness, chose not to see.

Gogol had had higher hopes for *Selected Passages from Correspondence with Friends* than for any other work he published. The book's failure must have exceeded his worst nightmares. It was condemned by Gogol's erstwhile literary allies and by members of the Orthodox clergy, several of whom wrote to Gogol to accuse him of presumption and overweening pride. It took him almost six months to conclude that the book had been a miscalculation and that the moral transformation of Russia that he had hoped it would produce was not forthcoming. When he did realize it, his reaction had a strongly masochistic tinge. "It is painful to read these abject, shameful self-accusations, these obsessive reiterations of the words 'a slap in the face' [Gogol had repeatedly compared the reaction to his book to receiving a public slap in the face]," Mochulsky wrote. "There is something pathological in Gogol's frenzied self-lacerations."

Now Gogol felt the need to go to Jerusalem more than ever. He embarked late in January 1848 and traveled to Palestine, encountering revolutionary uprisings in Malta and Sicily along the way. The year 1848, still remembered as the "Springtime of the Peoples," was marked by a flurry of revolutions and attempts to replace monarchies with republics throughout much of Europe. By the time Gogol arrived in Jerusalem, the government of Louis-Philippe had fallen in Paris. Within less than a month there were uprisings in Prussia, Austria, and Hungary. Many of Gogol's friends back in Russia saw these events as a hopeful sign, possibly foreshadowing greater freedom in Russia as well. But Gogol regarded the events of 1848 as the approach of the total disintegration of human society. "No one can bear the terrifying anguish of this fatal transitional period," he wrote to Danilevsky on September 21, 1848. "And almost everyone has nothing but night and darkness around him."

Gogol's old classmate from Nezhin, Konstantin Bazili, who had once played Starodum to Gogol's Mrs. Prostakova in Fonvizin's *The Minor*, was now the Russian consul in Beirut. He obtained leave from his duties and escorted Gogol to Jerusalem. But the mystical experience for which Gogol had hoped did not come about. The arid Palestinian landscape was nothing like the paradisiac Land of Milk and Honey he had imagined. Feeling depressed over his creative impotence, over the reception of *Selected Passages*, and over current events in Europe, Gogol went through the motions of visiting the Holy Land in a daze. "My journey to Palestine was undertaken as though to enable me to recognize and to see with my own eyes how hard-hearted I am," he wrote to Zhukovsky. "I was granted the grace of spending a night at the Savior's Sepulcher, I was granted the grace of partaking of communion, which was placed on the Sepulcher instead of an altar—and with all that I did not become any better." Gogol could not even remember later whether he had prayed at the Sepulcher or not.

The journey to Jerusalem yielded no sign of divine grace or guidance. Gogol decided to terminate his stay abroad and to return to Russia permanently. His mother and sisters found him withdrawn, depressed, morose. He stayed in Odessa on the Black Sea for a while, sharing a residence with Pushkin's younger brother, Lev. He visited St. Petersburg, where he was received by younger writers like visiting royalty. Gradually, he overcame his depression. In October of 1848 he settled permanently in Moscow, at first at Pogodin's. "Orthodoxy and Autocracy are in my home," Pogodin noted ironically in his diary on November 19, 1848. "Gogol had a midnight mass celebrated—does he expect to ascend the throne?" At the end of the year, Gogol moved to Count Alexander Tolstoy's house on Nikitsky Boulevard. This was to remain his home for the rest of his days.

Count Alexander Tolstoy had served as the governor of two different provinces before he met Gogol in the early 1840s. Later in his life he was the Ober-Procurator of the Holy Synod, a position that was subsequently occupied by the sinister Konstantin Pobedonostsev, the originator of some of the more repressive policies of Alexander III and Nicholas II. Of all Gogol's male friends, only Count Tolstoy could share Gogol's religious and mystical interests fully and uncritically. He is the addressee of a number of letters in *Selected Passages*, including the majority of those on religious topics. The Moscow home of Count Tolstoy and his wife, née Princess Anna Gruzinskaya, was spotlessly clean; their marriage, a sexless, fraternal relationship, since the spouses valued cleanliness and chastity above all other virtues. When Count Tolstoy was told that one of Sergei Aksakov's grown-up sons was still a virgin, he knelt in front of him in public, bowed to the ground, and then asked for permission to kiss him. Only religious literature and religious music were permitted in the Tolstoy home. According to Gogol's sister Annette, her brother told her that Count Tolstoy secretly wore a hairshirt under his clothes. Church dignitaries and monks were frequent visitors at the Tolstoys'; the conversation often turned to miraculous portents and wonder-working icons. But, on the other hand, except on fast days, the Tolstoys served excellent and abundant meals and always had available a profusion of chocolates and pastries from a nearby German bakery. All in all, it must have been a congenial environment for Gogol.

And indeed, Gogol's first year of residence at the Tolstoys' marked a definite recovery from his depressed and depressing state during the past two years. His health improved, he attended the theater and social functions, and he began work on a new version of *Dead Souls*, Part II (the earlier, almost completed version he had apparently destroyed in either 1843 or 1845). He visited Alexandra Smirnova and her husband in Kaluga and at her country estate, getting his first good look at the Russian provinces he had described in *Dead Souls* and at Kaluga society, which he had earlier sought to improve through his advice to Smirnova in "What Is a Governor's Wife?" His Moscow friends were delighted that he had recovered from his dejection and was again writing.

In the 1840s Gogol kept up a steady correspondence with Iosif Vielhorsky's mother and his two younger sisters, Sophia and Anna. He gave Sophia advice on the conduct of her marriage to Count Vladimir Sollogub, consoled her when her child died, and discussed literary matters with Anna. In March of 1846, Anna Vielhorskaya sent Gogol a copy of the novel *Poor Folk* by the new and much acclaimed writer Fyodor Dostoyevsky, about whom Yazykov and Pletnyov had also written Gogol. Gogol failed to see the derivation of Dostoyevsky's first book from "The Overcoat" or its covert polemicizing with his story. In fact, he could not even finish the book: "I began reading *Poor Folk*," Gogol wrote to Anna Vielhorskaya on May 14, 1846, "read about three pages and took a peek at the middle, so as to get an idea of the style and manner of the new writer. . . . The author of *Poor Folk* shows talent, his choice of subject speaks well for the qualities of his heart, but one can also see that he is still young. There is still much verbosity and not enough inner concentration. It would all have been far more likely and possessed greater

Gogol and Anna Vielhorskaya

strength if it were more compact. However, I say this without having read the book, having only leafed through it."[46] As this letter shows, Gogol thought more highly of the novella "The Foster Daughter" by Anna's brother-in-law, Sollogub, than of *Poor Folk*.

Throughout the decade that followed Iosif's death, Gogol frequently stayed with the Vielhorsky family in Paris and Nice and at various German spas; he also made a point of visiting them whenever he was in St. Petersburg, where they regularly resided. The last such visit took place in the second half of September 1848, just after Gogol returned from Jerusalem. He stayed at the Vielhorskys' home as their house guest and he accompanied the entire family to their country residence in order to help celebrate Sophia Sollogub's nameday on September 17. During that stay, Gogol became alarmed at the mood of Anna Vielhorskaya. Ordinarily of as studious and intellectual a disposition as her late brother, Iosif, Anna had suddenly become interested in the worldly whirl, taking up dancing and card playing and attending numerous parties. As Gogol's letter to her of October 29, 1848, makes clear, the change in her mode of life was caused by her desire to meet the right man: "You see that society has given you nothing: you were searching in it for a heart able to respond to yours, you thought you would find a man with whom you could live out your life hand in hand,[47] but all you found was pettiness and triviality." In the course of their encounters in September of 1848, Anna both shocked and frightened Gogol by declaring to him: "I would like to be seized and carried away by something. I have no strength of my own" (Gogol's letter to Alexandra Smirnova of October 14, 1848).

At this stage of his life, Gogol had come to accept with equanimity the marriages of such male friends as Zhukovsky and Danilevsky. But in Anna Vielhorskaya's case he reacted exactly

Gogol and Anna Vielhorskaya

the way he did when one of his own sisters expressed an interest
in marriage. He wrote to Smirnova (who was in St. Petersburg
just then), asking her to see Anna as often as possible and to distract her from her frivolous mood by engaging her in religious
discussions and instilling Russian patriotism in her. The same
concern with Anna Vielhorskaya's patriotic feelings and their
role as a possible antidote to the social distractions of St. Petersburg recurs periodically in his letters to her during the following
year. He had particularly high hopes that reading *Domostroi*
might convince her of the superiority of traditional Russian
ways to the Westernized mores current in the court circles in
which the Vielhorskys moved. Gogol went on corresponding
with Anna, as well as with her sister and mother, until the spring
of 1850, at which time their correspondence and apparently all
further contact between Gogol and the Vielhorskys suddenly
ceased.

Most of Gogol's biographers and numerous other sources tell
us that his break with the Vielhorskys was occasioned by the
proposal of marriage Gogol allegedly made to Anna Vielhorskaya, which her parents supposedly found offensive in view of
Gogol's lack of title and his undistinguished family origins.
Among recent commentators, Victor Erlich alone shows a
healthy skepticism and expresses doubts that the proposal was
ever made. And indeed, the surprising thing is not that such an
idea could have occurred to Gogol (Peter Tchaikovsky's proposal to Desirée Artôt, which she turned down after friends had
informed her of his homosexuality, and his subsequent ill-fated
marriage to Antonina Milyukova suggest a plausible line of reasoning that may have guided Gogol), but, rather, the flimsy historical evidence on which this widely asserted episode in Gogol's
biography rests.

Apart from Vladimir Sollogub's statement in his memoirs that

Gogol and Anna Vielhorskaya

his sister-in-law was the only woman with whom Gogol was in love (a claim as substantial as Sergei Aksakov's and Yazykov's convictions that Gogol was having a love affair with Alexandra Smirnova), the sole source for the story of Gogol's proposal to Anna Vielhorskaya is one single paragraph in the four-volume *Materials for Gogol's Biography* compiled by Vladimir Schoenrock (or Shenrok) between 1892 and 1898. One of Gogol's earliest biographers, Schoenrock gathered a great deal of useful factual data on Gogol and published it in what Vikenty Veresayev has described as an "inept, disheveled, self-satisfied, and verbose book." Interviewing the surviving relatives of the Vielhorsky family in the 1890s, Schoenrock was told that there was a family tradition that Gogol had sought Anna Vielhorskaya's hand in marriage. On the basis of this information Schoenrock proceeds to describe Gogol's gradual infatuation, the astonishment of Anna's parents, and the outrage of her German-born mother at Gogol's presumption. Then, within the very same paragraph, Schoenrock reverses himself: "Actually, all Gogol did was to address an inquiry to the Countess through Alexei Venevitinov, who was married to the Vielhorskys' oldest daughter, Apollinaria Mikhailovna. Knowing the views of his in-laws, Venevitinov understood that the suit couldn't be successful and frankly said so to Gogol."[48]

Schoenrock's manner of writing about the Vielhorsky family and especially about Countess Luise Karlovna reflects the anti-aristocratic and anti-foreign bias of the utilitarian and Populist critics who dominated Russian literary scholarship at the end of the nineteenth century. This manner has been revived in Soviet times. Soviet commentators never fail to mention that Luise Vielhorskaya was born Princess Biron (the name is also spelled Biren and Bühren; most Russians are sure to associate it with Ernst Johann Biron, the sinister German favorite of the Empress Anna Ioannovna, who was responsible for a reign of police ter-

Gogol and Anna Vielhorskaya

ror during the 1730s). In this way Iosif Vielhorsky's mother, who was in fact Gogol's affectionate friend and correspondent for ten years, is made to appear a haughty German aristocrat who ruined her daughter's chances for happiness and offended and humiliated one of Russia's greatest writers.

Gogol's later biographers have chosen to read the paragraph in Schoenrock to mean that Gogol had actually made the proposal and been rejected; some of them have expanded Schoenrock's information into extended accounts of Gogol's developing love for Anna and his pain at being rejected by her mother.[49] But all Schoenrock says is that Gogol sounded out Alexei Venevitinov about the matter and was told by Venevitinov that he did not have a chance. If that was *all* that happened, there was no way for the proposal to be turned down and no real cause for all the Vielhorskys, including Gogol's close friend Sophia Sollogub, to stop corresponding with Gogol and to drop him on the spot after ten years of affectionate friendship and regular correspondence.

Schoenrock was also the first to publish an undated letter from Gogol to Anna Vielhorskaya which he and the annotators of subsequent editions of Gogol's letters interpret as being Gogol's reaction to having his marriage proposal turned down (that is, the proposal that Schoenrock himself says was never made). The letter is invariably dated "Spring 1850," apparently because there exists a warm and friendly letter from Gogol to Anna's sister Sophia Sollogub, dated May 29, 1850, in which Gogol sends his best regards to Luise and Anna, and it is assumed that the letter to Anna must have been written later than that. The letter in question begins:

> It seemed essential to me to write to you at least a part of my confession. As I began it, I prayed to God to allow me to tell nothing but the truth. I wrote, corrected, crossed out, and

began all over and saw that what I had written must be torn up. Do you actually need my confession? Perhaps you will look coldly at what is close to my heart or from the wrong point of view, and then everything will appear in the wrong light and what has been written to clarify matters will only confuse them. A totally frank confession should belong only to God. I will tell you only one thing from this confession: I have suffered much since we parted in St. Petersburg.[50] My soul was in torment and my situation was difficult, more difficult than I can tell you. It was particularly difficult because there was no one to whom I could explain it, no one whom I could ask for advice or sympathy. I could not confide it to my closest friend, because my relationship to your family is involved and everything pertaining to your family is sacred to me. You would be unjust if you bear me a grudge for having surrounded you with murky clouds of misunderstandings.

The letter continues with Gogol's expression of regret that he and Anna have not lived near each other long enough, as this would have enabled them to determine the form their relationship should take: "Then you and I could see clearly what I should be to you. For, after all, I must be something to you— God does not bring people together so miraculously for nothing. Perhaps I am to be nothing but a faithful watchdog that guards its master's property in a corner."

Only wishful thinking could enable commentators to read this letter as that of a disappointed lover or suitor saying goodbye to the woman who had rejected him. What Gogol actually says is that something important, something that he holds sacred, connects him to Anna Vielhorskaya. He would like to confess to her the nature of this connection, but it is a personal matter and one that he fears might be misunderstood. It sounds very much as though he is talking of his relationship to her late brother. If, after writing this letter, he indeed made the confes-

"Eradication of Inborn Passions"

sion he found so hard to make either to Anna or to another member of the Vielhorsky family, it would indeed constitute a plausible cause for the entire family to sever all contact with Gogol, suddenly and for good. Within the mores of the Victorian Age, an admission of the nature of his love for the son would be much more valid grounds for such a brutal move than a mere inquiry into the possibility of marrying one of the daughters. The story about the marriage proposal could then have been concocted by Alexei Venevitinov to cover up the true cause for the break.

As already stated, the story about the marriage proposal is psychologically tenable. David Magarshack's hypothesis that Gogol was inspired by the example of the chaste and sexless marriage of his Moscow hosts, Count and Countess Tolstoy, and thought that Anna Vielhorskaya would make a good choice for a similar, "Old-World Landowners"-style union is quite shrewd. But, tempting as such a parallel might be, the evidence for Gogol's intention to marry Anna Vielhorskaya is scant, unconvincing, and self-contradictory. The wide acceptance of this episode as fact is an example of the habit some biographers have of manufacturing conventional romances when writing about the lives of sexually unconventional artists.

"Innumerable like the sands of the sea are the varieties of human passions," Gogol wrote in Chapter XI of *Dead Souls*,

and none of them resemble one another and all of them, lowly or beautiful, are first obedient to man and only later become his terrifying masters. . . . But there exist passions whose

"Eradication of Inborn Passions"

choice does not depend on man. They were already born with him the moment he was born into this world and he has no power to reject them. A higher design has brought them about and there is in them something beckoning, something that never falls silent throughout one's life. They are destined to fulfill an important earthly role. Whether in a macabre guise or as a radiant phenomenon that will make the world rejoice, they all were brought about for the sake of good, which is unfathomable by man.

These words were written after the death of Iosif Vielhorsky and before Gogol's involvement with Yazykov began. After the ordeal of publishing *Selected Passages* and the disappointing pilgrimage to Jerusalem, Gogol came to regard the less conventional aspects of his nature not as part of the higher design, but rather as a diabolical temptation, as machinations of the corporeal devil whose presence haunts a number of Gogol's last letters. On a copy of *Dead Souls* that belonged to one of the monks at Optina Pustyn, a monastery he often visited in his last years, Gogol wrote on the margin next to the passage cited above: "I wrote that in a state of delusion; it is nonsense. Inborn passions are an evil and every effort of man's rational will should be directed toward their eradication." The eradication of his inborn passions was one of Gogol's central preoccupations during the last three years of his life. The pain and difficulty of his constant inner struggle can be seen from the two undated entries made in his notebooks shortly after his return from Jerusalem:

Look and admire the beauty of your soul, false witness, perjurer, the greatest violator of law and sanctity who ever lived, you who hope to be a Christian and cannot sacrifice the earthly dust for the heavenly, valuing your contemptible worth [the rest is illegible].

Father Matthew Konstantinovsky

Have mercy, O Lord. Thou art merciful. Forgive me everything, sinner that I am. Make me remember that I live only in
Thee, O Lord; do not let me vest my hopes in anyone but
Thee, so that I may withdraw from the world into the sacred
corner of solitude.

From the time of his trip to Jerusalem on, Gogol formed no
new or close friendships with men other than monks or clergy-
men. He felt closest to religious-minded women. The names of
Father Matthew Konstantinovsky and Nadezhda Sheremeteva
head the list of people nearest and dearest to Gogol for whom he
intended to pray at Christ's Sepulcher. Following these two
names, we find "my entire family, Alexandra Smirnova, Shevyryov, Pogodin, Count Alexander Tolstoy, Pletnyov, Zhukovsky, and the Vielhorsky and Aksakov families." Except for the
Vielhorskys, these are, by and large, the people with whom
Gogol continued to associate until the end. Deprived of Sophia
Sollogub's and Anna Vielhorskaya's friendship and correspondence, he formed a close relationship with the sister of another
man he had once loved, Ekaterina Khomyakova, the sister of
Nikolai Yazykov (to whose death in 1846 Gogol reacted with
near indifference). Despite his continual wrestling with his inner
nature, Gogol kept working on the sequel to *Dead Souls* and on
a new religious book, *Meditations on the Divine Liturgy*,
throughout 1850 and 1851.

Father Matthew (or Matvei) Konstantinovsky, who heads
Gogol's list of people to be prayed for in Jerusalem, was brought
into his life by Count Alexander Tolstoy. This fiery provincial
preacher began his clerical career by serving in a series of small
villages, in each of which he sought to dominate all aspects of his
parishioners' lives. A priestly incarnation of Chekhov's authoritarian Sergeant Prishibeyev, Father Matthew would tolerate no

Father Matthew Konstantinovsky

parties, games, or singing of secular songs in his parish. Listening to sermons and singing religious anthems were the only forms of entertainment the villagers were allowed; even little children had to recite and sing prayers during their games. Count Tolstoy became aware of this priest during his tour of duty as the governor of Tver Province. He was so impressed that he had him transferred to the Church of the Transfiguration in the city of Rzhev, where Father Matthew was encouraged to work on converting Old Believers and returning them to the bosom of the Orthodox Church. The efforts of the energetic priest brought results. "Father Matthew's victory would have been even more fruitful," wrote Tertius Filippov, one of Count Tolstoy's pious friends, "if at the end of his life he had not participated, directly and assiduously, in persecutions of dissenters."

Gogol's initial contact with Father Matthew came when he sent him a copy of *Selected Passages* shortly after the book's publication. Attacked and berated from all sides, Gogol had hoped that this man of the cloth would understand his intentions and appreciate the book's religious message. He received instead a thunderous denunciation of his book. To judge from Gogol's penitent reply, most of Father Matthew's fire was concentrated against the fine essay on the significance of theater (Letter XIV). Addressed to Count Tolstoy, who considered all forms of theater sinful and immoral, the essay sought to demonstrate the theater's moral potential, arguing that since writers as great as Shakespeare, Molière, Schiller, and Goethe had written for it, and since St. Dmitry of Rostov, one of the most respected Orthodox saints, was a noted playwright of his time, theater could not be totally corrupting. But Father Matthew cared nothing for Gogol's examples. A religious book that encouraged people to go to the theater rather than to church was an abomination in his eyes. It seems he also feared that Gogol's worldly influence might deflect Count Tolstoy from his righteous ways.

Father Matthew Konstantinovsky

Father Matthew's critique of *Selected Passages* initiated a regular correspondence. After Gogol's return to Russia, Father Matthew was one of a series of churchmen whose spiritual guidance he sought, by correspondence or in person, in his endeavor to "eradicate his inborn passions." He paid several visits to the famous hermitage of Optina Pustyn, which was associated later on in the century with Dostoyevsky and Vladimir Solovyov and in the vicinity of which the excommunicated Lev Tolstoy wandered in indecision after running away from Yasnaya Polyana, just before catching the cold that led to his death at Astapovo. Gogol repeatedly asked Optina Pustyn's famed hermit Macarius for spiritual advice. But he was so vague and indecisive about stating the nature of his problems that Macarius finally lost patience with him and told him he was old enough to bear responsibility for his own life and decisions.

This was not the kind of guidance Gogol wanted. The stern, hellfire-and-brimstone Christianity of Father Matthew corresponded to his penitent mood more closely than the benign wisdom of Macarius. The fateful last encounter between the two men took place at the end of January 1852. Father Matthew came from Rzhev and was given a room at the Tolstoys'. He and Gogol had a long series of religious discussions. Other people in the house heard Gogol scream in the midst of one of their conversations: "Enough! Stop it! I cannot listen any more, it is too terrifying!" Everything indicates that at this point Gogol confessed to Father Matthew his innermost secret, the one he could not bring himself to confide to Anna Vielhorskaya or to the hermit Macarius or even to his personal notebook.

Asked by Tertius Filippov in 1855 or 1856 about Gogol's spiritual state on the eve of his death, Father Matthew replied: "He sought inner peace and inner cleansing." "Cleansing from what?" asked Filippov. "There was inner filth (*vnutrennyaya nechistota*) in him." "What kind?" "Inner filth, I say, and he tried to get rid

Father Matthew Konstantinovsky

of it, but could not. I helped him to cleanse himself and he died a true Christian," Father Matthew said. Accused by many of having contributed to Gogol's death and even of having caused it, Father Matthew never denied the accusation and never showed any signs of repentance. In the memoir of Father F. I. Obraztsov, Father Matthew's colleague and long-time friend, we read:

> Father Matthew, as Gogol's spiritual father who took it upon himself to purify Gogol's conscience and to prepare him for an honorable Christian death, demanded that Gogol repudiate Pushkin. "Repudiate Pushkin," Father Matthew demanded. "He was a sinner and a pagan." What had caused Father Matthew to demand such a repudiation? He said: "I considered it necessary." This demand was made at one of their last interviews. Gogol imagined his past and was afraid of the future. Only a pure heart can behold God, therefore anything that conceals God from the believing heart has to be removed. "But there was something else . . .," Father Matthew added. But what was it? It remained a secret between the spiritual father and his spiritual son: "A physician is not blamed when the seriousness of the illness makes him prescribe strong medicine for his patient." With these words Father Matthew concluded our conversation about Gogol.

In a letter to one of his Rzhev parishioners, a shopkeeper whose wife had died and who was considering remarriage, Father Matthew wrote that the Lord's taking the wife unto Himself meant that the man did not need a wife. He advised him instead of marrying to mortify his flesh: "You must surely know what mortifies the passions: eat as little and as rarely as you can, stop regaling yourself, cut out tea, drink only cold water, and only when you really want it, with bread; sleep less, talk less, and work more." For this kind of ascetic, fanatical mind, a confession of homosexual desires (surely the "inner filth" mentioned to Filippov and the "something else" that Father Matthew could not bear to mention to Father Obraztsov could not have been anything else) was enough to sentence a man to death. This was indeed what Father Matthew did. The "strong medicine" he prescribed was a fast that was actually a starvation diet, abstinence from sleep, and constant prayer.[51]

On February 5, Father Matthew returned to Rzhev. Gogol saw him off at the railroad station. The next day he wrote Father Matthew a brief, fond letter: "My heart wanted to thank you greatly, so greatly! But what's the use of talking? I was only sorry that we did not exchange overcoats. Yours would have felt warmer for me. Bound to you with eternal gratitude both here and beyond the grave, entirely yours, Nikolai." Throughout his life Gogol signed his letters even to his oldest and closest friends either "N. G." or "Gogol." The signature with his first name alone was reserved for his mother and sisters only. Only they and Iosif Vielhorsky are known to have addressed Gogol as "Nikolai." The affectionate tone of Gogol's last letter to Father Matthew, the unusual signature, and the desire to exchange overcoats (reminiscent of the eighteen-year-old Gogol's confession to Gerasim Vysotsky: "In a word, I become *you*") all suggest that in the dour, death-bringing priest Gogol may have found the last love of his life.[52]

Father Matthew's reply to Gogol's last letter, affectionate and uncharacteristically gentle, was written on February 12 and received by Gogol a few days before his death. He showed it to no one and hid it in the room where he died. It was found there some years later by Count Tolstoy's house manager, in whose family it was preserved. In the first paragraph of the letter, Father Matthew praised Gogol for his total frankness during their last encounters and urged him to be resolute in his striving to foil the Devil's wiles. The second and last paragraph of the letter reads:

Father Matthew Konstantinovsky

I thank you for [the idea of] exchanging overcoats. Summer is coming and you will not need mine, nor I yours. The Lord has seen your zeal toward me and it has already been accepted. Forgive me, my beloved in God! I somehow fear that you still might be vanquished by our mutual enemy. But I also sense a hope that you will not disgrace yourself before our Lord on the day His glory will become manifest. Let us pray for each other and [He] will hear you and fulfill our mutual desire. I wish you to realize as you taste the Holy Eucharist how good our Lord is. Farewell and guard yourself against that recalcitrant kind. May the Grace of God be with you always and everywhere; I pray for this. Loving you in Christ,

Archpriest Matthew

Before submitting totally to the regime prescribed by Father Matthew, Gogol made one half-hearted attempt to escape. He took a cab and had himself driven to a Moscow mental institution which, through a striking coincidence, bore the same name as Father Matthew's church in Rzhev: Hospital of the Transfiguration. The hospital was known as the residence of nineteenth-century Russia's most famous holy idiot, Ivan Yakovlevich Koreysha, widely revered among the less literate Muscovites as a prophet and seer. That Gogol could consider turning to this coarse and incoherent madman for solace or guidance is an indication of the fear and despair into which Father Matthew's death sentence must have plunged him. However, all that is known is that Gogol paced the hospital yard in indecision for a long time and then had the driver take him home.[53]

From February 6 on, Gogol reduced his food intake to several spoonfuls of watery oatmeal soup or of sauerkraut brine per day, occasionally supplemented with a few drops of wine taken in a cup of water. He spent most of his nights in prayer, allowing not more than two or three hours for sleep. To his friends' en-

Gogol's Death

treaties to eat more (the horrified Stepan Shevyryov knelt before Gogol and tearfully pleaded with him to have a meal), Gogol replied that he got all the nourishment he needed. He quickly became physically weak and had to stay in bed most of the time. On February 10, he wrote the last letter of his life. It was addressed to his mother. Not telling her what was happening to him, as was his wont, he pleaded that she pray for him and begged her to take care of *her* health. On the night of February 11, he had a fire built in the fireplace and burned what is assumed to have been the manuscript of the completed portions of *Dead Souls*, Part II, apparently in response to Father Matthew's earlier suggestion.

Alarmed at Gogol's condition and fearful of being held responsible, Count Tolstoy sought the help of the Metropolitan of Moscow. This high dignitary of the Church sent several priests to provide Gogol with spiritual counsel and ordered him to break his fast and to consult a physician. But Gogol merely replied to all clerical admonitions by saying: "Leave me alone, I feel fine." Getting no help from the Church, Count Tolstoy turned to medical science. Dr. Alexei Tarasenkov, one of the numerous physicians who attended Gogol in his last days, left a detailed memoir describing the ordeal by medical torture to which the dying writer was subjected.

Dimly sensing that Gogol's problem might have some sexual aspects, Dr. Tarasenkov questioned him on his relations with women. Gogol replied that he had never had any. Pressed further by the doctor, he admitted that he had once accompanied some friends to a brothel in his youth, but said he had not enjoyed the experience (this must have happened when he accompanied Danilevsky and Pashchenko on one of their brothel expeditions shortly after arriving in St. Petersburg from the Ukraine; the experience was later reflected in the brothel scenes of "Nev-

Gogol's Death

sky Prospect"). Asked by Dr. Tarasenkov about "self-abuse," Gogol replied that he did not indulge in it. Since the good doctor apparently knew of no other forms of sexual expression, he dropped this line of questioning as unpromising.

The grim farce of Gogol's medical treatment has been reported in detail by a number of biographers, most notably Vladimir Nabokov. It is an authentic horror story, as weird and macabre as anything Gogol's imagination had ever devised. There were three sets of doctors, each with a conflicting theory about the best mode of treatment. The official diagnosis was *gastroenteritis ex inanitione*, inflammation of the stomach and intestines due to inanition. The man was dying because he had abstained from food and sleep for two weeks. His doctors' idea of helping was to bleed him, repeatedly and profusely, and to attach live leeches to his nose and mouth and a corrosive mustard plaster to his back. Soapy suppositories were inserted by force into his anus, stinging liquids were dripped on his head, he was surrounded by hot loaves of freshly baked bread and plunged into icy baths. In a state of delirium, Gogol believed that he was already in hell and undergoing the torments that Father Matthew had promised him. During the last three days he screamed intermittently in a whining, piercing scream that could be heard throughout the Tolstoy house and in the street. When death came on February 21, it must have been a relief and a deliverance. Shortly before dying, he scribbled on a piece of paper: "What to do so as to remember with eternal gratitude in one's heart the lesson one has been taught?" His last feverish words were: "A ladder! Quickly, a ladder!" We can only hope that his imaginary ladder helped Gogol make his escape from that all-too-real hell his life had become. He died with a serene, peaceful expression on his face. On his tombstone were engraved the words he himself had cho-

Gogol's Death

sen, a verse from the Book of Jeremiah: "For I will laugh with my bitter speech."[54]

Several of Gogol's stories anticipate the circumstances of his death in an uncanny manner. Like the evil magician-father in "Terrible Vengeance," Gogol had been told that he was the greatest sinner who ever lived and like that magician he came to believe God wanted him punished and destroyed for having, as he put it in *Dead Souls*, the passions that were born with him and that he had no power to reject. Like Pulcheria Ivanovna in "Old-World Landowners," Gogol believed he had been given the signal that the time had come for him to die, and like her he stopped eating until death came. Like Poprishchin in "Diary of a Madman," he was subjected to atrocious tortures by people who thought they were helping him.

"Gogol committed suicide in 1852 at the age of forty-three," Alexei Remizov wrote in his book *The Fire of Things*. But his death was not only a suicide, it was also a ritual murder. The sentence was passed by an ignorant, fanatical priest in the name of God and Christianity and carried out by the medical science of the time, both parties prescribing the strongest medicine they could think of in order to cure a great writer of being what he was. That the victim collaborated in carrying out his own execution makes Gogol's case particularly harrowing, but not different in kind from those of other major artists victimized by Western civilization's willful ignorance of variant forms of sexuality and intolerance of sexual minorities. In this sense, Nikolai Gogol, screaming for the leeches to be removed from his nose, belongs in the same chamber of horrors with Peter Tchaikovsky standing knee-deep in the freezing water of the Neva River and hoping to catch the pneumonia that would deliver him from the unbearable marriage to a psychotic woman into which he had been pushed by social pressures. Oscar Wilde, incarcerated at Reading, is an obvious candidate for the same chamber, as is the film maker Sergei Paradjanov, in whatever psychiatric ward or forced labor camp he has been cast into by a regime that honors Gogol with monuments and ceremonies.

Illusion, deception, and mistaken identity were among the basic themes of Gogol's writings and of his life. They remained basic to the way his work was read, understood, and written about after his death. In 1854, a garbled translation of *Dead Souls* appeared in England under the title *Home Life in Russia*. Rather than tell the English public that this was a work of fiction by a celebrated writer, the publishers attributed it to an anonymous "Russian Noble" and offered it to the readers as an account of actual events, a book that "gives us an insight into the internal circumstances and relations of Russian society." With the publication of Nikolai Chernyshevsky's *Studies in the Gogolian Period of Russian Literature* in 1855-56, a standard Russian view of Gogol was established that did not differ all that much from the fraudulent claims of the English publishers of *Home Life in Russia*.

In his influential series of nine long-winded essays, Chernyshevsky vehemently rejected the idea that Gogol possessed any sort of imaginative faculty. Polemicizing with Shevyryov, who had compared Gogol's stories to the works of E. T. A. Hoffmann and Ludwig Tieck, he wrote: "It is superfluous to point out that Hoffmann does not have the slightest similarity to Gogol: the first makes things up, independently inventing fantastic adven-

---

tures typical of German life, while the second [i.e., Gogol] records verbatim either Ukrainian folk legends ('Viy') or well-known anecdotes ('The Nose'). Where is there any similarity?" The significance of Gogol for Chernyshevsky was that he introduced the dimension of social criticism into Russian literature (which is historically, of course, utter nonsense). This made Gogol's prose fiction the most important in Russian literature. Compared to it Pushkin's prose works, such as *The Tales of Belkin* and "The Queen of Spades," were for Chernyshevsky mere trifles.

The impact of *Studies in the Gogolian Period of Russian Literature* was enormous. It asserted the reputation of Belinsky as a major critic, confirmed the Belinskian view of Gogol as a critical realist, and, by insisting that Gogol and Lermontov were the first Russian prose writers of any consequence, it deleted from literary history the entire achievement of Russian Romantic prose, relegating to obscurity for almost a century such attractive and significant writers as Vladimir Odoyevsky, Nikolai Pavlov, and Antony Pogorelsky, among others. Until the very end of the nineteenth century, Gogol was universally regarded as the foremost social critic of his age and the originator of Russian realism. Considering how widely read and loved he was, it is incredible to what extent everything specifically and uniquely Gogolian was overlooked in the nineteenth century. His name was so generally associated with notions of the satirical and realistic that when Lev Tolstoy began publishing the first chapters of *War and Peace* in the 1860s, he was chided by some critics for treating the national ordeal of the Napoleonic invasion in inappropriately Gogolian terms.

The most meaningful and creative response to Gogol's artistic vision in the nineteenth century came not in the form of critical exegesis, but in the unique amalgam of the imitation of Gogol and debate against him in the early fiction of Fyodor Dostoyevsky. There is hardly another case in the annals of literature where a predecessor has had such a powerful impact on the artistic development of a major writer. Almost everything Dostoyevsky wrote while Gogol was still alive is a variation on and a response to some work by Gogol. *Poor Folk* (1845) is, as already stated, a refutation of "The Overcoat," *The Double* (1846) embroiders on the themes and characters of "Diary of a Madman" and "The Nose," *The Landlady* (1847) is a transposition of "Terrible Vengeance" to St. Petersburg, and *White Nights* (1848) is a sentimentalized correction of the Piskaryov portion of "Nevsky Prospect." After Gogol's death and after his own return from hard labor in Siberia, Dostoyevsky liberated himself from Gogol by writing his novel *The Manor of Stepanchikovo and Its Inhabitants* (also known in English as *A Friend of the Family*) in 1859. Borrowing the external framework of Molière's play *Tartuffe* and basing the novel's central figure of the despicable bigot and hypocrite Foma Opiskin on Molière's central character, Dostoyevsky made Opiskin speak in direct quotations from *Selected Passages* and in paraphrases from Gogol's other writings and known public utterances. This deliberate act of intellectual aggression finally enabled Dostoyevsky to cut himself loose from Gogol and to incorporate creatively what he had learned from him into his great novels of the 1860s and 1870s. The tragic and illusory St. Petersburg of *Crime and Punishment* (1866) could not have come into existence without Gogol's St. Petersburg tales, yet it is a wholly Dostoyevskian creation. In the critical articles of his last years, Dostoyevsky wrote of Gogol with love and admiration, singling out *Marriage* as a particularly enigmatic work, needing further deciphering to be properly appreciated.

Dostoyevsky was not the only nineteenth-century figure

Nineteenth-Century Views of Gogol

whose literary art reflected an awareness of Gogol's essence. It is there in the verbal exuberance of Saltykov-Shchedrin and Leskov and in the occasional absurdist touches in the plays of Pisemsky, Sukhovo-Kobylin, and A. K. Tolstoy.[55] But the majority of nineteenth-century Russian readers and critics saw Gogol as just another important realist, whose artistic method and vision differed little from those of Goncharov, Turgenev, or Tolstoy. Generation after generation of Russian revolutionaries honored Gogol as a powerful indicter of autocracy and serfdom. The anarchist Alexander Berkman, doing time in an American prison in the 1890s for an attempted act of political terrorism, placed Gogol's Taras Bulba alongside Turgenev's Bazarov and the revolutionary heroes of Chernyshevsky's *What Is To Be Done?* among the champions of freedom he wanted to remember.

The realization of who or what Gogol actually was began to dawn with the publication in 1893 of Vasily Rozanov's two essays, appended to his book on Dostoyevsky. Calling Gogol "a madman of genius" and describing his artistic method as caricature, Rozanov was the first to question the validity of seeing Gogol's writings in terms of realism only. Rozanov's speculations about Gogol's possible necrophilia are surely wrong, but they are the first suggestion ever made that there is a sexual substratum to this writer's work that at least deserves to be examined. In 1906 came Merezhkovsky's brilliant *Gogol and the Devil*, demonstrating once and for all the central importance of Gogol's religious and mystical views for any meaningful discussion of the stories, plays, and *Dead Souls*.

By the time of the centenary of Gogol's birth in 1909, the realization that earlier generations of writers and critics had misread Gogol had grown into a revisionist wave. That was the year Alexander Blok published his essay "Gogol's Child," which developed the notion that Gogol gave up the love of women because he himself was pregnant with a vision of a fantastic future Russia. Mikhail Gershenzon's "Gogol's Testament" pointed out that the utilitarian critics of the nineteenth century simply read their own ideas and preoccupations into Gogol's work, rather than trying to understand what he was actually saying. A special issue of the journal *Balance* (*Vesy*, also translated as *Scales*), honoring the centenary, contained an array of excellent essays by leading Symbolist writers and critics, including Valery Bryusov and Andrei Bely, documenting the thematic and stylistic richness and complexity of Gogol's art and pointedly rejecting the distortions and simplifications of the earlier tradition.

The Gogol centenary issue of *Balance* contained not only criticism, but also a piece of concrete evidence of the way the new realization and appreciation of Gogol's originality were altering and enriching the literary scene in the early twentieth century: a chapter from Andrei Bely's first novel *The Silver Dove*. In the prose of Russia's master novelists of the Symbolist Age (Bely, Remizov, and Fyodor Sologub, among others) Gogol's influence became paramount, being reflected not half-consciously, as it had been by Dostoyevsky, but with a full understanding of the literary dimensions and qualities involved. This influence was continued in the pre-revolutionary poetry of such Futurist poets as Mayakovsky and Khlebnikov and in the ornamental prose and rich, unbridled imagery of early post-revolutionary prose writers like Bulgakov, Babel, Zoshchenko, and Platonov, all of whom, in one way or another, trace their literary lineage to Gogol, both directly and also via Bely and Remizov.

The reinterpretation and re-evaluation of Gogol in the decade preceding the Revolution did not sit well with the radical tradition, since it contradicted the views inherited from Belinsky,

Chernyshevsky, and Dobrolyubov, the views that formed the thinking of Lenin's and Trotsky's generation and that were held to be sacrosanct and indisputable by all radical factions, from the anarchists to the Bolsheviks. Nevertheless, the creative momentum of discovering and understanding Gogol that was generated by the Symbolists continued unabated for almost a decade and a half after the October Revolution. Boris Eichenbaum's ground-breaking study of "The Overcoat" (1918) and Vasily Gippius's magnificent book *Gogol* (1924) revealed many essential, basic aspects of Gogol with such total clarity that subsequent critics could only wonder why no one had perceived them from the very beginning. Ivan Yermakov applied the Freudian method to Gogol, bringing into the open the sexual themes previously touched upon by Rozanov and Blok.

The Marxist approach had been brought to Gogolian studies even before the Revolution in Valerian Pereverzev's book *The Art of Gogol* (1914), in some ways still the best Marxist study on the subject. Pereverzev became one of the leading Gogolian scholars after the Revolution, but his uncompromising insistence on the importance of Gogol's social origins and of his reactionary political ideology brought charges of "vulgar sociologizing" by the late 1920s. With all that, Pereverzev, his opponent Nikolai Piksanov, and a number of other Soviet Marxist critics managed to bring valid new dimensions to the understanding of Gogol during the first post-revolutionary decade.

The year 1933 saw the publication of the novelist Vikenty Veresayev's exhaustive compilation of biographical materials on Gogol, which, although never again reprinted in the Soviet Union, has served as the basic source for every work on Gogol published in the West since that time (including the present one). One year later, Andrei Bely's thorough study of Gogol's style and language, *Gogol's Mastery*, appeared. Bely bent over backward in his book to pay lip service to the government-ordained cult of Belinsky and Chernyshevsky and to utter the requisite complement of Marxist clichés and platitudes. Yet his book could be published only upon the inclusion of a patronizing preface by Lev Kamenev. Kamenev, one of the party triumvirate who took over the Soviet government after Lenin's death and who was purged by Stalin before the end of 1934, expressed mild approval of Bely's work, but he also chided him for an insufficient grasp of dialectic materialism and warned the reader against taking the book too seriously.

In her book *Hope Against Hope* Nadezhda Mandelstam qualified Kamenev's introduction to Bely's book on Gogol as the government's notice to the intellectual community that party control of literary studies would henceforth be total: "This preface showed that, whatever the twists and turns of inner Party politics, the one thing that would never be permitted was normal freedom of thought. Whatever else might happen, the idea of indoctrinating people and watching over their minds would remain the basic line. Here is the high road, they told us, and we have marked it out for you, so why do you want to wander off on side roads? Why indulge your whims, if the only worthwhile tasks have already been set and their solution given beforehand?"[56]

While a certain amount of historical distortion is inherent in the Soviet treatment of all earlier writers, Gogol constituted a special problem for the official ideology because of his central position in the Belinsky-Chernyshevsky-Dobrolyubov scheme of the origins of Russian critical realism and because, unlike Tolstoy or Dostoyevsky, he is a writer whose work is traditionally read by Russian schoolchildren. Showing that Chernyshevsky's reading of Gogol was mistaken might suggest that not only Chernyshevsky, but also Lenin (whose thinking Chernyshevsky

Soviet Views

helped shape[57] and who owed his literary views entirely to articles by Belinsky, Chernyshevsky, and Dobrolyubov) might be wrong about something. Telling Soviet children and university students that one of their most admired national literary figures was a political reactionary, a religious mystic, and a precursor of Western modernist sensibility rather than a traditional realist (realism in the arts being equated in Soviet schools with progress, truth, and goodness) is obviously a questionable way of going about "indoctrinating people and watching over their minds," to borrow Nadezhda Mandelstam's phrase.

So four decades of brilliant scholarship, historiography, and imaginative criticism, ranging from Rozanov in 1893 to Bely in 1934, were declared a mistake and scrapped—including not only the works of the Symbolists, the Formalists, and the Freudian Dr. Yermakov, but all the valid Russian Marxist studies of Gogol as well. Nikolai Piksanov's fine introductory essay to the 1931 edition of Gogol's stories,[58] impeccably Marxist-Leninist ideologically, but containing the assertions that the Ukrainian peasants in the Dikanka stories are more operatic than realistic and that the letters on serfdom in *Selected Passages* simply brought into the open the conversations on this topic in the Gogol family, could not possibly have appeared in print in the Soviet Union after the late 1930s. In 1938, Valerian Pereverzev, the foremost Marxist Gogolian scholar, was arrested and sent to a labor camp.

The present state of Gogolian studies in the Soviet Union is comparable to the state of Soviet genetics when it was controlled by Lysenko. The authors of the official textbooks on Gogol that are compulsory in all schools and universities—Mikhail Khrapchenko, Nikolai Stepanov, Semyon Mashinsky, and the late Vladimir Yermilov (who helped hound Mayakovsky to suicide and who, in his book on Chekhov, turned that free spirit into a

---

fanatical, narrow-minded Stalinist in his own image)—have access to all of Gogol's correspondence, to an immense body of memoirs about him, and to the rich storehouse of critical exegesis that accumulated between 1893 and 1934. To keep repeating as they do that Gogol was a revolutionary democrat, an ideological ally of Belinsky and Herzen, and that his work is one vast and deliberately intended indictment of tsarist Russia and a call for revolutionary change, is to ignore and suppress nine-tenths of the available historical evidence and violently distort the rest.

One popular method of bolstering Gogol's image as a revolutionary is to cast doubt on the memoirs of his friends and contemporaries. Smirnova, Pogodin, Aksakov, and Annenkov may have known Gogol personally, the line goes, but, being either aristocrats or liberals, they did not have the proper revolutionary perspective for understanding his views or motives, as Belinsky supposedly did. Where Veresayev's 1933 collection of biographical materials strove to be as complete, detailed, and objective as possible, Mashinsky's analogous 1952 collection of memoirs about Gogol (*Gogol v vospominaniyakh sovremennikov*) is extremely selective, and offers texts that are riddled with censorship cuts. The commentary to the Mashinsky volume and the commentary to the Gogol materials in volume 58 of *Literary Heritage (Literaturnoye nasledstvo)*, both published to commemorate the centenary of Gogol's death, blame those of Gogol's opinions and interests that contradict his officially fostered image on his reactionary or liberal friends, the two categories being interchangeable in the Leninist view. According to this scheme, Zhukovsky, Aksakov, Smirnova, the Vielhorskys, and Count Tolstoy were all part of one vast conspiracy, the aim of which was to encourage Gogol's religious mania, misinform him about the true political situation in Russia, and keep him separated from his one true ideological ally, Vissarion Belinsky.

Soviet Views

This improbable cabal is thus blamed for the writing and pub-lication of *Selected Passages*, the drafts for the second part of *Dead Souls*, and anything else that Gogol did or said that does not fit the official image.[59]

The image requires that all religious or sexual dimensions in either Gogol's life or his writings be dismissed as irrelevant. Should the present study come to the attention of the Moscow *Literary Gazette*, for example, the reaction is so predictable that the opening paragraph of its review may be sketched out in advance: "Reactionary American Wall Street circles, in a futile effort to draw attention away from the economic crisis and the ever-growing unemployment problem, have commissioned a so-called 'scholar' from California to write a sensationalist ex-posé of one of Russia's best-loved classical writers and to slander him by imputing to him unnatural sexual perversions, which are brought about in Western countries by capitalist exploitation. The ordinary American working people, who, together with the rest of progressive mankind, love and honor the deeply realistic, freedom-loving literary art of Nikolai Vasilievich Gogol, are sure to see through this pornographic hoax that dares to mas-querade as scholarship, and to discern the true reasons behind such reactionary provocation."[60]

"You absolutely must have a husband, madam: the law re-quires it," Mr. Omelet informs the heroine of Gogol's sketch for *The Suitors*. An unwritten but rigidly enforced Soviet law requires anyone mentioning Gogol to say that he was a serious student of Ukrainian folklore, a conscientious observer and recorder of life in St. Petersburg and the Russian provinces, a proto-revolutionary, and, first and foremost, a realist. Any other approach will be instantly branded decadent, bourgeois, and—irony of ironies—reactionary. Popular illustrations, lac-quered plaques, and even cigarette case lids show Gogol wandering all over the Ukraine and interviewing peasants about their folk beliefs. A note to Zhukovsky's translation of Robert Southey's "The Old Woman of Berkeley" (in volume 2 of the four-volume edition of Zhukovsky's poems and translations, Moscow, 1959) states that similar themes occur in old Russian and Ukrainian legends and that it was on these legends that Gogol had based "Viy," rather than on Southey's poem, which it so obviously resembles. The very word "Viy" has recently made its appearance in Ukrainian dictionaries as a bona fide term from Ukrainian folklore, even though it is attested only in Gogol's story.

Viktor Vinogradov's standard study of the development of literary Russian[61] insists that the numerous neologisms and various other verbal coinages found in *Dead Souls* and the plays (which were so ably documented and analyzed in Bely's book). were in fact existing expressions which Gogol overheard and recorded for posterity (realist writers do not go around inventing their own language). Several detailed studies of Gogolian references in the writings and speeches of Lenin have appeared, all of them arguing that since Lenin mentioned and quoted him with approval, Gogol's revolutionary commitment must be considered beyond doubt.[62] Examples could be multiplied ad infinitum.[63] But perhaps the simplest way of understanding to what extent Gogol's person, biography, writings, and posthumous reputation have been confiscated and co-opted by the Soviet state is to visit the grave at the New Virgin Cemetery in Moscow, where his remains now are. The cross that marked the original burial has been replaced by a pillar, surmounted by a bust of a benignly smiling Gogol. Instead of the biblical quotation from the book of Jeremiah that Gogol wished inscribed on his tomb, the text on the memorial now reads: "To the Great Russian Literary Artist Nikolai Vasilievich Gogol from the Government of the Soviet Union."

Gogol in the West

No other figure in the history of Russian literature has attracted so many commentators who themselves were or are practicing literary artists. It is to these creative writers—Rozanov, Merezhkovsky, Blok, Bryusov, Bely, and Forsh—much more than to the critics or scholars, that we owe our modern awareness of Gogol's full originality and complexity. This tradition of creative reinterpretation has been continued in two important books by major exiled Russian writers, Vladimir Nabokov's *Nikolai Gogol* (in English, first published in 1944) and Alexei Remizov's *The Fire of Things*, a brilliantly idiosyncratic reading of Gogol (with some additional brief chapters on Pushkin, Lermontov, Turgenev, and Dostoyevsky) by one of his leading twentieth-century disciples. This book, one of the most significant studies of Gogol ever published, was typeset and printed privately in Paris in an edition of three hundred copies by Remizov's friends in June of 1954. The two important (and widely divergent) books on Gogol's religious and spiritual dimensions, Konstantin Mochulsky's and V. V. Zenkovsky's (Paris, 1961), were also written by émigrés. Essays on Gogol by Russian-born scholars who live in the West, most notably Dmitry Čiževsky and Leon Stilman, belong in any list of basic Gogoliana.

In recent decades, the task of exploring Gogol has been inherited by the West. While in the Soviet Union a philistine government policy forces commentators to keep on praising Gogol for holding views that they know he never held and for influencing people he is known never to have influenced, American, British, German, French, Dutch, and Italian scholars, who are free to build on the achievements of the Russian criticism of 1893-1934, have been steadily enlarging the scope of our understanding of

Gogol in the West

Gogol in their literary studies, biographies, and essays. Among the most fascinating by-products of the new understanding of Gogol outside the Soviet Union is the emergence of his biography as a subject for fictional or dramatic treatment by foreign writers who find his imagination congenial to their own twentieth-century mentalities.

Gogol's Death, a one-act play by the Croatian writer Ulderiko Donadini (1894-1923), first appeared in 1921.[64] It is a wittily Gogolian but also highly topical (for its time) reconstruction of the last few hours in Gogol's life. Gogol is shown breaking off his relationship with an admiring young woman from the highest social sphere (apparently based on the figure of Anna Vielhorskaya) so that he can dedicate himself fully to Christ. He is then visited by characters from his writings. Chichikov is now working openly for the future revolution, disregarding his creator's intentions and wishes, by exposing the corruption of the existing system. The new regime of the future is described by Chichikov as a redressing of past abuses: Akaky Akakievich will be made Minister of Welfare; Major Kovalyov will get to march in a magnificent parade which His Excellency the Nose, driven in a splendid carriage, will review. Khlestakov visits Gogol disguised as Nicholas I, but is unmasked when, to Gogol's horror, he steps out of his role and asks for a small loan. To cheer Gogol up, Chichikov and Khlestakov show him a vision of his future Fame. She is an empty-headed, heavily made-up coquette willing to dance and go off with anyone who asks her. Left alone and in utter despair, Gogol is addressed by Christ from an icon: "Abandon everything and follow me." Gogol burns the manuscript of *Dead Souls*, Part II, and quietly dies.

Donadini's brief play obviously shows a finer grasp of Gogol's life and of the meaning of his writings than the traditionalist Russian approach, whether nineteenth-century or Soviet, ever

did. Equally imaginative and authentically Gogolian is Tommaso Landolfi's 1954 novella "Gogol's Wife."[65] It shows Gogol
secretly married to an inflatable rubber doll named Caracas,
who gradually assumes a human identity and tries to run
Gogol's life. The Finnish playwright Paavo Haavikko combined
ingredients from Donadini's play and Landolfi's story with some
ingenious ploys of his own in his 1960 full-length comedy about
Gogol's confrontation with characters from Dead Souls, some of
them still struggling to be conceived and to find their way into
his book.[66]

These three remarkably Gogolian treatments of Gogol's life by
three writers from three diverse cultures demonstrate the imme-
diacy with which Gogol can speak to the twentieth-century consciousness. Various developments of the past half century in the
arts of the West have served to bring Gogol closer to us, to make
him even more of a "modern instance" than Philip Rahv had
realized when he wrote his essay "Gogol as a Modern Instance"
in 1949.[67] In many ways Gogol is somehow more alive today
than almost any other nineteenth-century writer. American college students who have not studied Russian literature frequently
assume that Gogol lived in the twentieth century (they may
possibly confuse his name with that of either Gorky or Babel). A
New York newspaper, announcing the local opening of an Italian
film based on "The Overcoat," indicated that Gogol was to be
present at the premiere. A young literary scholar who recently
tried to see Gogol's old apartment at 126 Via Sistina (formerly
Via Felice) in Rome was told by the concierge: "He's not there.
He died."

But it is not only Gogol's personality and writings that are
acquiring new life today. His religious tragedy, which can now
be seen as indissolubly linked with his psychosexual orientation,
may also be seen with greater clarity now. His sense of guilt

drove him to embrace the dogmatic, punitive form of Christianity expounded in "Terrible Vengeance" rather than the humane and constructive Orthodox Christianity of his contemporary and friend Alexei Khomyakov. This form of guilt still haunts many men who cannot reconcile their sexual natures with traditional Western attitudes. Both the comedy and the tragedy of Gogol's wonderful literary art can be fully appreciated only when we perceive the price in pain and self-repression that had to be paid for bringing this art into existence.

NOTES

ANNOTATED MINI-BIBLIOGRAPHY
OF GOGOL IN ENGLISH

INDEX

Notes

1. Rozanov was the writer who did more than anyone else to make sexuality a respectable topic for literary investigation in Russian literature of the early twentieth century. For a self-professed sexologist, however, he could be amazingly naive. His 1911 book *Moonlight People* is ostensibly a study of homosexuality. For Rozanov this concept entails only the lack of desire for members of the opposite sex. Nowhere in the book is the possibility of physical desire for a member of one's own sex explicitly mentioned. What the book seems really to be about is celibacy, since in Rozanov's view all homosexuals are celibates and vice versa. This enables him to list as homosexuals ("moonlight people," in his terminology) any number of early Christian saints, hermits, and nuns who voluntarily gave up sex.

   In his essay on the Maximilian Harden case ("Nechto iz tumana 'obrazov' i 'podobii,' " *Vesy*, March 1909, pp. 56-62; the Harden case was the trial in Berlin of some homosexual former friends of Kaiser Wilhelm II), Rozanov ridiculed the medical experts who testified at the trial that homosexual inclinations are the result of decadence and degeneration. Throughout this essay, he defended homosexuality as a valid and time-honored alternative form of sexual expression. But he also insisted that because of the high intellectual caliber of the Berlin defendants, their homosexual involvements could not possibly have had any physical manifestations. Citing the dialogues of Plato as his ultimate authority, Rozanov argued that physical sexual contact between persons of the same sex and spiritual, intellectual, and emotional attachment to a person of the same sex are two entirely different, discrete phenomena, which never have been and cannot possibly be combined in one and the same relationship.

2. Vladimir Markov, "The Poetry of Russian Prose Writers," *California Slavic Studies*, 1 (1960), 77-82. A somewhat different version of the same essay in Russian appeared in *Vozdushnye puti*, 1 (1960), 135-178.

3. A number of commentators (most recently, F. C. Driessen and Victor Erlich) have designated Ludwig Tieck's story "Liebes-

zauber" as Gogol's principal model for "Saint John's Eve." Actually, the two works are connected only by two particular details of their respective plots: the murder of an innocent child as the price paid for magic help in winning a loved one in marriage; and the amnesia following this crime, which is lifted only after the wedding, with the return of memory leading to a bloody dénouement. Gogol may well have borrowed these two plot elements from Tieck's story, which was published in a Russian translation in 1827. But even so, he made a highly characteristic change in the situation he found in Tieck. In "Liebeszauber" the crime is committed by the young woman who is in love with the hero and who allows a witch to murder the little orphaned girl she is raising as her ward. In Gogol's story the witch remains a female, but both the perpetrator of the crime and the little victim become males.

The similarities of "Saint John's Eve" to the libretto of *Der Freischütz* go beyond particular details and extend to the entire plot outline (except for the final outcome), the characters' situations, their motivations, and their course of action. Furthermore, the rustic and operatic milieu of Weber's opera and its straightforward, uncomplicated protagonists are far closer to the general conception of Gogol's story than the verbally subtle, psychologically complex world of Tieck's highly sophisticated story.

4. Because an ignorant translator at the turn of the century did not know how to derive the town's name from its adjectival form, the actually existing Sorochintsy has been replaced in the English version of the title of Moussorgsky's opera with a nonexistent "Sorochinsk." A similar mistranslation, likewise sanctioned by custom and usage, is the subtitle of Tchaikovsky's Second Symphony, known in English as the "Little Russian" Symphony. For most speakers of English, this means a "little" symphony which is also Russian. In the nineteenth century, in accordance with the chauvinistic policies of the Romanov rulers, "Little Russian" was the officially approved term, used in oppo-

sition to "Great Russian" and meaning simply "Ukrainian." Isn't it time to correct the title of the opera to *The Fair at Sorochintsy* and that of the symphony to "The Ukrainian"?

5. All English translations of *Evenings on a Farm near Dikanka* and all biographical and critical studies of Gogol in English give the name of the narrator as "Rudy Panko." No reader can possibly be expected to realize that this beekeeper (who sounds rather like a baseball player in this guise) is *not* named Rudolf and that Panko is *not* his surname. "Rudy" comes from an uncritical transliteration from the Cyrillic of the Ukrainian adjective *rudyi*, "red-haired." Panko is the affectionate Ukrainian diminutive of Panas (i.e., Athanasius). So the English version corresponding to the original would be something like "Red-haired Tony" rather than the quasi-Germanic outfielder we usually get.

6. The Dutch literary scholar F. C. Driessen quotes this particular passage in his book *Gogol as a Short Story Writer* (The Hague, 1965) and asks himself and the reader whether it might indicate any sort of homosexual orientation in Gogol. But despite this passage and the other evidence for Gogol's homosexual leanings scattered throughout the book, Driessen finally denies the possibility of homosexuality because he is committed to a rather pat Freudian explanation of Gogol's sexual problems—he postulates an Oedipal sexual fixation of the writer on his mother and a concomitant identification with his father, whom Gogol supposedly tries to placate by lavishing affection on substitute fathers, such as Pogodin and Pushkin (this entire scheme is supported by a reading of "Woman" which is accepted in toto as a reflection of Gogol's actual emotions and experiences).

7. This last point is the interpretation of "Viy" offered in Semyon Mashinsky's commentary to that story in volume II of Gogol's *Collected Works in Six Volumes* (Moscow, 1959).

8. E.g., L. Zemlyanova, "On Freudian Distortion of Russian Literature in Contemporary American Literary Scholarship," *Russkaya literatura* (Leningrad), 2 (1959), 226-234.

9. Clarence Brown in "The Not Quite Realized Transit in Gogol" (*Mnemozina. Studia literaria russica in honorem Vsevolod Setchkarev*, Munich, 1974, pp. 42-45) points out two other similar juxtapositions of seemingly unrelated elongated items in Gogol, one of which is subtle and the other crude: the barber's comparison of the human nose to a loaf of bread in "The Nose" and Lieutenant Pirogov's anecdote about the unicorn and the cannon in "Nevsky Prospect."

10. Marina Tsvetaeva must have had Homa Brut's nocturnal ride in mind when she wrote her folklore-based narrative poem "Sidestreets" ("Pereulochki"), in which the seduction of the hero by a sorceress is conveyed in terms of a wild gallop, with the woman as the rider and the man as her steed.

Another twentieth-century Russian poet whose work contains significant parallels to "Viy" and to the whole of the *Mirgorod* cycle is Mikhail Kuzmin (1875-1936). As Michael Green has pointed out in his essay "Mikhail Kuzmin and the Theater" (*Russian Literature Triquarterly*, Ann Arbor, no. 7, Winter 1974), "the theme of a male partnership endangered by a female interloper . . . appears with obsessive frequency in Kuzmin's work." The outcome of female interference is fatal to the relationship between males in only one instance in Kuzmin's writings, however: in the musical comedy *The Venetian Madcaps* (English translation by Michael Green in the same issue of *Russian Literature Triquarterly*), where a seductive actress causes a young man to murder his male lover. In Kuzmin's other plays (e.g., *The Dangerous Precaution*), novels (e.g., *Wings*), and stories (e.g., "Aunt Sonya's Couch"), the female competitor is usually routed and the union between the males is allowed to culminate in a happy love affair. Both Gogol and Kuzmin obviously regarded the female presence as threatening, but Kuzmin, who accepted and admitted his own homosexuality, saw ways of coping with the threat. Gogol never came to terms with his sexuality the way Kuzmin did, and consequently kept visualizing the female presence in his protagonists' lives as not only threatening, but actually lethal.

11. In the original Russian of Gogol's note about the folklore origin of "Viy" there is a curiously tautological formulation: *veki na glazakh* ("eyelids on his eyes"). Commenting on this phrase, Leon Stilman asks "but where else?" Where, indeed?

In his book *In the Shadow of Gogol* (London, 1975), which I read after completing the present study, Abram Tertz (Andrei Sinyavsky) singles out "Viy" as Gogol's most erotic piece of writing, permeated with "perverted visual sensuality." The following passage strikes me as especially perceptive: "Viy's elongated eyelids, which see right through and kill, and which combine utter subterranean blindness with clairvoyance, cast their shadow over the entire text of the story, which is possessed by a lust to see what is concealed and prohibited, and which is suffused with eroticism and, if you will, a state of erection of the sense of sight" (p. 501).

12. George Siegel's study, "The Fallen Woman in Russian Literature" (*Harvard Slavic Studies*, 5, 1970), examines this progeny in greater detail. As Siegel puts it, "in one way or another all the 'literary prostitutes' in 19th-century Russian literature come out of 'Nevsky Prospect.' " In addition to the instances cited in the present study, Siegel discusses similar situations in poems by Nekrasov and Nadson, and in novels and stories by Garshin, Vsevolod Krestovsky, Gorky, and Kuprin.

13. "Diary of a Madman" is called *Zapiski sumasshedshego* in Russian. It is a title that inaugurates a long series of similarly titled works by nineteenth-century writers. The filiation is concealed from those who read these works in English and who have no way of knowing that Turgenev's *Sportsman's Sketches*, Dostoyevsky's *Notes from the House of the Dead* and *Notes from the Underground* (a total mistranslation, since the Russian title means "diary written in a basement"), and Tolstoy's "Journal of a Billiard Marker" all begin in Russian quite identically as *Za-*

piski... ("Diary of ... "). A literary tradition that is self-evident in Russian has thus been obliterated in translation.

14. Wolfgang Kayser, *Das Groteske: Seine Gestaltung in Malerei und Dichtung* (Hamburg, 1960); English translation, *The Grotesque in Literature and Art* (Bloomington, 1963); Yuri Mann, *O groteske v literature* (Moscow, 1966); Victor Erlich, *Gogol* (New Haven and London, 1969). Erlich did use the term "surrealism" in connection with Gogol on an earlier occasion. See his "Gogol and Kafka" in *For Roman Jakobson* (The Hague, 1956).

15. See Patricia Allderidge, *The Late Richard Dadd* (London: The Tate Gallery, 1974), for reproductions of such Gogolian canvases and watercolors as "Portrait of a Young Man" (p. 89), "Crazy Jane" (p. 109), "The Child's Problem" (p. 113), and "The Feller's Master Stroke" (p. 131), with their precise and recognizable detail seen in incongruous combinations or from an impossible perspective. Like Gogol, Dadd alternated his surrealistic productions with others that are recognizably realistic or conventionally romantic.

16. Boris Eichenbaum, "Kak sdelana 'Shinel' Gogolya" ("How Gogol's 'Overcoat' Was Made") in his book *Skvoz' literaturu* (Leningrad, 1924) (the essay was originally written in 1918). D. Čiževsky, "Zur Komposition von Gogols 'Mantel,' " *Zeitschrift für slavische Philologie*, 14, nos. 1-2 (1937). A shorter version of this essay in Russian (with references to the Devil censored by the journal's editors, brought up in the Positivist traditions of the Russian dissident intelligentsia) appeared in the émigré journal *Sovremennyya zapiski* (Paris), 67 (1938). English translations of the Eichenbaum and Čiževsky essays appear in *Gogol from the Twentieth Century: Eleven Essays*, ed. Robert Maguire (Princeton, 1974). See also John Schillinger, "Gogol's 'The Overcoat' as a Travesty of Hagiography," *Slavic and East European Journal*, 16, no. 1 (1972).

17. Gogol's explanation that the name Bashmachkin is derived from the word for shoe, *bashmak*, has gone unchallenged

by scholars and has been accepted without comment by all the translators. But by the ordinary processes of Russian family name formation, *bashmak* would yield Bashmakov; its diminutive form *bashmachok* would result in the name Bashmachkov. Bashmachkin can only come from the nonexistent feminine form *bashmachka*, which would mean either "contemptible female shoe" (not a woman's shoe, but a shoe that is itself of feminine gender) or, even less probably, "a woman involved with shoes."

18. Elizabeth C. Shepard, "Pavlov's 'Demon' and Gogol's 'Overcoat,' " *Slavic Review*, 33 (June 1974). The sophisticated and highly original stories of Nikolai Pavlov (1803-1864) were enthusiastically received by Gogol, Pushkin (who devoted to them a brief but admiring essay), and Lermontov. Like so many other interesting phenomena of nineteenth-century Russian literature, Pavlov's work was swept under the historical carpet by the intolerant utilitarian critics of the 1860's, whose narrow views he refused to accept. Later generations remembered Pavlov only as the husband of Karolina Pavlova, Russia's finest woman poet of the nineteenth century. There has been a mild revival of interest in his work in the Soviet Union in recent decades.

19. The complete Russian title of this work is *Teatral'nyi raz"ezd posle predstavleniya novoy komedii*, i.e., "audience leaving the theater after the performance of a new comedy." Using a dramatic form that is closer to a modern screenplay than to the conventional forms of nineteenth-century drama, Gogol records in this dialogue the reactions of various members of the audience and the press after the first performance of *The Inspector General* and concludes by offering his own opinion of the diverse comments.

20. "Khlestakov," in Yury Ivask, *Khvala* (Washingon, D.C., 1967), p. 55.

21. The letter-reading scene in *The Inspector General* bears a striking resemblance to the dénouement of Molière's *Le Misanthrope*. Gogol may have borrowed this device directly from

Molière, whose plays he apparently knew but little, did not particularly like, and read only after Pushkin had given him a scolding for speaking of Molière with disdain. But the stratagem of ending a play by reading a letter in which most of the characters are ridiculed by someone they considered a friend also occurs in Bogdan Elchaninov's comedy *The Punished Giddypate* (*Nakazannaya vertoprashka*, 1767), a witty transposition of Celimène's final humiliation from *Le Misanthrope* into eighteenth-century Russia.

22. For a detailed account of Meyerhold's production and the critical responses to it, see K. Rudnitsky, *Rezhisser Meyerhold* (Moscow, 1969). An English translation of this fascinating book has been announced by Ardis Press.

23. The original Russian is *Zakon ispolnil*. Although here, as in several other passages in both *The Suitors* and *Marriage*, the implication is that compliance with the law is the principal raison d'être for matrimony, the word *zakon* may also refer to Divine Law (which was the way Constance Garnett understood it in her translation of the play) or, possibly, the law of nature. According to Vladimir Dahl's standard dictionary of Russian usage, *zakon* was also used as a synonym for "marriage" or "matrimony" in certain provincial dialects. Dahl's dictionary also provides the correct definition of the word that Gogol chose for the title of this play. Most Russian-English dictionaries define *zhenit'ba* as "marriage." Dahl points out that it can refer only to a man's marriage. Russian possesses a different word for a woman's marriage (*zamuzhestvo*), and still one more word for marriage, *brak*, which does not refer to any specific sex and may be used with reference to both men and women.

24. In an earlier publication, written before I had studied the earlier versions of *Marriage*, I described Kochkaryov's activity as an example of a gratuitous project for a project's sake (Simon Karlinsky, "The Alogical and Absurdist Aspects of Russian Realist Drama," *Contemporary Drama*, 3, no. 3, Fall 1969). I now see that things are a bit more complicated than that.

25. In English translations of *The Gamblers*, the crucial line about queens/ladies and deuces/couples has been either eliminated or distorted. In the Constance Garnett-Leonard Kent volume, the stage direction appears as: *Snatches up the pack and flings it at the door. The cards fly to the floor.* The elimination of Adelaida Ivanovna's name and of the mention of the queens and deuces epitomizes the way Gogol has been systematically flattened out and trivialized by his English translators. Alexander Berkman's translation, published in New York in 1927 (with an introduction by Isaac Don Levine which claimed that Pushkin and Gogol were the first Russian writers to introduce "a Western strain" into Russian literature) does something rather interesting to this stage direction. Berkman translates it as: *Grabs up the deck and throws it violently against the door—aces and kings fly about.* The adverb "violently" has been arbitrarily added; the ladies and the couples have been replaced by aces and kings who "fly about" instead of falling down or collapsing.

Berkman, a famous figure in the turn-of-the-century Anarchist movement, tells of his first encounter with male homosexuality in his *Prison Memoirs of an Anarchist.* He initially reacted to it with fear and revulsion, typical of the Russian nineteenth-century radical tradition. His later experiences in an American prison made him take a less abstract attitude to varieties of human behavior and eventually made him more tolerant and understanding of the emotional and physical involvements between the other inmates. Berkman's odd tampering with Gogol's text suggests that he was aware of the deeper implications of the line and possibly did not consider his English and American readers quite ready for them.

26. Donald Fanger, "The Gogol Problem: Perspectives from Absence," in *Slavic Forum: Essays in Linguistics and Literature,* ed. Michael S. Flier (The Hague, 1974).

27. Helen Muchnic, "A Long Nose Argued with Its Owner," *The New York Times Book Review,* December 23, 1973.

28. E.g., George Weinberg, *Society and the Healthy Homo-*

sexual (New York, 1972), and Dennis Altman, Homosexuality: Oppression and Liberation (New York, 1973).

29. Dr. Howard J. Brown, Professor of Medicine at the New York University School of Medicine and the former high-ranking Health Services administrator in Mayor John Lindsay's cabinet who in 1973 revealed his homosexuality in a front-page story in the New York Times, particularly stressed the high price in tension and nervous pressure he had had to pay during his administrative career due to the constant need to hide and the fear of discovery. Dr. Brown's sudden death from a heart attack at the age of fifty also may well have resulted from the strain under which most of his life was lived.

30. The transcription of the name as Vielhorsky was the one preferred by the members of the Vielhorsky family. Other sources spell the name as Velgorsky, Wielhorski (which must have been the original Polish spelling), Veligurski, etc.

31. The Russian custom of considering "Nights at the Villa" a work of imaginative fiction, and of ascribing the love scenes between men that it contains to sensibilities peculiar to the Romantic age, has its exact parallels in the English tradition of explaining away the similar scenes and sentiments in Shakespeare's sonnets in terms of Renaissance sensibilities rather than homosexuality. In his introduction to the sonnets in the 1974 edition of the Riverside Shakespeare, Hallett Smith writes: "The attitude of the poet toward the friend is one of love and admiration, deference and possessiveness, but it is not at all a sexual passion. Sonnet 20 makes quite clear the difference between the platonic love of man for man, more often expressed in the sixteenth century than in the twentieth, and any kind of homosexual attachment" (p. 1746). For a commentator of this type, nothing short of an explicit physical seduction will ever qualify as an expression of homosexual sentiment. And yet, were it a question of a relationship between a man and a woman, no one would have dreamt of denying that an attitude that involved love, admiration, and

possessiveness constitutes a bona fide heterosexual attachment.

32. A number of recent commentators have shown at least an awareness that "Nights at the Villa" provides an important key to the problem of Gogol's sexuality. Driessen included the entire text in his book, with the telling mistranslation of the phrase "We will remain in bed for only half an hour" as "You'll just stay in bed for half an hour." Driessen saw no proof of Gogol's homosexuality in this fragment, but only further evidence for his thesis of Gogol's Oedipal fixation on his mother. Leonard J. Kent, in the introduction to his edition of *The Collected Tales and Plays of Nikolai Gogol* (New York, 1969), points out that the amorous attachment between the two men in "Nights at the Villa" is described in far more convincing terms than Gogol could ever achieve in his descriptions of love scenes involving men and women. Kent believes that this might indicate that Gogol may have had homosexual fantasies and adds that this is "wholly consistent with his literary fascination with corpses."

Henri Troyat, in his book *Divided Soul: The Life of Gogol* (New York, 1973), recognizes that the relationship between Gogol and Vielhorsky was a full-fledged love affair, but finds it necessary to speculate that Gogol could experience such an emotion only because the other man was ill and dying. The approaches of both Kent and Troyat betray the influence of Rozanov's turn-of-the-century theory about Gogol's necrophilia. Thais S. Lindstrom, on the other hand, in her recent book *Nikolay Gogol* (New York, 1974), shows that she is clearly aware of Gogol's homosexual orientation and of the importance of "Nights at the Villa" for documenting it. She chooses, however, to leave the subject to "the domain of the psychiatrist" (p. 130).

33. See N. G. Mashkovtsev, "Istoriya portreta Gogolya," in *N. V. Gogol'. Materialy i issledovaniya*, ed. V. V. Gippius (Moscow and Leningrad, 1936), vol. II. Reprinted, with additional material, in Mashkovtsev's book *Gogol v krugu khudozhnikov* (Moscow, 1955).

34. For a discussion of Belli and Gogol, James Joyce's later enthusiasm for Belli, and the text of Belli's sonnets, see the chapter on Belli in Eleanor Clark, *Rome and a Villa* (Garden City, N.Y., 1956).

35. In *California Slavic Studies*, 6 (1971).

36. Karolina Pavlova was the foremost Russian woman poet of the time. Gogol was indifferent to her work, while Yazykov expressed his admiration in a number of verse epistles addressed to her.

37. Gogol had presented Yazykov with a walking cane.

38. The following revealing statement by Eric Bentley seems to suggest a possible psychological motivation for Gogol's selection of Yazykov as the object of his affections:

Thus when a man is attracted by a man, but fears to be considered homosexual, and therefore makes the assumption that he is heterosexual—it is "normal" to be heterosexual and he considers himself to be "normal"—he is forced by his own logic to believe that the attraction is not homosexual. Since credulity might be strained if the *other* man did confess to homosexuality, diplomacy, if not logic, at this point recommends a heterosexual partner. "Since the man who attracts me isn't gay, it is clear that it isn't the gay thing that interests me. He and I are special. An exception. No *-ism*, no *-ity* can define us. We just are. We just love." This sophistry, like all sophistry —what else is sophistry for?—is full of good things, huh? Philosophically speaking, its motivation is more dubious: a need to evade the truth. As a stalling operation it is of course successful. The affair with a straight man is bound to fail, and thus any possible coming to terms with homosexuality is shelved.

Quoted from Rictor Norton, "An Interview with Eric Bentley," *College English*, 36, no. 3 (1974), 301.

39. Quoted from a variant manuscript version of Yazykov's letter that is dated January 9, 1843, in *Literaturnoe nasledstvo*, LII (Moscow, 1952), 644 (and in the biographies of Gogol by Magarshack and Troyat, which quote it). As this version shows, Yazykov was still waiting for the autumn months and for December and January to pass when he wrote it, so it must have been written in the fall of 1842. I am extremely grateful to Professor Evelyn Bristol, the American Yazykov specialist, for providing me with this text, which she found in the Yazykov collection at the Pushkin House in Leningrad. Professor Bristol believes that the portion of the letter that contains this quotation was erroneously combined in the archive with a page from another letter that was dated January 9, 1843, at the end.

40. Carl L. Proffer, *The Simile and Gogol's "Dead Souls"* (The Hague, 1967).

41. On Gogol's continuing concern with linguistic and phonetic phenomena throughout the text of *Dead Souls*, see Simon Karlinsky, "Portrait of Gogol as a Word Glutton, with Rabelais, Sterne, and Gertrude Stein as Background Figures," *California Slavic Studies*, 5 (1970). In his essay "On Gogol: Escape from Loneliness" ("O Gogole: vykhod iz odinochestva," *Mosty*, Munich, 12, 1966) George Ivask qualifies Gogol's entire *oeuvre* as one continuous "feast of Russian language," a qualification which Ivask applies equally to Gogol's comical and lyrical sides. Gogol's unique linguistic flair, says Ivask, gives him a verbal imagination and powers of depiction unmatched by any other Russian writer to this day.

42. Olga Forsh, *Sovremenniki (The Contemporaries)* (Leningrad, 1935), p. 158. Originally written in 1922, this novel is, apart from Mashkovtsev's study of Gogol's relationship with Alexander Ivanov, the only source printed in Russian that shows, in unobtrusive yet unmistakable terms, the author's awareness of Gogol's homosexual orientation. Gogol's relationship with Iosif Vielhorsky, as reflected in "Nights at the Villa," is

seen by Olga Forsh as the central, most significant emotional event of Gogol's entire life. *The Contemporaries* is one of the series of historical novels about literary figures written by Olga Forsh (1873-1961) during her fifties and sixties.

43. Before the Revolution, Nikolai Klyuev (1887-1937) was the leader of a group of peasant poets, two of whom—Alexander Shiryaevets and Sergei Yesenin—were at various times his lovers. While utilizing the literary traditions of Russian poetry, Klyuev and his group were opposed to the urban intellectual culture, advocating in their work a kind of peasant separatism and the preservation of the traditions of Russian village life. Klyuev's claim to be spokesman for the Russian peasantry was taken very seriously by figures as diverse as Alexander Blok, Empress Alexandra, and Nikos Kazantzakis. Hailing the October Revolution ecstatically for its promise of equality for the peasants and freedom for dissenting religious sects, Klyuev sang Lenin's praises and celebrated the demise of the intelligentsia in his poetry of 1917-1919. By 1922, however, he had taken a strong stand against the new regime's militant atheism, had become apprehensive about the destruction of peasant traditions by imminent urbanization and collectivization, and had become alarmed at the possibility of industrial pollution disfiguring the pristine Russian countryside and endangering its wildlife.

For voicing such sentiments in his two powerful long poems of 1922, "The Fourth Rome" and "Mother Sabbath" (in the first of which he also celebrated his love affair with the minor novelist Nikolai Arkhipov, making no bones about the physical nature of their relationship), Klyuev was branded a reactionary kulak in the offical Soviet press, a label that is still attached to every mention of his name in the Soviet Union today. Vilified in the press throughout the 1920s, Klyuev was arrested in 1933 for writing the magnificent epic poem "Pogorelshchina," which the authorities chose to qualify as "kulak propaganda," and sent to a labor camp, where he died four years later. The text of "Pogorelshchina" survives only because a copy was given by Klyuev to an Italian literary scholar who took it out of the country and preserved it.

While lacking the easy charm and popular appeal of his disciple Yesenin (who in 1916 addressed several passionate love lyrics to Klyuev and who is much better known in the West because of his brief marriage to Isadora Duncan), Klyuev is a far more profound and original poet. An excellent two-volume collection of his work and of biographical and critical writings about him, edited by Gleb Struve and Boris Filippov, was published in the West in 1969.

44. In his paper "Gogol and Psychological Realism: *Shinel'*," read at the International Conference of Slavists at Banff, Canada, on September 5, 1974.

45. Konstantin Mochulsky, *Dukhovnyi put' Gogolya* (Paris, 1934), p. 43.

46. Gogol's complaint about Dostoyevsky's verbosity was later to be echoed by Lev Tolstoy and Anton Chekhov, who were speaking of the great novels of Dostoyevsky's maturity, which Gogol did not live to read.

47. This periphrase for marriage is one Gogol had previously used with reference to himself and Yazykov in the letter quoted on p. 216.

48. V. I. Shenrok, *Materialy dlya biografii Gogolya* (Moscow, 1898), IV, 739-740. Quoted in Vikenty Veresayev, *Gogol v zhizni* (Gogol in Life) (Moscow and Leningrad, 1933), p. 419.

49. E.g., Vladimir Seduro, "Dostoyevsky i Gogol," *The New Review* (*Novyi zhurnal*) (New York), no. 117 (1974), 91.

50. This phrase casts further doubt on the accepted dating of the letter. Gogol last saw Anna Vielhorskaya in September of 1848. In his letter to her of October 29, 1848, and in his letter to Smirnova of November 18 of the same year Gogol was worried and concerned about Anna's spiritual state. After that, their correspondence assumed a more even tone. The words "since we parted in St. Petersburg" would make more sense if one assumes that they were written in the fall of 1848, rather than two years

later. Furthermore, Gogol's severing of all contact with the Vielhorsky family was not as final as is usually asserted: in his letter
to Smirnova of January 1, 1852, he wishes a Happy New Year to
all the Vielhorskys, something he was not likely to do if there
had been a total break on both sides.

51. Late nineteenth-century biographers were likely to depict
Father Matthew Konstantinovsky as an evil genius who en-
hanced Gogol's morbid mood by bringing out his fanatical religiosity. This view was so patently influenced by the anticlerical
bias of Russian criticism of the time that in the early twentieth
century a counter-reaction set in, and a new trend developed that
minimized Father Matthew's role or denied it. In 1931, Vasily
Gippius, annotating his edition of letters and documents by and
about Gogol (*Gogol v pis'makh i vospominaniyakh*, Moscow,
1931) wrote: "Undoubtedly M. Konstantinovsky encouraged
Gogol's ascetic mood; but the notion of his exceptional influence
on Gogol has been greatly exaggerated."

The true picture of the relationship between the writer and the
priest emerged with the publication of Veresayev's exhaustive
documentation in his *Gogol in Life* (*Gogol v zhizni*) in 1933,
from which the statements of Tertius Filippov and Father Obraztsov are quoted in the present study. Mochulsky makes a
heroic effort to whitewash Father Matthew and to represent him
as a naive, kindly village priest. To this end, he unfortunately
had to resort to highly selective quotation of Veresayev's documentation and to omit a great deal of material that did not support his conception. Nor does Father Matthew's brand of ascetic
and intolerant Christianity seem typical of the Russian Orthodox tradition, as Mochulsky maintains, being more akin to the
outlook of the Old Believers in Russia (whom Father Matthew,
ironically, opposed and persecuted) and of such denominations
as the Puritans and the Calvinists in Western Protestantism.

52. The theme of a male homosexual seeking death or other
forms of punishment at the hands of the man he loves in order to

avoid admitting his homosexuality has been treated in a number of literary works in the West during the second half of the twentieth century, among them Julien Green's play *Sud (South)* and Tennessee Williams' story "Desire and the Black Masseur." A work that offers some interesting parallels to Gogol's case is James Purdy's novel *Eustace Chisholm and the Works* (New York, 1967). At the end of the novel, one of its principal characters, the former coal-miner and soldier Daniel Haws, unable to face his homosexuality and recognize his love for the appealingly depicted college student Amos Ratcliffe, re-enlists in the army and deliberately submits to the humiliation and torture inflicted on him by the sadistic Captain Stadger. Although the religious dimensions of Gogol's relationship with Father Matthew are missing from the situation in Purdy's novel, the torture and eventually the murder of Haws by Stadger are spoken of by the latter in terms of protecting Haws and saving him from his vice. Ultimately, the author shows the relationship as a disguised and twisted love affair between Stadger and his willing victim.

53. Olga Forsh's novel *The Contemporaries* has it that Koreysha refused to receive Gogol. Koreysha was an authentic celebrity throughout the nineteenth century. Many works of Russian literature mention him. He appears as a character in the third novel of Lev Tolstoy's semi-autobiographical trilogy, *Youth;* Chekhov mentions him in his letters as a synonym for the abdication of all reason and rationality.

54. The Church Slavic text, from Jeremiah 20:8, corresponds to the Greek Septuagint version. The passage comes out very differently in the Vulgate and modern English translations.

The legend that Gogol was not dead, but in a cataleptic trance, at the time of his burial has cropped up persistently in the twentieth century, most recently in a poem by Andrei Voznesensky and in Andrei Sinyavsky's book cited in note 11 above. The various versions claim that when Gogol's grave was opened, his skeleton was found (1) lying face down, (2) on its side, or (3) on its hands and knees. There seems to be no factual confirmation for these stories. Their source is probably the passage in the "Testament" section of *Selected Passages* where Gogol voices his fear of being buried alive and awaking in his coffin and asks that he not be buried until decomposition sets in.

55. See my paper "The Alogical and Absurdist Aspects of Russian Realist Drama."

56. Nadezhda Mandelstam, *Hope Against Hope*, trans. Max Hayward (New York, 1970), p. 156.

57. For a thorough demonstration of Chernyshevsky's impact on Lenin, see the book of Lenin's one-time associate Nikolai Valentinov, *The Early Years of Lenin*, trans. Rolf H. W. Theen (Ann Arbor, 1969).

58. Reprinted in Piksanov's collection of essays *O klassikakh* (On the classics) (Moscow, 1933).

59. Minimizing undesirable and unacceptable views of admired pre-revolutionary or foreign artists by blaming these views on the artist's associates is a widespread Soviet practice. It is currently being applied to Igor Stravinsky to achieve his posthumous "rehabilitation" in the Soviet Union. Cf. Aram Khachaturian's explaining away Stravinsky's criticism of nineteenth-century Russian composers as being inferior to some of their Western colleagues and his indictment of some Soviet musical policies: "Of course, in such cases, one should not take [his] statements too seriously, not only because there arise frequent contradictions between them and the actual content of his work, but also because a number of businessmen were bustling around Stravinsky during his final years, trying to speak on his behalf" (*I. F. Stravinsky, Stat'i i materialy* [Essays and Documents], ed. L. S. Dyachkova and B. M. Yarustovsky, Moscow, 1973, p. 10).

60. Those who follow the *Literary Gazette's* responses to Western scholarship dealing with Russian literature will know that this is neither an exaggeration nor a parody.

61. V. V. Vinogradov, *Ocherki po istorii russkogo literatur-*

nogo yazyka XVII-XIX vv., 2nd ed. (Moscow, 1938). English version, *The History of the Russian Literary Language from the Seventeenth Century to the Nineteenth*, adapted by Lawrence L. Thomas (Madison, 1969).

62. "Gogol in Lenin" by the arch-Stalinist historian Militsa Nechkina, in *N. V. Gogol: Materialy i issledovaniya* (Documents and studies), ed. Vasily Gippius (Moscow and Leningrad, 1936), II, 534-572, is typical of this genre. The study demonstrates that, like most educated Russians, Lenin frequently mentioned Gogolian characters. His particular favorites were Afanasy Ivanovich and Pulcheria Ivanovna from "Old-World Landowners," whose names he used as synonyms for anyone backward or reactionary. Also frequently mentioned were Manilov and the "lady pleasant in every respect" from *Dead Souls*, to whom Lenin likened a whole array of adversaries. Any liberal, Populist, Constitutional Democrat, or Menshevik who did not agree with Lenin was promptly accused of Manilovism. Lenin often ironically likened male opponents to Pulcheria Ivanovna and the "lady pleasant in every respect," obviously choosing female characters to render the comparison more contemptuous and humiliating.

63. Two basic publications should be mentioned at this point: *N. V. Gogol v russkoy kritike* (Gogol in Russian criticism) (Moscow, 1952), an anthology supposedly comprising everything of value written about Gogol up to that time, which devotes the lion's share of its pages to Belinsky and Chernyshevsky, restricting the twentieth-century contributions to articles by Korolenko, Nemirovich-Danchenko, and Lunacharsky that rehash standard nineteenth-century views; and *N. V. Gogol: Seminariy* (The Gogol seminar) (Leningrad, 1962), an annotated bibliographical guide compiled by Ella Voytlovskaya and Anatoly Stepanov, which instructs Soviet college teachers how to indoctrinate their students with the official view of Gogol and how to train them to reject all evidence that contradicts this view.

64. *Gogoljevu smrt,* in Ulderiko Donadini, *Novele Romani Drame Kritike Eseji* (Zagreb, 1968). Originally published in the journal *Kritika,* 2, no. 2 (1921).

65. "La moglie di Gogol," in Tommaso Landolfi, *Ombre* (Florence, 1954). English translation by Wayland Young in Landolfi, *Gogol's Wife* (New York, n.d.).

66. *Nuket,* in Paavo Haavikko, *Kaksi näytelmää* (Helsinki, 1960).

67. Philip Rahv, "Gogol as a Modern Instance," in Donald Davie, ed., *Russian Literature and Modern English Fiction* (Chicago, 1965).

Annotated Mini-Bibliography
of Gogol in English

I. ENGLISH TRANSLATIONS

STORIES AND PLAYS

The Collected Tales and Plays of Nikolai Gogol, trans. Constance Garnett, ed., with an introduction and notes, by Leonard J. Kent. New York: Random House, 1964.

This volume contains the complete Dikanka stories, *Mirgorod*, the five St. Petersburg cycle stories, "The Carriage" (as "The Coach"), and the three completed plays. The translations, taken from the five-volume edition of Gogol's collected works translated by Garnett and published by Alfred A. Knopf between 1923 and 1929, were revised by Kent for this edition. Garnett occasionally misread and misunderstood Russian. Not all of her misreadings have been eliminated by Kent's revision, though many were. But despite her mistakes, she had a greater affinity for Gogol's style and treated his stylistic peculiarities with more sympathy and respect than the more recent translators of his work into English have. There is a striking contrast between Garnett's translations of Gogol and David Magarshack's versions of *Dead Souls* and the stories, now widely available in paperback. Magarshack's understanding of the language is superior to Garnett's. Readers and critics who are not familiar with Gogol's originals often prefer Magarshack's translations as being more "readable." They do not realize that this "readability" is achieved at the cost of systematically flattening and trivializing Gogol's texts, toning down or eliminating his surrealistic imagery, and converting his wild humor into something cute and coy.

To her everlasting credit, Constance Garnett understood that Gogol's stories come in distinct, thematically interconnected cycles and that each individual story is best appreciated when read within the context of the cycle in which Gogol placed it. Except for Ovid Gorchakov's

---

translation of the Dikanka cycle (*Evenings near the Village of Dikanka*, stories ed. by Rudi Panko, trans. Ovid Gorchakov; New York: F. Ungar, 1960), other currently available collections of Gogol's stories make mincemeat of the author's intentions by offering the reader a hodgepodge of stories from the three cycles, chosen according to no discernible principle. Thus, the volume selected and translated by Ronald Wilks (*Diary of a Madman and Other Stories*, Harmondsworth, Eng.: Penguin Books, 1972) throws together "Diary of a Madman," "The Nose," "The Overcoat," "The Two Ivans," and "Ivan Fyodorovich Shponka and His Aunt." The selections by Andrew MacAndrew and Magarshack are equally arbitrary and illogical.

At this writing Random House has unaccountably allowed the Garnett-Kent volume to go out of print (temporarily, let us hope), leaving the field to its inferior competitors.

PLAYS

I have seen no rendition of any of Gogol's plays into English that does full justice to their verbal brilliance and conveys their surrealistic essence. Constance Garnett is far more timid in her translations of the plays than she is in her treatment of Gogol's prose fiction. Bella Costello's translation of *Marriage* (New York: Barnes & Noble, 1969) is one of the more attractive versions of Gogol's plays that exist in English, but she too succumbs to the general trend to "correct" (i.e., to simplify) Gogol for easier accessibility. The renditions of *The Inspector General* by B. G. Guerney, Andrew MacAndrew, F. D. Reeve et al. range from barely acceptable to plainly inept. Ideally, the translator of Gogol's plays into English should have the verbal flair and audacity of a James Joyce or a Gertrude Stein. Only when such a paragon does come along will we get Gogol's plays in English with their flavor and color undiluted.

In addition to the numerous translations of the plays, there also exist "adaptations" in which the text of a literal translation is rewritten by persons who cannot read the originals. The purpose is to make the plays easier to stage in English. While these "adaptations" depart even further from Gogol's text than the available translations, some of them (e.g., those of Eric Bentley, whose versions "for the Anglo-American theater" of *Marriage, From a Madman's Diary*, and *The Gamblers* will be published by Crofts Classics, Northbrook, Ill., late in 1976) are indeed more playable and more effective on the stage.

A translation of *After the Play* (*Teatral'nyi raz"ezd*) was published in *Tulane Drama Review*, Winter Issue, 1959.

DEAD SOULS

Of the numerous translations of this novel currently available, the one by Bernard Guilbert Guerney is by far the best. The paperback edition (*Dead Souls*, New York: Rinehart, 1948) is preferable to the earlier hardback (New York: Press of the Readers Club, 1942) with its inappropriate title (*Chichikov's Journeys; or, Home Life in Old Russia*, which combines the title forced on Gogol by the censorship with the title of the fraudulent London edition of 1854) and its odd inclusion of passages from earlier drafts that Gogol himself had discarded.

SELECTED PASSAGES

Selected Passages from Correspondence with Friends, trans. Jesse Zeldin, Nashville: Vanderbilt University Press, 1969.

This volume makes an important Gogol text available in English for the first time and in its entirety. It is, however, handicapped by the frequently incompetent translation (Gogol's famous behest to the landowners to burn some paper money in front of their serfs emerges in this translation as advice to "deplore currency") and uninformed commentary (Zeldin has trouble identifying the Vielhorsky family and has no notion of the nature of Gogol's relationship with them).

LETTERS

Letters of Nikolai Gogol, ed. Carl R. Proffer, trans. Carl R. Proffer in collaboration with Vera Krivoshein. Ann Arbor: University of Michigan Press, 1967.
  A volume of fragments and "selected passages" from Gogol's personal correspondence. The commentary to these fragments is informative and, except in sexual matters, knowledgeable.

MEDITATIONS ON THE DIVINE LITURGY

The Divine Liturgy of the Eastern Orthodox Church, trans. Rosemary Edmonds. London: Darton, Longman and Todd, ca. 1960.

II. CRITICAL BIOGRAPHIES

Erlich, Victor. *Gogol.* New Haven: Yale University Press, 1969.
Lavrin, Janko. *Gogol.* New York: E. P. Dutton, 1926.
  The most outdated and least reliable of the biographies.
Lindstrom, Thais. *Nikolay Gogol.* New York: Twayne Publishers, 1974.

Biographies

Magarshack, David. *Gogol: a Life.* New York: Grove Press, 1957.
Nabokov, Vladimir. *Nikolai Gogol.* Norfolk, Conn.: New Directions, 1944.

A brilliantly idiosyncratic reading of Gogol's life and writings (reduced to *Dead Souls, The Inspector General,* and "The Overcoat," with the rest apparently regarded as unworthy of attention) that tells us almost as much about Nabokov as it does about Gogol.

Obolensky, Alexander P. *Food-Notes on Gogol.* Winnipeg: Trident Press, 1972.

A curious attempt to tell the story of Gogol's life and examine his writings in terms of his culinary interests and preoccupations.

Setchkarev, Vsevolod. *Gogol: His Life and Works,* trans. (from the German) by Robert Kramer. New York: New York University Press, 1965.

The most scholarly, reliable, and balanced introduction to Gogol that is currently available in English.

Troyat, Henri. *Divided Soul: The Life of Gogol,* trans. from the French by Nancy Amphoux. Garden City, N. Y.: Doubleday, 1972.

Like Troyat's earlier biography of Pushkin, this is a semifictionalized embroidery on Vikenty Veresayev's collection of biographical materials (the notes invariably refer to entries in Veresayev's book rather than to the original sources they claim to cite). Because of the wholesale utilization of Veresayev's materials this is the most detailed of the biographies. It is also probably the most readable one. But Troyat's numerous fictional embellishments and his arbitrary reconstructions of Gogol's mental processes, which are offered to the reader as if they were established facts, undercut whatever value the book might have had as either history or scholarship.

Bibliography

III. CRITICISM

With one exception, critical works mentioned in the text and the annotations to the present volume are not listed below. The interested reader will find useful bibliographies of Gogol criticism in Leonard J. Kent's edition of *The Collected Tales and Plays of Nikolai Gogol* and in Carl R. Proffer's edition of *Letters of Nikolai Gogol*.

Debreczeny, Paul. *Nikolay Gogol and His Contemporary Critics*. Transactions of the American Philosophical Society, vol. 56, pt. 3. Philadelphia, 1966.
   An account of the reception of Gogol's work by the Russian critics of his time.
Fanger, Donald. *Dostoevsky and Romantic Realism: A Study of Dostoevsky in Relation to Balzac, Dickens, and Gogol*. Cambridge, Mass.: Harvard University Press, 1965.
Garrard, John G. "Some Thoughts on Gogol's 'Kolyaska.' " *PMLA*, 90, no. 5 (October 1975), 848-860.
   Ostensibly a study of the critical reception of "The Carriage," this essay is also a good examination of Gogol's artistic method and its reception by leading Russian writers and critics.
Hughes, Olga Raevsky. "The Apparent and the Real in Gogol's 'Nevskij Prospekt.' " *California Slavic Studies*, 8 (1975), 77-91.
   A perceptive analysis of "Nevsky Prospect."
Maguire, Robert A., ed. and trans. *Gogol from the Twentieth Century: Eleven Essays*. Princeton: Princeton University Press, 1974.
   This important book makes available in English a wide selection of Gogol criticism written in Russian in the early twentieth century, which is of course the finest Gogol criticism that exists. Among the authors represented are Merezhkovsky, Bryusov, Pereverzev, Yermakov, Vy-

323

Criticism

acheslav Ivanov, Vasily Gippius, Eichenbaum, Čiževsky, Alexander Slonimsky, and Leon Stilman (including his two essays discussed in the present volume, "The All-Seeing Eye in Gogol" and "Brides, Bridegrooms, and Matchmakers," the latter translated by Maguire under the title "Men, Women, and Matchmakers"). The editor's introductory essay, "The Legacy of Criticism," is an important and illuminating contribution in its own right.

McLean, Hugh. "Gogol and the Whirling Telescope." In *Russia: Essays in History and Literature*, ed. L. H. Legters, pp. 79-99. Leyden: E. J. Brill, 1972.

_____ "Gogol's Retreat from Love: Towards an Interpretation of *Mirgorod*." In *American Contributions to the Fourth International Congress of Slavists*, pp. 225-244. The Hague: Mouton, 1958. (Discussed on pp. 59-61.)

Rowe, William Woodin. *Through Gogol's Looking Glass: Reverse Vision, False Focus, and Precarious Logic*. New York: New York University Press, 1976.

Todd, William Mills. "Gogol's Epistolary Writing." In *Columbia Essays in International Affairs*, pp. 51-76. New York: Columbia University, 1970.

Index

Index

Index

Index